The Politics of Public Memory in

TURKEY

Modern Intellectual and Political History of the Middle East
Mehrzad Boroujerdi, *Series Editor*

Mustafa Kemal Atatürk with his then-wife Latife Hanın.
Courtesy of the Anatolian Civilization Museum.

The Politics of Public Memory in

TURKEY

EDITED BY

ESRA ÖZYÜREK

Syracuse University Press

The paper used in this publication meets the minimum requirements
of American National Standard for Information Sciences—Permanence
of Paper for Printed Library Materials, ANSI Z39.48–1984.∞™

For a listing of books published and distributed by Syracuse University Press,
visit our Web site at SyracuseUniversityPress.syr.edu.

ISBN-13: 978-0-8156-3131-6
ISBN-10: 0-8156-3131-6

Library of Congress Cataloging-in-Publication Data

The politics of public memory in Turkey / edited by Esra Özyürek.—1st ed.
  p. cm.—(Modern intellectual and political history of the Middle East)
Includes bibliographical references and index.
ISBN 0–8156–3131–6 (hardcover : alk. paper)
1. Turkey—History. 2. Collective memory—Turkey. I. Özyürek, Esra.
DR471.P65 2006
  956.1—dc22   2006031225

Contents

Illustrations

Contributors

Ayfer Bartu Candan received her Ph.D. in anthropology at the University of California, Berkeley. Currently she is an assistant professor in sociology at Boğaziçi University in Istanbul. She has published numerous articles on cultural heritage and archeology in Turkey.

Aslı Gür is a Ph.D. candidate in the Department of Sociology at the University of Michigan. In addition to representations and institutions of nationalism, she has worked on the politics of cultural appropriation between empires in the nineteenth century. She is currently writing her dissertation, a comparative historical study of the transculturation of French and American educational institutions in the late Ottoman Empire.

Kimberly Hart received her Ph.D. degree in anthropology at Indiana University. Her dissertation is about conceptions of time and tradition among villagers in western Anatolia. She has published articles on weaving and political iconography in Turkey.

Aslı Iğsız received her first M.A. in French language and literature in Hacettepe University, Ankara, and her second M.A. in Near Eastern studies at the University of Michigan. Currently she is a Ph.D. candidate in comparative literature at the University of Michigan. Her dissertation is about the memory of the Turkish-Greek population exchange and the political economy of the cultural production.

Nazlı Ökten received her B.A. in sociology at Boğaziçi University in Istanbul. Currently she is a graduate student in political sociology at Sorbonne University and a lecturer of sociology at Galatasaray University in Istanbul.

Esra Özyürek received her Ph.D. in anthropology at the University of Michigan. Currently she is an assistant professor in anthropology at the University of California, San Diego. She has published articles on the ideologies of the state, images of Atatürk, publicity and privacy, gender, and Islam in Turkey. Her book *Nostalgia for the Modern: State Secularism and Everyday Politics in Turkey* was published earlier in 2006.

Cihan Tuğal received his B.A. at Boğaziçi University in Istanbul and his Ph.D. in sociology at the University of Michigan. Currently he is an assistant professor of sociology at the University of California, Berkeley. Tuğal has published articles on Alevis, Islam, urban culture, and poverty. He is currently working on a manuscript concerning the religious, spatial, and socioeconomic dimensions of the Islamist movement in Turkey.

The Politics of Public Memory in

TURKEY

1

Introduction

The Politics of Public Memory in Turkey

Esra Özyürek

In the popular 1990 novel *The Black Book* by the Nobel prize-winning Turkish writer Orhan Pamuk, a middle-aged Istanbulite named Galip travels through layers of his memory as he searches for his wife, who has suddenly abandoned him. He suspects that she is playing one of their childhood games of hide-and-seek and is somewhere in Istanbul with their cousin, the journalist Celal. In the novel, every object, word, and face becomes a sign from the past for Galip to decipher in order to make sense of the present. Throughout the novel Galip searches for his wife and himself in the multilayered space and time of the city as well as in Celal's cryptic newspaper essays. Early on, Celal predicts that the Bosporus River that cuts through the city will soon dry up and reveal the thousands of years of history buried underneath:

> On the last day, when the waters suddenly recede, among the American transatlantics gone to ground and the Ionic columns covered with seaweed, there will be Celtic and Ligurian skeletons openmouthed in supplications to gods whose identities are no longer known. Amidst mussel-encrusted Byzantine treasures, forks and knives made of silver and tin, thousand-year-old barrels of wine, soda pop bottles, carcasses of pointy-prowed galleys, I can imagine a civilization whose energy needs for their antiquated stoves and lights will be derived from a dilapidated Romanian tanker propelled into a mire-pit. (Pamuk 1994, 15)

Throughout the 1990s and into the 2000s, citizens of Turkey, much like the determined Galip, have been sorting through the rich layers of their history, long covered by the river of a modernist, future-oriented vision. And like Pamuk's evaporating Bosporus, their belief in the future has been drying up. Today many in Turkey curiously excavate through the remnants of their past in order to find clues to help them understand or control the present. Upper-class urbanites frequent antique shops to buy pieces of furniture that their grandparents discarded or "dealers" stole from the deserted homes and churches of Greeks and Armenians. Expensive restaurants invent and serve "Ottoman" food to local customers. Memoirs, historical novels, and films become best sellers and sources of unending public discussion in newspapers and on television. Newly married couples recover the long forgotten black-and-white pictures of their grandparents in their youth and use them to decorate their homes. Middle-class women take private lessons to learn the Ottoman script.

While nostalgia and its industry are on the rise all over the world (Lowenthal 1985; Boym 2001), the shapes they take in Turkey are especially intriguing (Özyürek 2006). In 1923, the newly founded Turkish Republic committed to a modernist future by erasing the memory of its immediate Ottoman past. Now, almost eighty years after the establishment of the Republic, the grandchildren of the founders have a different relationship with history. New generations utilize every effort to remember, record, and reconcile the imagined earlier periods. The multiple and personalized representations of the past with which they engage allow contemporary Turkish citizens to create alternative identities for themselves and their communities. As opposed to its futuristic and homogenizing character at the turn of the twentieth century, Turkish nationalism today utilizes memories and generates diverse narratives for the nation as well as the minority groups.

The changing nature of Turkish relationships with the past offers a unique context to study the complex nature of public memory in Turkey. Contributors to this volume come from diverse disciplines of anthropology, comparative literature, and sociology, but they share a common understanding that in contemporary Turkey representations of the past have become metaphors through which individuals and groups define their cultural identity and political position. The contributors explore the ways people challenge, reaffirm, or transform the concepts of history, nation, homeland, and Republic through acts of memory. The volume demonstrates that memory can be both a basis for cultural reproduction and a source of resistance to it.

Turkish society is frequently accused of being amnesiac. Many locals complain that there is no social memory in Turkey. When I mentioned to friends and acquaintances in Turkey that I was working on a book on public memory, many times they affirmed my efforts by saying: "It is really important that you are writing a book on this topic. Lack of memory is one of the most important problems we have in this country." Indeed, the Turkish Republic was originally based on forgetting. Yet, at the turn of the twenty-first century, cultural practices are replete with memory, and people relentlessly struggle over how to represent and define the past. The growing laments about amnesia attest to the shared desire to have even more memory in Turkey.

Administered Forgetting During the Early Republic

In *The Book of Laughter and Forgetting,* Milan Kundera writes: "Forgetting is a form of death ever present within life . . . but forgetting is also the great problem of politics. When a big power wants to deprive a small country of its national consciousness it uses the method of organized forgetting. . . . A nation which loses awareness of its past gradually loses its self" (Kundera 1980, 235). The kind of administered forgetting Kundera talks about has been integral to politics in Turkey, especially during the foundation of the Republic. Organized amnesia, however, was self-administered by the Republican reformers, rather than imposed by the external "big power" Kundera warns against. The founders of the new regime decided that in order to build a new identity for the new nation, they first had to erase the Ottoman legacy. After six hundred years of rule over the Middle East, North Africa, and Eastern Europe, the Ottoman Empire had been partitioned by the Allies following the end of World War I. The Turkish Republic was founded by a group of former Ottoman soldiers who organized an independent republican movement in the country. The new regime established itself as a homogenous and secular nation-state that rejected the multicultural heritage of the Ottoman Empire and its emphasis on Islam.

In the 1920s and 1930s the new Turkish government occupied itself with a series of reforms, initiating new and state-administered ways of dressing, writing, talking, and being for the new citizens of the Republic. These reforms have commonly been interpreted as measures of Westernization and secularization. Although the Republican officials did aim at establishing closer ties with Europe and placing religion under state control, another major motive for their reforms was to sever ties with the Ottoman past. Erasing the everyday habits and memories of the immediate past allowed the Turkish government to establish itself as the founder of a new era, although it was a direct inheritor of the six-hundred-year-old Ottoman Empire.

The new government exerted the first attempts of erasure on the bodies of citizens, possibly the deepest site of memory inscription. In 1925, merely two years after the Republic was established, the Parliament passed a law banning men from wearing fezes and obliging them to wear Western hats with brims.[1] The hat reform was so abrupt that when the law passed, there was not a large enough supply of male hats in the country. Family albums include pictures of men who proudly posed for the camera with any kind of hat they could find, including fedora, safari, or wicker hats, and sometimes with no hat (Baydar and Çiçekoğlu 1998). Although the law did not abolish veiling, many women took their veils off, and those who did not were subject to attacks on the streets.[2] Female students were required to wear shorts and join gymnastics demonstrations in the stadiums. The new bodies of the Republic had to learn new habits of moving to accommodate their new outfits.

The second rupture with the recent past took place in regulating time. In 1926 the new Republic adopted the Western clock and calendar and trans-

---

1. Mustafa Kemal Atatürk legitimized the hat reform with the following words in a speech in 1927: "Gentlemen, it was necessary to abolish the fez, which sat on the heads of our nation as an emblem of ignorance, negligence, fanaticism, and hatred of progress and civilization. [It was necessary] to accept in its place the hat, the headgear used by the whole civilized world; and in this way, to demonstrate that the Turkish nation, in its mentality as in other respects, in no way diverges from civilized social life" (in Lewis 1968, 268).

2. Many elderly retired teachers whom I interviewed for my dissertation research told me how young men in neighborhoods would rip off veiled women's clothing (Özyürek 2006).

formed the way Turkish citizens experience time in a day, month, and year.[3] The abandoned Islamic calendar was lunar and thus eleven days shorter than the solar year. Because it is very difficult to calculate how dates in the Islamic calendar correspond to the Gregorian calendar, the Ottoman past became difficult to locate on yet another level.[4] Many of the elderly citizens I interviewed still had a hard time converting dates to the Common Era calendar, even though they have been living with the new calendar for more than seventy years. Thus, events that predate 1926 appear as if they belong to a different temporal zone. The new calendar in Turkey made it possible for the Turkish Republic to move from the "Oriental" flow of time, which the reformers disdained, toward an "Occidental" one, to which they aspired.

The most powerful way in which the Republican officials disconnected with the past, however, was through administering the script reform of 1928 and the language reform of 1932. The government replaced the Arabic script with the Latin one over a period of three months. The alphabet reform did not bring the expected increase in the level of literacy to the nation, but it did make it impossible for the new generations to read anything written before 1928. In order to couple the script reform with the language reform, Mustafa Kemal Atatürk founded the Turkish Language Institute in 1932. Its members worked relentlessly for three years to replace all the foreign words in the language with "pure Turkish" words collected from Anatolia and Central Asia or at other times simply with invented words. Although the language reform slowed down after 1935, the changes were so dramatic that it is quite difficult for an educated person to understand a text written before 1928, even if it is transliterated into Latin script.

Another reform that split connections with the past was the 1934 "law of last names." At that date all Turkish citizens were required to drop their family, tribal, and location names and religious titles, and adopt a last name. The Republican officials were actively involved in the naming process. They vetoed

3. This reform is reminiscent of the way the leaders of the French Revolution adopted a new calendar to mark the beginning of a new time (Ozouf 1988).

4. Historians use books and computer programs in order to figure out the correspondence between dates in the Muslim calendar and dates in the Gregorian calendar.

many names on the basis that they were not Turkish or appropriate as last names, and they simply recorded other names in their books (Türköz 2001). The law of last names divided larger families into smaller groups and made it difficult for younger generations to follow their genealogies through official documents. The law also baptized the citizens for their new lives, purifying them of older connections with units larger than a nuclear family.

Despite the well-organized efforts to foster forgetfulness, the new Republic could not completely erase the memories. Even though past experiences conflict with the nationalist history, they coexist in individual memories. According to Martin Stokes, revoking "old ways" has a political function: "Remembering becomes both a problem and a matter of cultural elaboration. This is not because the state is incapable of making people forget but because the politics of forgetting paradoxically demands the preservation of a variety of things to demonstrate the necessity of their having been forgotten" (Stokes 2000, 240). As early as the first decade of the Republic, unpaved village roads, the old education system, and veiling practices were commonly compared in official posters to new, modern city scenes (Bozdoğan 2001). Such visual images repeatedly remind citizens of what they should leave behind and forget about desiring. At the same time, these efforts have also prevented the old ways from totally disappearing, at least from memories. In contrast to the famous French historian Pierre Nora's frequently cited concept of "sites of memory," where "a residual sense of continuity exists" (1996, 1) with the past that is lost to modern people, Turkey became awash with "sites of forgetting." Such sites are marked with a residual sense of rupture that should be constantly remembered to prove that the break actually took place.

Rise of Memory at the Turn of the Twenty-First Century

If the turn of the twentieth century is marked as an age of forgetting for Turkish citizens, the turn of the twenty-first century is one of nostalgia for people in Turkey and elsewhere. *Nostalgia,* a term that originated in the seventeenth century to name the symptoms of homesick Swiss soldiers (Lowenthal 1985), is now a widespread feeling shared by millions of people around the world. From the Taliban in Afghanistan (Roy 1994) to discontented postreform workers in China (Rofel 1999) or postsocialist citizens of Germany (Berdahl 1999), large groups of people yearn for an imagined past. A widely held belief about nostalgia is that since modernity could not fulfill its promises for a better and freer life, nations marginalized in the global order now look back at the past fondly. In other words, modernity finished with the end of hope for tomorrow, and since then people look to the past rather than the future for their utopias (Huyssen 1995).

Another popular explanation about the new orientation toward the past holds rapid social and technological transformations of the modern age responsible. Pierre Nora, the leading figure of this approach, argues that rapid changes cut people off from their past. In the modern world people lose an embodied sense of the past, and their access to earlier periods only becomes possible through archived, alienated, or dutifully followed histories rather than orally transmitted memories. He argues, "What was left of experience, still lived in the warmth of tradition, in the silence of custom, in the repetition of the ancestral, has been swept away by a surge of deeply historical sensibility." Thus, he states, "memory is constantly on our lips because it no longer exists" (Nora 1996, 1).

Although illuminating, both explanations define memory in negative terms, seeing it as a mere replacement for something lost, a belief in tomorrow or a real tradition. Essays in this volume go beyond such a replacement approach and suggest at least three ways in which memory is constructive of new sets of relations in the Turkish context. Each contributor, in his or her own way, demonstrates that memory is both productive and a product of political struggle in the present. Some authors (Bartu, Hart, and Iğsız) point to the power of memory in turning communal objects and concepts into commodities for personal ownership. Others (Gür, Iğsız, Ökten, Özyürek, and Tuğal) discuss the ways in which memories create identities and help members of the nation come to terms with the past and with national traumas, by either highlighting or concealing them.

The Politics of Public Memory

It was the French sociologist Maurice Halbwachs who in the mid-twentieth century first introduced the idea of memory as something shared by a unit larger than the individual. According to Halbwachs, memory is collective, and it is not possible for an individual to remember something that is not already collectively inscribed. He claims, "One may say that the individual remembers by placing himself in the perspective of the group, but one may also affirm that the memory of the group realizes and manifests itself in individual memories" (Halbwachs 1992, 40). Thanks to his Durkheimian approach, Halbwachs was able to see how memory serves the present goals of society, such as maintaining and strengthening group membership. The same emphasis on the cohesive nature of the group, however, also inhibited him from paying attention to differences within society in terms of the memories individuals and groups own and promote.

Halbwach's understanding of the shared aspects of memory was influential among Anglophone scholars in the 1990s. Although contemporary scholars are more reluctant to use his phrase "collective memory," other terms, such as *social memory* or, more recently, *cultural memory,* are frequently used with similar connotations. The concept of collective memory is useful in discussing how "identification and knowledge of a particular place, stories, songs or poems, and crafts or artistic forms help form a basis of common identity, a sense of community, and especially the continuity of the past into the present," as Kimberly Hart writes in this volume. Based on her research on time and identity in an Anatolian weaving village, Hart suggests that collective memory is embedded in practices, objects, and land. The idea of tradition, on the other hand, involves a conscious remembering and careful performing of past practices.

Because the terms *collective, social,* and *cultural* all emphasize the shared nature of culture and memory, the rarely used phrase *public memory* is an apt descriptor of the events analyzed by several of the contributors to this volume. My use of the term *public memory* is inspired by Arjun Appadurai and Carol Breckenridge's definition of *public culture.* In the first issue of the journal *Public Culture,* Appadurai and Breckenridge claim they chose the term *public culture* over more commonly used phrases such as *folk culture* or *mass culture* because, they argue, the term *public culture* is less embedded in Western dichotomies like high versus low, elite versus mass, or popular versus classical. Furthermore, it better expresses their desire to consider culture as a "zone of cultural debate" or "an arena where other types, forms, domains of culture are encountering, interrogating, and contesting each other in new and unexpected ways" (Appadurai and Breckenridge 1988, 6).

Phrases that are frequently associated with memory do not present the same problems as those coupled with culture. For example, there is no common distinction between high or low or elite or mass forms of memory. Yet, there is a generally accepted distinction between individual and social memory, and also between memory and history. Such divisions suggest that individual memories can be diverse, yet social, collective, cultural, or written memories are shared by all members of the group. The phrase *public memory*, on the other hand, connotes both the shared and the contested aspects of memory at the same time. As many of the contributors to this volume demonstrate, public memories are comprehensible for most members in the group. Yet, this does not mean that all members share these memories or agree with them. Rather, different groups and individuals in society promote their own versions of memory in order to serve their interests in the present (see chapters by Bartu, Özyürek, and Tuğal).

Chapter 6, "Public Memory as Political Battleground," for example, demonstrates that in the late 1990s Islamist and secularist politicians, intellectuals, and citizens shared the idea that the foundation of the Turkish Republic was a crucial turning point for the history of the nation. The two parties, however, contested the foundational intent of the Republic. Islamists challenged the secularist memory of the foundation by longing for what they remember as the religious nature of the founding days. They retrieved pictures of Atatürk that showed him praying with religious leaders, traveling with his veiled wife, and making statements praising Islam. As in the example of the Islamists, nostalgia creates legitimate political space in which marginalized groups can engage in critiquing the present through redefining the past.

In chapter 4 of this volume, "Remembering a Nine-Thousand-Year-Old Site," Ayfer Bartu Candan similarly demonstrates how different groups that relate to the archeological site of Çatalhöyük emphasize their unique relationship with the location to claim ownership. Her rich analysis attests to the impossibility of making a simple division between official and unofficial versions of memory, since representations of the past are much more complicated than such a dichotomous split can reveal.

Commodification of Memory

An extensive public dispute about memory arose in Turkey as politicians and citizens debated the best way to market Istanbul's global service industries and tourism companies. During the 1994 local elections, the major issue of debate among candidates revolved around how to replan the city and, more importantly, what kind of heritage to emphasize among the multiple layers of history in the city while marketing the city to global investors (Bartu 1999a; Bora 1999).

As the case of Istanbul demonstrates well, memory and nostalgia turned into effective engines of late capitalism at the turn of the twenty-first century. Kathleen Stewart once noted that nostalgia runs with the economy of which it is a part (1988, 227). Today it might be more appropriate to rephrase her words as "nostalgia runs the economy of which it is a part," particularly because nostalgia is quite successful in turning commonly shared objects, concepts, and spaces into commodities (Özyürek 2004a). In contemporary Japan, for example, nostalgia creates desire for tourism and for so-called traditional objects by keeping Japan "on the verge of vanishing, stable yet endangered" (Ivy 1995, 65). In Turkey, on the other hand, nostalgia commodities allow people to reconnect with a past that has already vanished.

Entrepreneurs have creatively used the emergent nostalgia for the Ottoman Empire to sell furniture, houses, novels, films, and food. They have invented a curious new category, "Ottoman food," to market pricey menu items consisting of commonly consumed homemade dishes such as vegetarian appetizers, meat dishes cooked with vegetables, pickles, and fruit desserts. More recently the same dishes are also sold in Istanbul as Greek food, recalling the Ottoman residents of the city, and for even higher prices (Iğsız 2001). As Aslı Iğsız points out in chapter 8, new markets are emerging for music, literature, and movies, reminding contemporary Turks of the multicultural past of the Ottoman Empire, and Cihan Tuğal describes in chapter 7 how diaspora Armenians are reminded of the homeland they lost. Another lost past, namely the pure and traditional village life, also makes urbanite Turkish and international customers willing to pay high prices for handwoven and naturally dyed rugs. Kimberly Hart notes in chapter 2 how, by purchasing rugs, Turkish and global consumers seek to connect with pastoral village life, which they imagine as their past.

Memory, Trauma, and Identity

Memory is also productive of social relations by managing identities and helping individuals and groups come to terms with the suppressed or commemorated traumas of the past. Today many scholars agree that both individual and group identity becomes possible through claiming and remembering sameness over time and space (Boyarin 1994; Gillis 1994). Memory not only helps individuals form membership in groups but also helps them create a sense of their past, present, and future (Fentress and Wickham 1988; Tuğal 2002). This is precisely why nation-states spend so much effort on institutions of memory, such as museums (Bennett 1995; Duncan 1995; chapter 3 in this volume), monuments (Savage 1994), national history-writing projects, commemorations (Bodnar 1992; chapter 5), and founding myths (Ben-Yehuda 1995): to create a sense of imagined community for the nation. But what about events that are too painful to remember or represent in the present? How do nations and their states deal with their public traumas?

Foundation of a nation-state is commonly a traumatic experience because it brings a rupture with the past (Antze and Lambek 1996). The process that led to the foundation of the Turkish nation-state and national identity included traumatic events where religious minorities were massacred, deported, or encouraged to migrate in the name of establishing a homogenous national identity. The three major traumas of the early twentieth century involved the massacre of Armenians and other Christian groups in Anatolia in 1915 (Akçam 2004; Dadrian 1999), deportation of some two million Orthodox Christians out of their homes in exchange for a smaller Muslim population from Greece in 1923 (Hirschon 1998), and the infamous wealth tax of 1942, when Christian and Jewish citizens of the Turkish Republic were so heavily taxed that they had to sell all their belongings to pay their taxes (Akar 1999; Bali 1999; Aktar 2000). As a result of such policies, religious minorities in the country decreased dramatically. Whereas non-Muslims constituted 19.1 percent of the population at the beginning of the twentieth century, at the end of the century that number had dropped to a mere 0.2 percent (Courbage and Fargues 1997).

The memory of such traumatic events, where people killed their neighbors and stole their property, live on in the silenced memories of the individuals who experienced them (Yalçın 1998). In the 1990s, however, those events became the center of public attention. *The Singles of Salkım Hanım* (Salkım Hanım'ın Taneleri), the novel and then the feature film depicting the tragedy of the wealth tax, received substantial public attention (Bali 2001). Likewise, the question of whether the 1915 massacres of Armenians can be defined as genocide became one of the most intensely discussed issues of public debate in the 1990s and early 2000s.

Memories of foundational traumas serve different groups in distinct ways. First, recall of earlier traumas creates a legitimate space in the present to acknowledge the ongoing suffering. Throughout the late 1980s and the 1990s, Turkey experienced a civil war between the Turkish army and guerrillas of the Kurdish Workers Party (PKK). According to Turkish official reports, a total of thirty thousand citizens died in the fighting. At the time, individuals could get into trouble if they publicly discussed the present misery of the Kurdish people. As Aslı Iğsız notes in chapter 8, leftist publications and music houses have utilized the past traumas of the Anatolian people to talk about the present tragedy. By alluding to a pre-twentieth-century nostalgia, when different peoples of Anatolia lived peacefully side by side, they can make an indirect critique of the ongoing oppression of the Kurdish population and identity.

The memory of foundational traumas has a different role for the victimized groups. In the 1990s, the Armenian and, to a lesser extent, the Jewish community in Turkey also started to come to terms with their ordeals (Baer 2000). Such memories are utilized more effectively by the Armenian communities in diaspora than those in Turkey. In chapter 7, "Memories of Violence, Memoirs of Nation," Cihan Tuğal argues that massacre memoirs written by and for Armenians especially in the United States are crucial for them to imagine Armenians as a community. He also notes that memoirs are more successful than histories in illustrating the complexity of representing the past and the difficulty of finding a meaningful explanation for violence.

Not all traumas of the Turkish nation-state are silenced. In chapter 5, "An Endless Death and an Eternal Mourning," Nazlı Ökten analyzes a commemorated national trauma in Turkey: the death of the founding father, Mustafa Kemal Atatürk. She argues that the never-ending mourning for the leader and the relentless recall of his death makes him immortal. As such, he becomes an ever-present figure of the Turkish public sphere and defines its legitimate boundaries. Ökten argues that because the memory of Atatürk has occupied a central place in Turkish political culture for more than sixty years, it is difficult for Turkish citizens to debate and create new grounds of political legitimacy that go beyond the teachings of the leader.

Memories in and of Turkey Beyond the National Boundaries

One of the earliest aims of the new Turkish Republic was to replace the living memories of a multicultural and heterogeneous Ottoman Empire with a written history of the unified nation that is limited by the newly drawn national boundaries. In chapter 3, "Reading the Stories in Three Dimensions," Aslı Gür demonstrates how during the early Republican years, history writing and archeology aimed to establish connections with people who lived in Anatolia thousands of years earlier. Archeological excavations and displays of the 1930s fulfilled two goals. First, by defining earlier civilizations in Anatolia such as the Hittites and Sumerians as Turkish, they legitimized the Turkish state's exclusive claims on Anatolia. Moreover, the same findings established historical connections between contemporary and ancient residents of Anatolia. The "territorial kinship," to use Gür's term, that was established between Turks and the Hittites aimed to replace other kin relationships Turkish residents had established with Greeks, Armenians, Iranians, and Arabs.

Although Aslı Gür's study in chapter 3 of contemporary Turkish museum visitors demonstrates that the idea of territorial kinship with ancient civilizations is still popular, official efforts to replace lived memories with a distant history has not been fully successful. Memories about imperial territories and times when people of different ethnic and religious backgrounds lived together are still alive in Turkey and among diasporic Anatolian communities such as Armenians and Greeks. Elif Ekin Akşit (2001) argues that first-generation Republican women integrate nostalgia for the early Republic with fond memories of their Greek and Armenian neighbors, who were erased from the national narrative of early Ankara. The personal narratives of these women do not form a conscious resistance to the nationalist narrative. But contemporary interest in music and novels from pre-population-exchange days has engendered criticism of homogenizing policies and national boundaries. Such cultural products are consumed mainly by younger generations who never personally experienced such coexistence, and thus gives these people new political identities defined in the context of the 1990s. In a similar vein, Cihan Tuğal's study in chapter 7 on massacre memoirs written by and for Armenians in diaspora demonstrates that memory-based cultural products work both to make and break territorial identities.

History of the Book

The Politics of Public Memory in Turkey already has a publicly shared past. An earlier and quite different version of it was published in Istanbul by ıletişim Publication House in the summer of 2001. I was inspired to put together a volume on the politics of public memory in Turkey when I started to take note of rapidly increasing interest in the past both by lay citizens and academics. Young scholars of Turkey, such as the contributors to this book, have no doubt been influenced by the lively discussions of memory in world academic circles. I believe that such interest in the past also has something to do with being members of the third generation of the Turkish Republic. The first and second generations followed the modernist and future-oriented vision of the Turkish Republic and turned their backs to the past. For the third generation, however, the futuristic modernization project and the erasure of the past already belong to history. Like many others in Turkey, contributors to this volume define themselves through competing memories of the past instead of the predetermined narrative of the modernist vision. One way they explore some of these memories is to write about them.

The attention the original volume received motivated me to revise the book for English readers. Although the basic idea behind the two volumes is the same, the content is quite different. In its second incarnation, the book has benefited greatly from the public and private discussions that followed publication of the first volume. Moreover, it has been revised for readers who are not necessarily intimately familiar with Turkey. Some articles are substantially revised, and some others are new. A few articles published in the Turkish version are not included in the English version. Thus, the present volume is more like a reminiscence of the original volume than its repetition.

Family and friends helped me through the process of putting the first and second versions of the book together. I owe the greatest thanks to Asena Günal, who encouraged and enabled me to publish the original book. I am also grateful to Mary Seldan Evans of Syracuse University Press for her continual support. As always, Ellen Moodie carefully combed through this introduction and my contribution to the volume. Above all, *The Politics of Public Memory in Turkey* became possible only through the enthusiasm and active engagement of the contributors during the lengthy process of book production.

2

Weaving Modernity, Commercializing Carpets

Collective Memory and Contested Tradition in Örselli Village

Kimberly Hart

> The imagination has become an organized field of social practices, a form
> of work (in the sense of both labor and culturally organized practice), and
> a form of negotiation between sites of agency (individuals) and globally
> defined fields of possibility. . . . The imagination is now central to all
> forms of agency, is itself a social fact, and is the key component of the
> new global order.
>
> Appadurai 1996, 31

Perched on the side of a mountain in the Yuntdağ region of western Turkey,
Örselli village is the center of the Yuntdağ cooperative, a sister to the DOBAG
carpet-weaving project *(Doğal Boya Araştırma ve Geliştirme Projesi,* or Natural
Dye Research and Development Project). The village is uniquely poised as a
location to explore ideas about time and identity because DOBAG has revitalized traditional carpet weaving and reintroduced natural dyeing. In addition to
aiding the villagers economically, the project draws upon an imaginative reinvention of ideas about tradition that are accepted by the people in Örselli as
marketing tools but not as markers of a cultural identity. This essay explores
how the people in Örselli are in the process of coming to terms with modernization, which they experience through material change, and the intersection
of their identities, founded on a homogenous national ethnicity, with an international Muslim community.

When I began my two-year ethnographic research in the village, I was initially surprised to discover that, in addition to introducing significant material, infrastructural, and ideological change, interpretations of the past, carried out in the carpet-weaving project, were highly contested and charged with notions of tradition and modernity. The commodification of traditional weaving contributes to politically charged tensions over the past because it has created a space for contested ideas about cultural identity. These issues emerged in encounters between the villagers and foreign and local researchers, dealers, and tourists. In this essay, the term *tradition* is used not as a conscious or literal enactment of the past, but rather as a component of political ideology against which ideas of modernity are conceptualized and within which people and things are compartmentalized in a global hierarchy of value (Herzfeld 2004). As Michael Herzfeld argues in the case of Greece, "Craftspeople know . . . that their engagement with tradition is a double-edged sword. It exalts them . . . but it also serves to marginalize them from some of the most desirable fruits of modernity" (Herzfeld 2004, 5). In Örselli village, the production of "traditional" carpets in a women's cooperative creates the economic conditions for an improved living standard, which enables peasants to acquire some of the trappings of modernity. The cooperative, however, heightens the villagers' awareness that they are engaged in the commodification of ideas of tradition, which traps them in a performance of authenticity for tourists, dealers, and other visitors.

The foundation of the DOBAG cooperative in 1981 in Örselli village transformed local weaving practices, but it should not be held solely accountable for the commercialization of weaving. Many of the villages in the mountainous and arid Yuntdağ are settlements of former nomads, or Yörük, who have a long history of weaving, herding, and cheese making (J. Anderson 1998; Böhmer 1983; Brüggermann and Böhmer 1983; Black 1985). Until about twenty years ago, textiles, in the form of carpets, sacks, bags, kilims, prayer rugs, and pillows made in rural households, were essential furnishings and the key components of the *çeyiz* (dowry or trousseau; (Atlıhan 1993; Bayatlı 1944a, 1944b, 1945a, 1945b). Although textiles were a necessity and could be construed as traditional in terms of their design and function, they always had a potential market value; they were always a potential commodity. Carpets in particular had a recognized value, and many women carefully preserved carpets in their trousseaux and sold them when the family faced hard times. It is therefore difficult to identify a time when carpet weaving was noncommercial in the Yuntdağ. Weaving today, however, is very different from the first half of the twentieth century. Today it is a cottage industry, devoted entirely to commercial production. Textiles are no longer important household furnishings, and aside from their commercial value, they are not typical components of dowries and slowly have begun to lose their practical function. On an ideological level, however, carpets have value insofar as they are labeled as being "traditional."

Over the past forty years, the region has gradually lost its isolated character due to the construction of roads, the establishment of schools, the increased availability of medical care, and the spread of institutionalized Islam in village mosques, led by imams trained by the state. Villagers have begun to settle in Manisa, the market city to the south, although few have ventured farther afield, and in general, money has become important, desired, and necessary, even for those who want to stay in the village and lead a modest existence. Education pulls the children away, the elderly and the pregnant need medical care outside the village, and all the older people in the village desire to make the once-in-a-lifetime journey to Mecca. In addition to creating a newly mobile population that can imagine long journeys, a significant commute, or permanent resettlement, these activities all require payment in money, as does purchase of the latest appliances, including television sets, satellite dishes, cell phones, refrigerators, gas stoves, and washing machines. Carpet weaving has provided a substantial share of the necessary cash. It is not the commercialization of weaving, increased mobility, or increased consumption, that have become politically sensitive issues, but rather the ideological frameworks within which these activities take place. The commercialization of carpets through the cooperative rests upon the sustained fiction that villagers are leading an authentically rural, isolated, and impoverished existence, governed by tradition.

Development and Ideas of Tradition

The DOBAG project has two cooperatives, one based in Ayvacık and one in the Yuntdağ. The project was developed by Harald Böhmer, a German chemist who moved to Turkey in 1960, and Josephine Powell, an American photographer researching Anatolian flatweaves who moved to Turkey in the mid-1970s. The project is administered by Marmara University in Istanbul. While the project came from "outside," the villagers were active in establishing the cooperative in their village. Today, they organize production on a day-to-day basis. During 2000 and 2001, when I was conducting my research, the entire village was concentrated on this industry, and in general people were working hard to make money, to send their children to school, and to establish their older children in marriage.

While the villagers focus on the future of their families and the day-to-day work of weaving, the carpet-weaving business relies upon an implicit vision of the past, and especially of tradition. The carpets are traditional, in other words, and they are constructed as "antiques of the future," which significantly contributes to their marketability abroad. DOBAG has been well documented by researchers and textile specialists (Anderson 1998; Böhmer 1983; Ger and Csaba 2000; Glassie 1993; Mason 1985; O'Bannon 1990; Thompson 1986). In general, most researchers focus on how a moribund cottage industry has been revitalized. The "return to tradition" (Anderson 1998) implies that the villagers went "back" to something old and revived it; that is a very different orientation to work and perceptions of time than that experienced by the villagers who make the carpets and organize the business as an entrepreneurial strike into the future. The question of whether or not the project is based on a "backwards" or "forwards" motion is related to an "inside/outside" dichotomy. While the villagers know their side of the story, of how DOBAG was founded, and the interfamilial dynamics and power struggles over authority, money, and knowledge, the version of DOBAG that reaches the ears of academics, dealers, and tourists focuses entirely on the outside players. For this reason, the revitalization of weaving, and especially the development of natural dyeing, has been almost wholly attributed to the work of Harald Böhmer (Anderson 1998; Garrett 1988; Ger and Csaba 2000; Landreau 1978; Mason 1985; O'Bannon 1990; Thompson 1986; and conversation with Harald Böhmer and Josephine Powell). In these narratives, the villagers appear passive, the recipients of a German man's careful study of "traditional" and "lost" knowledge of Anatolian natural dyes.

If one judges on the basis of dealer lore, the movement towards natural dyes, which began with DOBAG during the 1980s, has transformed the carpet market. One finds that non-DOBAG dealers in the middle to low end in the covered bazaar in Istanbul, are quick to call all carpets *kök boya,* natural dyed, even when they obviously are not. Natural dyes have entered the realm of dealer lore and are used to construct ideas of value and authenticity (Spooner 1986). In fact, even ordinary textiles, such as head scarves, obviously dyed with chemical dyes, often have *kök boya* printed on the edge, as a mark of quality. The association of *kk boya* with quality has been one of DOBAG's victories.

It is logical to ask why the villages ceased using natural dyes if the dyes were essential to the revitalization of the textile market. Beginning in the late nineteenth century, the knowledge and use of natural dyes throughout Anatolia deteriorated, as chemical dyes, which act quickly and produce striking colors, became readily available (Thompson 1986; Böhmer 1983; Brüggermann and Böhmer 1983). Hawley, the writer of a travelogue, wrote in 1918, some of his observations of weavers in Izmir:

> Once weavers spun their own wool, brewed their own vegetable dyes, and wove patterns embodying ideal thought and subtle symbolism. Now in two large establishments at Smyrna (modern Izmir), the weavers tie knots with machine-spun yarn, which is colored with chemical dyes prepared in the laboratories of Germany, as they follow patterns furnished by their own employers, patterns of older rugs woven in Asia Minor, Persia, or China, or new patterns largely influenced by European taste. (Hawley 1918, 93)

In the Yuntdağ, weavers never dyed their own wool. Itinerant dyers arrived in villages to dye spun wool. Villagers in this region still refer to colors dyed with chemical dyes in their old carpets and kilims by the name of the itinerant dyer. Of course, most manufactured textiles are made from chemically dyed yarns. These tend to be relatively colorfast. Itinerant dyers, however, never seem to have learned fully how to use mordants to prevent the colors from running. Unlike the workshop in İzmir that Hawley observed in the 1910s, which used wool dyed in Germany, village weavings were made with wool and cotton dyed by itinerant dyers. The colors faded to bland and unattractive grays, and the colors ran. Technical problems caused by the dyers, as well as the color schemes favored by the village weavers, caused the market for those textiles to erode. Villagers continued to make them, but there were few buyers. In the meantime, the knowledge of natural dyeing deteriorated. As the market was flooded with cheap manufactured carpets, kilims, bags, and sacks, handmade items disappeared into the hands of collectors. As many said, *"Bunlar çıktı, eskilerle değiştirdik"* ("These [machine-made goods] came, and we changed them for the old ones"). Woven items were made because they had a functional use and not because they were traditional or regarded as special or better. In fact, as the new market blossomed with machine-made textiles, the new textiles were regarded as special because they were different and new.

Memory, Tradition, and DOBAG

Now that the DOBAG has been thriving in the Yuntdağ for more than twenty years, the excitement has begun to wear off, and ideas and feelings about memory and tradition in Örselli have intensified and become political. While conducting my research, I asked about the past because I wanted to know how people had lived in the village during prior generations. This, I thought, would be useful for understanding the social and economic changes. Material change was an important detail in narrations because it set a physical scene, and made the listener aware of the kind of world, which the characters experienced. When someone was telling a story, another person would often add, "That was when we didn't have a road," or "This was before electricity came to the village." The story often had only a tangential relation to material change, but would be told to explain, for instance, why, someone had lit a torch ("because there were no street lights") or what was the significance of cherries (they could only be bought in the market in Manisa, a five-day trip). No one implied that access to convenient sources of power, such as electricity, and accompanying appliances, such as televisions, refrigerators, and cell phones, changed human relationships. That is, they did not explain the social changes, which that had occurred in the village as being a result of new appliances or sources of energy. While visitors to the village are amused by the apparent juxtaposition of modern technology and rural life or balk at what they perceive as its corrupting effects, the villagers do not feel corrupted.

While material changes play an important role in village narratives, ideas of tradition play a role in the narratives of researchers, dealers, and tourists. On the surface, there appears to be a connection between village narratives that employ material change as a pivot around which social transformations are recounted and visitor narratives that employ ideas of tradition, since both sets of ideas (technology and tradition) contain an implicit reference to time. The anthropologist, June Anderson, sums up this perspective in her book on DOBAG, entitled *Return to Tradition*: "In villages today, very little has changed in the technology of carpet making since its early beginnings; women still use the drop spindle for spinning, and weave on the same type of loom as their ancestors did. Villagers shear sheep, card the wool, and dye the skeins much as their forebears did in ancient times. These traditional folkways have survived to this day, an unbroken link with the past." (J. Anderson 1998, 1).

The reality is quite different. Villagers weave today, as they did in the past, but everything about the weaving, from the designs to the uses and the markets, has changed—not just once but countless times. Looms used to produce carpets in the Yuntdağ cooperative are, with few exceptions, metal and not traditional wooden ones. Wool is carded by machine because no one will do this time-consuming and tiring work by hand. Wool is dyed with plants, as it was before the introduction of chemical dyes during the late nineteenth century, but only because Harald Böhmer studied natural dyeing techniques and taught villagers in western Turkey the recipes. Traditional folkways, in other words, exist in relation to contemporary technology, wage-labor, and commodified "traditional" village carpets.

Despite these conflicting narratives about the history of the project and differing impressions about how to describe rural village life today, the villagers are extremely happy to receive visitors. The entire village is focused on the business of weaving and selling carpets; any outsiders, regardless of their nationality or profession, are referred to as "customers." Yet many journalists, documentary film makers, and researchers are not interested in buying carpets; they come to collect information, images, and stories. These people are regarded with some skepticism, especially when they fail to buy a carpet, but everyone hopes that news of the village and of the cooperative will help sell more carpets. DOBAG has a handful of dealers who sell in their own exclusive shops in California, Norway, Ireland, and Australia. The dealers all discovered DOBAG and "fell in love," as one dealer expressed to me, with the project. Initially, dealers were not experts in textiles. Until recently, when the market became tight, most dealers sold DOBAG exclusively. They have devoted a great deal of time and effort as well as money in creating a business around DOBAG carpets and therefore need to gather images and information that help them sell carpets.

In many respects, the dealers and the village carpet makers identify with each other. The dealers' discourse on tradition is not particularly threatening because it is regarded as a way to promote business. The dealers, who have had long-term working relationships with the villagers, are trusted. Tourists usually go to DOBAG villages through groups organized by dealers. These visits are well orchestrated and everyone works to create a positive village experience for the tourists, the majority of whom are older Norwegian textile enthusiasts or Americans looking for an interesting travel adventure. The tourists' perceptions of the village are not particularly important or threatening to the villagers, either, because everyone hopes they will buy carpets and spread the word about the local hospitality and pleasant way of life. Local researchers and journalists, because they can speak Turkish and because their ideas about the local world are readily communicated, are regarded with skepticism. These visitors tend to be the least likely to buy a carpet. Hence, the villagers have concluded that Turkish people do not want to spend their money on such "traditional" objects as carpets. As one weaver expressed very forcefully, "Rich Turks want to take a holiday in America, not buy one of our carpets!" The juxtaposition of a trip to America, the quintessential "modern" place in the imagination of many Turkish people, with a village carpet illustrates a common village perception that "traditional" things, as well as the people who make them, are not respected or highly regarded. They assume that only foreigners value carpets.

While one might argue over whether weaving is traditional or modern, the ideology of tradition, the "unbroken link with the past," is useful for dealers, tourists, and researchers, in that it creates a basis for marketing carpets, fulfills customers' romantic ideas, creates a framework within which visitors make sense of their travel experience, and, for researchers, provides a ready-made narrative. The idea of tradition gives the narratives of researchers, dealers, and visitors to Örselli a structure and creates meaning within their discourse of time and development. The ideology, however, does not have the same meaning in the narratives of villagers. Viewing weaving as "traditional" or "modern" relates to the perspective of the researcher and relater, whether villager, dealer, tourist, or another researcher. Weaving in the Yuntdağ can be regarded as traditional in many ways. Textiles once furnished the house and formed the primary content of dowries; a component of a nomadic heritage, they related to the local herding economy. Today, however, weavers consider their work the equivalent of factory labor, even though it is a cottage industry. For this reason, they complain bitterly about the lack of health insurance and social security. This is not to say, however, that villagers are unaware of the role of the ideology of tradition, which is highly charged with class distinctions.

The point of village narratives about the past is to demonstrate change, whereas the goal of the narratives of dealers and visitors is to eliminate change. The villagers, by rejecting the association with "tradition," are working to insert themselves into the modernist narrative of historical discourse, and to claim their identities as Turks and not as Yörük, nomads. The visitors and researchers, on the other hand, want to attach the idea of tradition not only to the carpets but to the villagers as well. As journalists, tourists, researchers, and dealers describe the village they see before them, they have two different nostalgic reactions, both of which are predicated on an idea of tradition and of purity. This is, as Renato Rosaldo expresses it, "a particular kind of nostalgia, often found under imperialism, where people mourn the passing of what they themselves have transformed" (Rosaldo 1989, 108). In the first reaction, they praise the wholesome purity of village life, and while they praise the village, they express a feeling of sadness for all that is lost in urban Turkey. The second reaction is also tinged with sadness. They bemoan the apparent lost of purity in the village, which they see in modern appliances in the village, cell phones, televisions, and satellite dishes. These appliances, they feel, will corrupt rural society from the outside. In both reactions, the past is pure, the past is traditional; all that is modern is corrupt and corrupting. Visitors are inspired with an emotion that stems from a misinterpretation of both urban and rural societies in Turkey. Their heavy feelings of nostalgia for worlds they do not know and do not understand are increased by guilt over "ruined" purity.

Paradoxes of Tradition and Memory

In contrast to nostalgia, which connects visitor narratives of the present to the past, the villagers are connected to the past through collective memory. As discussed by historians and anthropologists, memory, or, as it is dealt with in this essay, "collective memory," is generally distinguished from history, as a practice, whether physical (as in craft and ritual) or oral (songs, stories, poetry), in which knowledge is transmitted from one generation to the next (Bahloul 1996, 128; Boyarin 1992; Yerushalmi 1982). In the transmission of memory, identification and knowledge of a particular place (Bahloul 1996), stories, songs or poems, and crafts or artistic forms help form a basis of a common identity, a sense of community, and especially the continuity of the past into the present. In this sense, memory does not have to be written; it can be expressed and transmitted orally or through action, and may be taught without recourse to records. The elderly are the most obvious link to the past through their stories, but people also engage with memory in other ways, through socializing their children, through their work, by living in a landscape steeped in the past, and, as already indicated, through objects—such as carpets.

A paradox of tradition and memory in Örselli is that the people have ambivalent feelings about the past and deny any connection to it, but simultaneously demonstrate a strong sense of collective identity. Village life has a rhythm structured by Islamic practice, changing seasons, and major life events marked by rituals and memory inscribed in the land. The people express a strong sense of collective identity and communal solidarity, grounded in part in a nonverbal demonstration of collective memory. One example of how collective memory is inexplicit but inscribed is in place-names for fields, wild pastures, wells, and watering holes. People experience the land, its small formations, as being inscribed with human history. This history is consciously remembered in the names of places and the ownership of property (fields, trees, wells, gardens, pastures). Although the land is inscribed with the signs of memory, the exact details are often forgotten; this is particularly surprising in the case of wells and watering holes created after a person's death as a good deed *(hayır yapmak)*. One would think that these useful places (water being very scarce) would help people remember the person being commemorated. However, when I asked, for example, for whom a well was dug, the person usually had been forgotten unless he or she had died in the past decade. Also surprising was the nonchalance that accompanied such forgetting. While I was surprised that everyone forgot, my informants were surprised that they should be expected to remember. The memory of specific individuals was expected to vanish. In fact, the people in Örselli demonstrate that remembering specific individuals is not important and may even be negative, as it isolates individuals and forces them to recall the past.

Similarly, history, which relies upon inscribed information and on details of individuals' lives, is regarded with suspicion. The ambivalence with which people view remembering the dead relates to the emphasis villagers put on the fleetingness of life, and the human illusion of stability in the face of divine, absolute, and incomprehensible order. When I asked about the deceased and life in the past, many older people began sadly to make remarks about *"yalan dünya"* (world of illusion) and *"kim geldi, kim geçti"* (who has come, who has gone). Many also asked, surprised and somewhat upset, "Why do you want to talk about those people who are dead now?" The "world of illusion," a phrase and sentiment often used in Turkish folk music, describes the spiritual orientation of villagers. They imagine this world to be an illusion but the afterlife to be real. *Yalan dünya* questions our notion of reality on a fundamental level. It also expresses the hubris of human beings who, each in their individual worlds, imagine that their thoughts, feelings, pains, and pleasures are important. Stacked up against the inevitability of death, the incomprehensibility of existence, and the relentless predictability of one's own life, individual concerns are insignificant; from the villagers' standpoint, all people really are living a lie. In a very complex way collective memory entwines daily life (work, environment), belief systems, a relationship to the past, and a process of forgetting individual lives. Furthermore, collective memory should be distinguished from the expectation that people have a coherent, chronological narrative of the past. This fixed chronology is not memory, but history. In this sense, the codified past is history in which memory and tradition are lost.

While there is a strong sense of collective memory in the village, it does not take the form of explicit ideas of tradition or history. For instance, although weaving is an important industry in the village, no one acknowledges or wants to acknowledge that women have been weaving in the village for many generations and that their weaving demonstrates the connection between the past and the present. The connection with the past can be seen in the mosque, which has many old carpets; they illustrate both the history of weaving and the practice of donating a carpet to the mosque as a good deed upon the death of a mother or father. Although weavers show their knowledge of a practice, which that has passed to them from their female ancestors, weaving is not acknowledged as having important roots. Villagers are even reluctant to admit that weaving might express a group or local identity, even though the cooperative is careful to include only regional designs in its repertoire. The designs that are included in the DOBAG collection have more to do with marketability than authenticity. For instance, every girl had a *deve halt* (camel carpet) in her dowry. This carpet is never woven today because it has no commercial value; it does not look traditional enough to be a "traditional carpet." Today, old carpets are used for design reference, and village weavers often look at old carpets in mosques in neighboring villages for new design ideas. These textiles act as reference works on design, drawn upon for new weavings, thereby synthesizing design and artistic forms across generations. However, looking at old things, such as carpets, to get ideas for new ones, marks a disjuncture with older practice. Now people look for a pattern they hope will sell. With a breakdown in the utility of textiles, other than as a source of income, designs became dislodged from specific places and began to travel more freely as women wove designs they liked or that were new to them.

This relaxed attitude about locally characteristic or "traditional" design is similar to the easy relationship people have with new technology. Just as designs are resurrected and become valuable because they sell, the villagers follow the latest fashions, tossing out obsolete practices and things as new ones come along. They never go out of their way to maintain an old practice if a newer, easier method appears. In the past, for instance, cheese was packed in earthenware jugs and put in the river *(dere peyniri)*. Today cheese is packed in plastic jugs and put in the refrigerator. The elderly will remark that "*dere peyniri* tasted much better than today's cheese," but no one goes to the trouble to recreate an old cheese. From the village perspective, a person who would carry difficult-to-obtain and heavy earthenware jars packed with cheese to the river would be wasting time and energy. Perhaps in time some enterprising individual will begin recreating this cheese for the exclusive market in regional specialties.

The implementation of these practices is motivated by practical and not ideological concerns. Not only do people in the village seem uninterested in maintaining old practices, they seem threatened by the possibility that some aspect of their lives could be labeled as old or traditional, as though that could negatively reflect on them. Since they are not indifferent to such a possibility but rather react negatively to it, they show that ideas of tradition and modernity are ideologically charged. The people in Örselli village think of themselves as being on the cutting edge, and they disparage their neighbors in other villages as being *"geri kafalı"* (backward). The villagers' designation of their communal identity as modern is connected with their entrepreneurial spirit, which they have invested in the cooperative. Even their neighbors note that "Örselli is more *açık* (open)," a statement that implies both that Örselli residents are inventive and hardworking and that they are a little shameless in their readiness to expose themselves to foreign influence and money.

While some aspects of material change were adopted with alacrity, other transformations seem to have been accepted as inevitable. In these cases, the relationship with old things is expressed in a strangely passive manner. Women will say, for example, about carpets, that *"makinalar (makina halı) çıktı"* (machine-made carpets emerged). Or they may say, "I switched my carpets for machine-made ones" *("halılarımı makinalar ile değiştirdim")*. In fact, many did "switch" their handwoven carpets for machine-made ones. Itinerant collectors of old things *(eskici)* still travel to villages with plastic goods and machine-made mats and carpets to trade new for old. In their description of material change, the people of Örselli appear to imagine themselves as passive receptors *("çıktı"* emerged, *"geldi"* came, *"değişti"* changed) of whatever is new— machine-made carpets, woven plastic sacks, and so on. At the same time, they emphasize the convenience of machine-made things and plastic bags over handmade textiles, demonstrating the active role they take in trading in old things for new ones. Once I asked a young woman about whether she had in her dowry a particular handwoven bag that is used to carry food and water and has many other uses in the fields far from home, for example as a sitting mat, a pillow, or as protection for one's back against heavy firewood bundles. It seemed not only a traditional item, but one with a continuing variety of uses. When she said she did not have one, I naïvely asked what she would take with her to the fields. Her response was breezy and clear: "I'll take a plastic bag instead!" Like many young women, she was probably hoping that her marriage would take her out of the village and away from the chores that would require a woven bag. Having one in her dowry would not make her proud of her traditional heritage or identity, but rather would suggest the future drudgery of village labor.

While visitors, researchers, and dealers all travel the rocky road to Örselli for carpets, weaving is only grudgingly recognized as being connected to the past in any significant way. People in the village usually argued that they keep sheep and weave in order to live, because they lack arable land. They did not acknowledge a historical tradition, even though they know that their grand-parents did more or less the same types of work that they do today. This con-nection seemed accidental to them; if suddenly their village were transported to a region with good farmland or other amenities, like a factory, they believed they would toss aside the work they do now and pick up new skills immedi-ately. That is, their identity was disconnected from what they do every day: herding sheep, weaving carpets, and making cheese. They did not regard these practices as having an inherent value or as having an explicit significance, at least insofar as they made verbal claims to identifying with the past. They were also actively denying their nomadic heritage. As a young Turkish scholar told me recently, many urban people in Turkey are offended when she says that Turks were nomadic. Not only do they not care about that history, but they feel they are being insulted. As Herzfeld notes a similar reaction among arti-sans in Greece: "In general, artisans and modernity appear increasingly to be viewed as categorically incompatible with each other, except in the sense that quaintness can itself become a resource for enterprising artisans in a world in which it seems to be in short supply" (Herzfeld 2004, 60). The villagers in Örselli are reacting to the nostalgic impulses of visitor narratives, which ossify them in a cultural museum. They further suspect that these well-meaning im-pulses would shut them off from being recognized as full citizens of the state. Denying the past helps strip them of cultural difference, which interferes with their allegiance to a national, homogenous, and modernist Turkish identity.

Müzelik: Objectifying the Past

The cooperative, which brought a measure of prosperity to the village, has re-arranged the stratification of social order. The effects of increased income are evident in the structure of houses across the three distinct generational groups in the village. The generation of elders have simple one—or two-room houses, while members of the middle generation have three-room houses, and those of the youngest generation have four rooms. The quantity of household goods also differs markedly across the generations. These inequalities demonstrate in material terms how generations have had access to varying levels of income. The houses also show how previous generations have invested as much as they possibly can to establish their children in marriage, which is interpreted as a meritorious act. For those left behind, the stratification of levels of consumption affects their conceptualizations of time and tradition, as the objects surrounding them remind them.

One indicator of tension about the idea of the past in the village is in the concept of *müzelik,* meaning "a museum piece" or "an old thing." The term might seem to imply remembering, since museums are often thought of as places where memories are stored, but used colloquially, it means old, objectified junk. One day I visited Fatma, who is about sixty-five years old, and she used the term *müzelik* with special effect to describe her house. This is because she lives in one of the few traditional houses, and Harald Böhmer, with only the best of intentions and with the greatest respect for both Fatma and her house, takes visitors to meet her and see what all houses used to be like, about twenty-five years ago. Visitors are curious and respectful, but Fatma still suffers.

Fatma has a two-room stone house with an earthen roof. The outer room is empty except for her loom, which is beside the window, giving her natural light for weaving. The inner room has an open hearth. The central area is used for all the household activities: eating, sleeping, sitting, and cooking. In the back of the room there is a raised platform stretching from wall to wall. In the middle of the platform is a single pole *(direk),* which supports a curtain. The curtain stretches to the right wall of the house and covers a line of sacks, filled with wheat and bulgur. Behind the sacks is the *banyo* (bath), a tiny booth with a wooden door and a drain to the outside, the *yüklük* or bedding pile, and next to that, Fatma's *çeyiz sandığı,* her dowry chest. To the left are shelves with simple kitchen utensils. This is the cooking section. The floor is covered with overlapping carpets, kilims, and blankets. One sits on *minder* (floor cushions). A high shelf runs along the entire room, and *torba* (bags) are hung on hooks along with a few sparse pieces of clothing. Fatma's house, unlike similar houses of other elderly women, is fully functioning and well kept. At the same time, its interior is quintessentially traditional, in that it resembles a nomadic tent (Atlıhan 1993, 77; J. Anderson 1998, 68). Everything is packed away neatly and only brought out for some purpose.

Fatma is deeply ashamed of the same qualities that visitors like about her house. As I sat with her, she said repeatedly, *"Benim ev çirkin!"* (My house is ugly). When I asked why it is ugly, she paused for a few moments and then said: *"Eski, eski bir ev"* (It's an old house). I said, "For that reason you find it ugly?" She confirmed that, nodding her head. As with all the old people who protested that their houses are old and ugly, I pointed out that her house is made of stone with an earthen roof and is cozy in the winter and cool in the summer, unlike the stifling hot and freezing cold brick and tile of newly built homes. Everyone immediately agrees that their homes are more comfortable than the new ones, but they still express shame over living in an old-style house. I drew the floor plan of Fatma's house, and all the while she and her husband argued about whether their house was ugly or not. In the end, Fatma admitted that she is embarrassed when tourists come to see her house. It is not the house itself that she finds problematic but rather showing it to people. Fatma tends to mutter and occasionally interject, *"müzelik!"* when she feels that she and her things are being singled out as being "old." She finds this process of objectifying her house, dating her, and also, importantly, showing how she is too poor to fill in the hearth, tile the roof, and buy furniture very disturbing.

A house, then, demonstrates a connection to the past, just as the land is inscribed with memory and carpets are visual texts of design traditions. In the case of houses, the connection is not useful or relevant and in fact points out how the owner cannot afford a new house. As the past becomes *müzelik*, it obfuscates experience and confuses an order that people in the village believe must happen: that old things must make way for the new. The names of people who die are forgotten, and no one attempts to attach a memory of a person to a place. When people die, their houses are allowed to fall apart and crumble. A bride, everyone says, would never "enter" an old house *(gelin girmez)*, meaning that although many of the older women in the village took over an old house when they married, standards have risen and only the new houses are regarded as suitable today for a bride. The past, in other words, is in the past, finished and irrelevant.

The people in Örselli seem to demonstrate a wariness that any discussion of the past will lead to objectification, which will become an obfuscating historical narrative. It is better, from this perspective, to allow the past to be buried by time and forgetfulness. The past, if it is selectively forgotten, cannot be a source for historical narration or a basis for generalized abstractions, because it is gone. In effect, the past is preserved by forgetting. The lives of those who are dead are not threatened by interpretation in the present. If details are forgotteon, they cannot threaten the present or prevent people from adopting a new, more convenient, or more comfortable life.

"You Have No Nice Traditions"

While the people in Örselli share a sense of collective memory, they do not objectify their lives or their practices as being traditional. They do not self-consciously create an historical narrative, that would single out their region as special. Instead, they selectively forget individuals, tribal names and references, and accounts of the past. This process of forgetting enables them to insert themselves into a national narrative of Turkish history and primes them as full citizens of the republic, where they will be able to have the same advantages and services as any other person.

DOBAG has politicized ideas about the past in the village because it markets the carpets each household weaves as traditional. Researchers, tourists, and dealers therefore assume that not only are the carpets traditional but so are the people. They also assume that by visiting one can discover tradition, living representations of the past. As Rosaldo writes in his essay, "Imperialist Nostalgia," we need to ask who is doing the reflecting, who needs to reimagine, reinvent, research, and remember. Rosaldo suggests that the ones who remember are those who are detached: the historian and the anthropologist (Rosaldo 1989, 108). In Örselli there are many others who likewise attempt the trip from a contemporary modern present into a traditional world of the past: the casual visitor from the city below who is exploring the mountains; the tourist led by a dealer who has flown halfway around the world; the journalist and documentary film maker who command the weavers to perform for the camera; and the researcher looking for a subject for her thesis. The meeting, which takes place on village soil, is not always comfortable as conflicting conceptualizations of time, memory, history, tradition, economy, society, and life itself clash. A pleasant consensus might be ethnographic fictions; in relation to her ethnographic work in Algeria, Joelle Bahloul discusses how her informants may have altered their stories because they knew how they would be used. "My ethnographic fiction entered my informants' reality and fiction and reality merged in the writing project. Collective memory claimed to become a historical discourse while being written from an outsider's viewpoint" (Bahloul 1996, 8). The project of research then, whether historical or ethnographic or some combination of the two, may be implicated in these dangerous processes, in objectifying, in contributing to obfuscating discourses in essentialisms, and in imperialist nostalgia. These meetings are often painful for both villagers and visitors, as illustrated in the following story.

An Ethnographic Story

It was the end of December, the holiday after Ramazan, and the village was filled with relatives from Manisa. I was sitting with ten or twelve people in the only warm room in the house where I lived with the president of the cooperative and her husband. A fire was burning in the wood stove, and the television was on. Suddenly, unexpected visitors arrived, a woman and two men. The visitors did not introduce themselves, and no one asked their names. The woman merely mentioned that she was a friend of Şerefe Atlıhan, the quality-control expert from Marmara University, whom everyone has known for many years. The woman had come to look at the rugs to do research. She said she was looking for Mehmet, the director of the cooperative, and she needed to see a loom. A few of us had been leaning against the warps on a loom, using it as a backrest. The woman pulled out a camera, and we got out of her way so she could photograph it.

The researcher took her snap shots and began quizzing Mehmet, the director. Aysu and Emine, the president and key manager of the cooperative, were waiting to be noticed by this researcher. There were many other women in the room as well who weave, and they too were apparently invisible. The researcher was interested in carpet weaving, for what end we did not know; presumably she was interested not only in the product but also in the process, which would entail asking a weaver—a woman—about weaving. She did not ask, however; she was focused on things as signs of a traditional village life.

Without being polite—and in the village politeness is highly valued—she mentioned that she wanted to see the rug depot. In order to go, she needed some help from Mehmet, the director, who was casually stretched out with the rest of us on the floor. It was clear he was not going to leap up for this woman. She asked him if the women were happy with the cooperative and about various traditions, clothing, and music. She asked if the village was old, "at least four hundred years old?" Mehmet said it was. For half a second, I wondered why he agreed so readily, since I knew he did not know, or at least he had not known when I asked. It was at this juncture that a discussion about time and tradition began. The researcher began to complain about how "they" do not have any "traditions" in this area, no nice clothing, no *davul* and *zurna* (drum and reeded instrument) at weddings. I was debating whether or not I would reveal myself, when I blurted out, "Well, why do you think these traditions are so important?" The question threw her off. She seemed to think that it was self-evident that traditions exist and are a good thing. Although I had blown my cover, I decided I would ask about this issue of traditions, which had in fact irked me considerably.

After explaining who I was and what I was doing there, a conversation began. As an example of this question of tradition, I told her that when I had talked to elderly women in the villages about traditional clothing, specifically a garment called the *üçetek* (literally, "three skirts"), I got many different responses. Some women said that the *üçetek* was annoying, too hot, or too expensive, but others remembered it fondly as much prettier that modern clothes. Some described in vivid detail girls strutting down the path to the well with the long colorful tassels of their *arkaleş* (small pieces of flatweave) swaying under the earthenware jugs on their backs. Their lively and nostalgic descriptions touched on how attractive and even sexy girls were when decked out in multicolored clothing with swaying, jangling, heavy beads and sequins. Still other women, I told the researcher, had patted various parts of their bodies and said that the *üçetek* "wanted" this and that, indicating the many layers, the weight, and the heat of all the cloth. Moreover, I remarked, the fact that all these different responses came out of a single village shows how everyone has different ideas and different memories about clothing. I was about to point out that if everyone's views about clothing varied so significantly, so too would their ideas about other things, such as this hazy notion of "tradition," when Mehmet, the director, got excitedly joined the conversation.

Mehmet began to analyze the *üçetek* and the practice of wearing clothing in practical and historical terms. He remarked that if I were dressed only in a shirt, sweater, *şalvar* (loose, pleated trousers), and head scarf (as all of the village women and myself were dressed in that room), and then I were to sit on the cold ground, I would be sorry that I was not wearing the *üçetek* and the *kuşak* (a triangular shawl worn with the *üçetek* around the waist). He was right, of course.

In essence, Mehmet was arguing that a common practice such as wearing certain clothing comes about because it has a function. When the *üçetek* lost its use-value, it ceased to be worn. The researcher turned to me to "explain" Mehmet's answer, seeming quite unaware that his response was utterly unrelated to her assertion that tradition is a steadfast code, inherently good and valuable, and is the basis of identity. From her perspective, when tradition vanishes, it has been corrupted from the outside. Her argument echoed ironically in the room because she represented in her body, mannerisms, and occupation the same kind of outside influence she was criticizing. She did not see that Mehmet was very clearly divorcing tradition, as an ideological construct, from practice. For the people in the village, it is not age that makes something like clothing valuable, but utility.

Finally taking notice of the women in the room, the researcher turned to Aysu, the president of the cooperative, and asked if there were any *üçetek* left in the village. Aysu said, very bluntly, that all the old *üçetek* had been burnt. Since I knew this was not true, I quietly concluded that Aysu was forestalling a search for old clothing. Moreover, her calculated bluntness and assertion of the violent fate of old traditional clothing seemed designed to shock the researcher. Predictably, the researcher was horrified that, with such apparent wanton disregard for the unquestioned value of the past, the villagers had burnt their heritage. In fact, the only *üçetek* left in the village were the wedding dresses of women who had married before 1970, when the white wedding dress first made its appearance and became the standard wedding costume for brides. Furthermore, because most women had very few items of clothing—generally one outfit to wear while the other was being washed—it would be unlikely that masses of old clothing could have survived. The villagers in the Yuntdağ had no surplus clothing, nor did they have finely made clothing. It was clear that this woman had never realized that poverty is stronger than "tradition."

The conversation about clothing was interesting because it immediately showed the very practical and experience-oriented knowledge of the villagers, in contrast to the woman's knowledge of "tradition," which was divorced from experience. She might have learned, as she claimed, about Anatolian traditions by visiting villages, and not just through books, but her knowledge, whether from conversation or texts, was still abstract and removed from practical understanding. It seemed she had no notion of the material reality of life in the villages, nor why clothing might have changed over time.

I asked her again, "What is the value of traditions?" A visitor from a coastal town who had studied at the university and whose family is originally from the Yuntdağ, jumped in and said that traditions are worthless if they are just nostalgic expressions. He said to the researcher that she "thinks it's nice in the village because it is different, but that she would think otherwise if she were to live here." He imagined that she thought the village was a natural, traditional place. She responded by saying that she "did not think it was nice here," which naturally astounded everyone. In her view, the village, with its tiled roofs, satellite dishes, and cell phones was a corruption of a "real" village. Perhaps becoming aware of her tremendous faux pas, she began to modify her position by saying that the *oya* (crocheted or needlework edging on head scarves) and carpets made today in the village are "traditional," which also served to justify her visit. I said that the carpets and *oya* are actually modern, which I knew she would not understand because she did not know what the purpose of carpet weaving was, nor did she make or wear *oya*. She would therefore have had no experience of how *oya* patterns travel around the country and are enthusiastically copied by women seeking the latest, newest, and most fashionable decoration for their head scarves. She also seemed to imagine that the carpets were the unthinking product of centuries of women weaving and not a product for foreign markets. It seems she had created her own nostalgic reality and was searching for signs of it in villages. She was disappointed when nothing seemed to match her expectations and excited when she found something appeared to confirm them. From the discussion that day, it was clear to me and to the other people in the room (but not to the researcher) that "tradition" is an assessment devised from the outside, after practice has disappeared. It also seemed that the ideological role of tradition is to create groundwork for the development of a historical consciousness.

Conclusion

The people in Örselli use "tradition" to objectify their lives and their experiences. Their work in founding the cooperative required trust in outsiders, new knowledge and techniques of natural dyeing, a strategic use of local design, and a clever use of ideas about tradition to market the carpets to dealers and tourists. The result is a business that has survived for more than twenty years, and new prosperity for village families, which has enabled them to buy consumer goods, educate their children, and make pilgrimage to Mecca. The villagers are pleased with the results of their hard work, although they are troubled by the objectification of tradition when applied to their lives.

Michael Herzfeld argues, as I quoted earlier, that craftspeople discover that, "engagement with tradition is a double-edged sword" (Herzfeld 2004, 5). In a world of mass-produced goods, crafts are replications of an imagined past, a literal objectification of ideas of authenticity or cultural markers of an exalted history. From the woven heritage of former nomads, textiles in the villages of the Yuntdağ evolved from essential household goods that furnished the house into commercialized knotted carpets for sale abroad. Once, textiles were as utilitarian as they were mysteriously beautiful. Now villagers struggle to hit on the right configuration of motifs and size and the correct juxtaposition of colors to appeal to foreign buyers. Everyday household goods are plastic bags, woven fiberglass sacks, and machine-made carpets and kilims. While new production textiles are not exciting to discerning collectors because they do not have the patina of age, DOBAG markets its carpets as "antiques for the future."

Villagers are confronted with a complex mixture of curiosity, quest for objectifying historical narratives, and authenticity in both material culture and village life through visitors, tourists, and researchers, who come to buy carpets and collect information on "traditional" carpet weaving. From the village perspective, the importance of these perceptions is ranked in relation to the probability that a visitor will buy a carpet. Unfortunately, Turkish visitors, whether journalists, researchers, or casual tourists, are the least likely to buy a carpet, the most likely to openly criticize the village, the most likely to insult the villagers with their notions of "tradition," and the most likely to be understood on all these counts because they speak Turkish. Dealers are well tolerated, because, like the cooperative workers, they are trying to survive by selling DOBAG carpets. Tourist narratives are the least likely to be understood, since the tourists do not speak Turkish. Tourists are not taken very seriously; they are foreigners, after all, and no one expects them to understand what is happening. Turkish visitors, therefore, are the most problematic because the villagers expect an ideological closeness with them. Both are presumably, from the village point of view, Turks and Muslims. Many visitors, especially researchers, understand how to be polite in the village setting, but those who do not, disappoint their hosts and cause them to reassess the other regions of Turkey and measure them up against the Yuntdağ.

While there is a heightened sensitivity about interpretations of tradition, the villagers live and work in an environment inscribed with collective memory. There is a truncated past that does not stretch any deeper than hazy memories of grandparents, yet also an inexplicit but strong collective identity, an embodied cultural memory in work and crafts. The result is the construction of a notion of the present that draws on an inexplicit reference to memory, a rejection of alternative ethnic and social identities, such as being Yörük, from the state-based one of Turkishness, and a forward-looking business in carpet production. Since DOBAG explicitly draws on a notion of tradition in carpet design, weaving techniques, materials, and natural dyes, it is not surprising that visitors (whether researchers, tourists, or dealers) expect to see a manifestation of tradition in the lives of the villagers. The resulting encounters are often uncomfortable. As Fatma suffers under the sensation that her home is being objectified as *müzelik,* other villagers have declared that they have "burned" all signs of the past so that any potential future connection between these objects and their lives will be impossible. This shows us that between the village and the urban regions to the south, an ideological and even a philosophical conflict arises over notions of memory and tradition. The villagers hoped to isolate the objectification of tradition and memory to the carpets. They find, however, that in the complex dynamics of ideologies and objects, in the global and national marketplaces of ideas (not only commodities), they are concerned by the very notions of tradition and authenticity they have used to gain new prosperity.

3

Stories in Three Dimensions

Narratives of Nation and the
Anatolian Civilizations Museum

Aslı Gür

Since its consolidation in the 1930s and 1940s, the cultural politics of the Turkish state has produced pervasive institutionalized narratives and symbols in the national public sphere.[1] The official ideologies have deeply touched the lives and the consciousness of the citizens through state interventions in mass media, literature, history writing, art, and education. Consequently, it is not surprising that state-sponsored representational practices that are inextricably interwoven with the official public imageries of nation, modernity, and development have long been paradigmatic issues for students of Turkish history. However, in the substantial scholarship on the relationship between nation-state and nationalist cultural reproduction in Turkey, two neglected lines of inquiry are striking.

First, few studies pay attention to the reception of the cultural products of the state institutions. Usually students of the cultural policies in the nation-building processes judge the power of nationalist discourses and narratives re-

1. I would like to thank Müge Göçek, Selim Deringil, George Steinmetz, Esra Özyürek, Julia Hell, and the fellows of the 2003–4 Global Ethnic Literatures seminar at the University of Michigan for their insightful comments on the various versions of this essay. I am particularly grateful to Ayşe Öncü for starting me off in this project and opening the doors of narrative analysis for me. I am also indebted to Nazan Atasoy for helping me formulate my interview questions, to Esra Özyürek for her unabated patience and encouragement, and to Tolga Könik, Yusuf Gür, and Zeynep Gür for their various kinds of assistance and support.

produced in the state institutions by their pervasiveness in the texts of the cultural products. The significance of the context and mode of interaction between these institutions and their target communities is neglected. The problem with such an approach is that, simply by not engaging with the question of reception, the ability of the receivers to interpret the products and the practices of schools, museums, and other state agencies regulating language, media, and collective memory is undermined. Thus, citizens are granted no agency to negotiate or subvert the messages encoded in the representational practices of these state institutions.[2]

How do the citizens experience the state's cultural politics amd institutions? How do they negotiate the meanings of the symbols and the narratives offered through museums, schools, canonical literature, and media? This study addresses these questions by focusing on one of the earliest cultural projects in the republic's history, the Anatolian Civilizations Museum (ACM), and its visitors. The ACM is significant to the state's nationwide museumification project, primarily because its foundation and development in Ankara and the discourse it embodies have been paradigmatic for later small-city museum projects in Anatolia. To understand the dominant narrative of the museum, this study first examines the institutionalization process is first examined from a historical perspective. After delineating the nature of the official cultural politics of the formative period and examining how they shaped the narrative of the museum exhibition, it explores the ways in which the dominant narrative mediates the visitor's experience of the museum through the special arrangements by which is its represented. Finally, an analysis of local visitors' narratives on their experiences of the exhibit provides insight into how the visitors engage with, reject, or negotiate the meaning of the museum's collection. Such an approach illuminates the current readings of the signification practices of the early years of the republic, providing access to a slice of the

2. Among the many definitions of *agency*, I base my conceptualization on Judith Butler's definition. Unlike other perspectives that focus on agency embedded in revolutionary forces and resistances that are often conceived as "outside" and "against" power, Butler conceptualizes *agency* as discursively proliferating through power networks with unintended consequences, operating "in a relation of contingency and reversal to the power that makes it possible, but to which it nevertheless belongs" (1997, 15).

collective memory. Ultimately, it enables us to explore popular critiques of the official narrative and to challenge the state hegemony on the regulation and definition of the cultural heritage.

Why should we study museums and their visitors rather than other public cultural institutions and their target audiences? This question brings us to the second line of inquiry that is neglected in the scholarship on the Turkish state's nation-building cultural projects: the study of archeological museums as public representations of official discourses on nation, modernity, and progress. The relatively small number of studies pertaining to the effects of official discourses about culture and history on the museumification processes in Turkey is particularly surprising in light of the fact that today, in almost every Turkish city, there is a local archaeological museum. Since the 1940s, more than fifty state-funded archaeological museums have been established throughout the country. The substantial resources devoted to the excavations and the exhibitionary practices in the early years of the republic—a period characterized by resource shortages and scarcity—is one of the major indicators of the significance that the state elite attached to the museumification of the archaeological findings as part of the nation-building projects of the time. Each year thousands of people in Turkey visit archaeological museums. Still, we know very little about how local visitors experience these spaces and how they read the stories museums tell in three dimensions. Therefore, studies of archaeological museums in Turkey are momentous, exploring them as sites where nationalism is signified, collective identities are mediated, and visitors imagine the nation, its past, and its future.

Since Benedict Anderson's call to pay attention to the significance of museums as representations of postindependence nation-states (1983), museum studies have flourished in cultural studies. British cultural studies, in particular, by focusing on how museums represent imagined pasts and perpetuate certain powerful discursive repertoires, underlined the influence of museums on collective memory and knowledge production in a particular community.[3] This approach has opened new venues for studying museums and highlighted the

---

3. For some of the best examples of museum representations of nationalism written from this perspective, see the volumes edited by Macdonald and Fyfe (1996); Boswell and Evans (1999); and Bal, Crewe, and Spitzer (1999).

role of their visitors in constructing and reproducing the meaning of the museum narratives. In a similar vein, this study places visitors' narratives at the core of analyses of the interaction between representations of official ideologies and the public, and demonstrates the significance of the people's active interpretation in terms of the ways in which state cultural products generate social effects.

Nationalism and Archaeology in Europe and in the Middle East

Scholars of archaeology and nationalism have demonstrated that postcolonial nationalist practices of archaeology emerge simultaneously as a reaction to colonial powers and as a celebration of young nations' newly achieved right to write their own histories. With the advent of the League of Nations and other attempts to organize the world internationally after the First World War, communities had to compete for sovereignty and independence over a given territory. Legitimization of their claims depended largely on a skillful mobilization of knowledge of the political and symbolic fields whose boundaries were set according to Wilsonian principles (notably the right to self-determination) and positivism. In such a context, it is hardly surprising that disciplines such as history, anthropology, and archaeology came to the fore as vigorous fields of national-identity construction.

Archaeological excavations and exhibitions of the archaeological artifacts are key practices in the spatio-temporal construction and representation of the nation.[4] What distinguishes the nation from other communities is that the community imagines its identity as tied to a territory and homogeneous within the national borders. Consequently, the historization of the ties imagined between the territory and the human collective living in it constitutes the core of nation-building projects and a crucial aspect of the nation-states' cultural politics. Archaeology, because of its integral relation to both land and culture,

---

4. Within the specific literature on how archeological practices have been interpreted for the ideological purposes of national and colonial history writing around the world, I find the volumes by Silberman (1989), Kohl and Fawcett (1995), and Meskell (1998) most profound and useful.

plays a special role in bridging the national territory and the imagined past of the nation.

Constructing archaeology as a practice of knowledge production independent from the nation-state's ideological intervention requires intense institutional and representational struggle. Nation-states have always found archaeology an attractive field in which to intervene, particularly for the discursive possibilities it opens up for the mobilization of official ideologies.[5] These interventions have had some positive results, such as the rapid progress the field has made as a result of the funding postcolonial nation-states have channeled toward its development. However, intervention has also established the dominant nationalist ideologies as the main frame of reference for interpreting archeological findings. Consequently, archeological discourses are frequently mobilized to provide a "scientific basis" for ethnic discrimination, racist politics, and culturally essentialist history-writing practices (Chernykh 1995; Silberman 1995).[6]

In the Middle East, archaeological practices and discourses on the prehistoric past had their start as British, German, and French endeavors to uncover the roots of Western civilization. Questions such as, "When was the first city

5. Some of the most interesting cases in which nationalist views seeped into the interpretation of the archaeological findings can be found in Sumathi Ramaswamy's 2001 essay on how Tamil nationalism has been reconstructed through the interpretation of the findings in the Indus Valley and in Neil Silberman's 1995 book on similar practices in Israel, Egypt, Cyprus, and Macedonia.

6. Nationalist archaeology should not be interpreted as a subverted version of an otherwise "purely scientific" discipline (Silberman 1995; Trigger 1995). In every period, contemporary political, economic, and social power relations influence all sciences, including archeology. For example, under the colonial regimes, archaeological practices were interrelated with the political and social dynamics of colonialism. As Michael Rowlands (1994) argues, colonial archeological practices that interpreted local prehistorical developments as part of the development of a world civilization, described civilization Eurocentrically. Thus, these practices provided ideological support for colonial enterprises and legitimated the civilizing missions of the European empires; by tearing apart the history of the geographical area to be colonized from its current inhabitants, they aided the contruction of essentialized differences between the colonizer and the colonized. For example, the particular way in which Mesopotamia was constructed through archaeological discourse provided the ideological context for colonization of the region by the British (Bahrani 1998).

built?" "Whose idea was it to use coins?" "Who sowed the first seed and started a settled, agrarian life?" "Where was the first poem composed?" motivated the earliest excavations. As one after another European archeologist uncovered ancient sites of life and settlement, the antecedents of what are deemed to be the pillars of Western civilization—the city, the monetary system, the state, literature, the archive, the library, and so on—emerged in the lands of "the Orient." The nineteenth-century Orientalist discourses defined European civilization in terms of its opposition to the Oriental Other; consequently, archaeological findings funded by the same Orientalist institutions that located the origins of European civilization in the lands of the Other highlighted a fundamental inner tension of the Orientalist discourses. This tension was often relieved by the proliferation of narratives based on another binary opposition, this time not between the Oriental and the Western but between the early inhabitants of Mesopotamia and Anatolia and the "Orientals" inhabiting the same territories today (Hodder 1998). A connection between the ancient civilizations and the "backward" people of the region was inconceivable within the Orientalist paradigm as this would indicate an inextricable link between the Orientals and the Europeans, conceptualized in many ways to be diametrical opposites of one another. Hence, the Orientalist discourses asserting incommensurable difference between East and West, and the contemporary power relations based on these discourses in the nineteenth century, were translated into a difference between the early and the current inhabitants of Mesopotamia and Anatolia through the anthropological, archaeological, and historical knowledge production of the period. Thus, the exceptional emphasis placed by the nationalist schools of archaeology in the newly emerging nation-states of the Middle East on the continuity between the current and earlier inhabitants of the national land should be understood against this political and cultural background.

The main motivations behind the local archaeological schools' reinterpretations of archaeological findings in light of nationalist discourses and the postcolonial projects of official history writing were both to react to the Orientalist history writing by subverting the claims of essential difference between Orient and Occident, and to appropriate the legitimating power of archaeological practices to claim a certain territory as rightfully belonging to their respective nations. Hence, the Orientalist framework that denied a link between the present nations inhabiting a particular land and the ancient peoples who lived in the same region thousands of years earlier was conceptually reworked into a primordial connection and continuity, linking these peoples across ages. This translation created a discursive space from which the postcolonial states in the Middle East challenged the European monopoly on "civilization" and located the new nations and their identities on the map of the "civilized world." In some cases, as in Turkey, the new nationalist archaeological discourses even enabled the new nations to claim a European identity on the basis of these constructed connections to the oldest known cultural formations in which a European past is arguably rooted.

History Writing, Archaeology, and Museumification in Turkey

The development of archaeology as a discipline and the laws regulating archaeological excavations in Turkey have been closely related to the interactions between the Ottoman and the European states since the nineteenth century.[7] In a fashion similar to European colonizers, Ottoman officials perceived archaeological excavations as symbolic practices of power in the imperial periphery. Osman Hamdi Bey, who was in charge of these early Ottoman excavations and sultans' collections, transported many artifacts from the Middle East to the imperial capital. These artifacts signaled the emerging European taste in the imperial court, and, as signs of modernity, they embellished the Ottoman court's window that was dressed for the Western gaze (Bartu 1997).

After the Turkish republic was founded in 1923, archaeological practices and museums continued to be seen as the success barometers of the Westernization project. Anti-imperialist and anticolonial sentiment, however, was also pervasive in the nationalist modernization discourse. Thus, the new regula-

---

7. For politics of museumification and antiquities in the Ottoman Empire, see Shaw (2003). The best sources for the historical development of legal procedures in Turkey pertaining to the artifacts and regulation of archaeological excavations are Atasoy (1983); Özdoğan (1992, 1998); Paksoy (1992); and Akın (1992). For the history of the discourses and methods in archaeology and the influence of these changes on Anatolian archaeology, see Hodder (1991, 1998).

tions and laws pertaining to archaeological excavations and findings became important issues where the state, on behalf of the nation, claimed responsibility and exercised the "nation's right to protect its own cultural heritage." To create a core cadre of Turkish archaeologists, the Turkish Ministry of Education sent a group of bright Turkish students to Germany and opened archaeology departments at the public universities.[8] Many "national" excavations were started, particularly at Hittite sites in Central Anatolia.[9] Consequently, museumification of the findings and their public display became immediate concerns. Upon the orders of the national leader and the first president of the republic, Mustafa Kemal Atatürk, the Ministry of Education and the Turkish Historical Society started planning a Hittite museum in Ankara. Thus, in the heart of the new nation was born the earliest museumification of Hittite artifacts: the Ankara Archaeological Museum (now renamed the Anatolian Civilizations Museum).

The Anatolian Civilizations Museum should be seen as a part of a larger project of rewriting Turkish history.[10] The major institutional form of this larger project, the Turkish History Foundation, started many studies on history and culture of the "Turks" specifically for the purpose of defining a homogeneous Turkish culture. At that time, the Kemalist historians traced the origins of Turkish identity to the Hittites. This official historical narrative was known as the Turkish History Thesis (or Atatürk's History Thesis). It purported to show a Turkish ethnic continuity in Anatolia since prehistoric times. According to the thesis, Hittites were part of the Turkic tribes who migrated from Central Asia to Anatolia. Narratives based on this thesis shaped most of

8. During this period the faculty of these departments was composed mostly of German professors, some of whom had fled to Turkey to escape Nazi persecution. For details, see Canpolat 2001.

9. Hittitologists estimate that Hittites migrated to Anatolia around 2000 B.C. However, when they first migrated and where they originally came from are still issues of debate. Hittites established the earliest known centralized authority in Central Anatolia along the River Kızılırmak and enlarged their area of influence as far as today's northern Syria. Their power faded after 1200 B.C. For further information on the Hittites and their art, see Gurney (1990); McQueen (1986); Darga (1992); Akurgal (1970, 1997); and Yener et al. (2002).

10. For the content and development of this larger project of historical narrative formation, see Berktay (1983); and Ersanlı (2003).

the anthropological, folkloric, and archeological projects of the 1930s.[11] In the aftermath of World War I, the motivation behind this argument was to make a case for a primordial Turkish existence in Anatolia and hence to support the claim that the Turkish nation-state should be recognized as the natural heir of Anatolia in the international arena.

Symbolic Turkification of pre-Islamic Anatolia was both a nationalist move and an attempt to counter Orientalist discourse. The Turkish nationalist archaeological discourses reinterpreted the chain of historical continuity constructed among European, Anatolian, and Mesopotamian civilizations by inserting Turkish culture into the chain. This provided a rich discursive repertoire for nationalist elites eager to construct a national identity that could claim historical connections with European culture (Bartu 1997). Consequently, the investigations that the Turkish Historical Society undertook to label the Neolithic civilizations in Anatolia as "Turkish" firmly articulated the Turkish state's cultural politics with the nationalist archaeological discourses in the postcolonial world.

Even though the museum was initially conceived along the lines of the Turkish History Thesis, by the time the renovation of the historic building hosting the exhibition was completed in 1968, the predominance of the Turkish History Thesis in nationalist history writing was fading.[12] The thesis and similar projects that focused on racial continuity in Anatolia were replaced by less racialized but still essentialist narratives, oriented more toward the discursive construction of the homeland along the nationalist lines. These narratives comprise a discourse demonstrating a resilience in the collective conscious-

11. The best primary source of information for the Turkish History Thesis is the transcription of the lectures that Afet İnan gave at the Turkish History Foundation Congress in 1933 (İnan 1933; İğdemir 1973). The most detailed account of the archaeological practices of the Turkish History Foundation in the 1930s can be found in the minutes of the Second Turkish History Congress in 1937.

12. Since different sections of the exhibition were opened at different dates, it is difficult to identify a definite opening date for the museum. I use the date 1968, the year in which the name of the museum was changed from the Ankara Archaeological Museum to the Anatolian Civilizations Museum, because only then did the museum take its final form. For more details on the formation and opening processes of the museum, see Bayburtluoğlu (1991) and Koşay (1979).

ness that the implausible Turkish History Thesis failed to show over the years. I refer to this discourse as the Anatolian Civilizations Discourse.[13]

The Anatolian Civilizations Discourse constructs the national identity around "the peoples of Anatolia," which is an imagined community across ages and which shares a common identity of "Anatolian-ness." In this imagery, the underlying assumption is that common exposure to the same nature and landscape produces essentially similar cultures regardless of diverse origins and historical change. The central signifier, Anatolia, does not simply signify a geographical region but is rather combined with another central signifier in nationalist discourse, "homeland." Thus, its meaning is intensified, and Anatolia signifies a political territory of the sovereign nation-state, the homeland of the Turkish citizens, and the birthplace of the homogenous national culture. In this sense, the predominance of the Anatolian Civilizations Discourse over the Turkish History Thesis marks a shift in the representations of Turkish nation building from an essentialism based on biologically conceptualized race to an essentialism based on a homogenized and territorially defined culture.[14]

What is, then, this discursively constructed Anatolian culture? The narrative usually starts with Paleolithic cave dwellers in the Antalya region in southern Turkey. It is an evolutionary narrative that ties scattered settlements and *höyük*s in Turkey to one another with a tale of the development of the state and the city in Anatolia: the two "pillars of civilization."[15] The emergence of the first forms of state and city are traced teleologically as the origins of a chain of cumulative progressive developments culminating in the present. In

13. For various practices and embodiments of Anatolian Civilizations Discourse currently in circulation in Turkey, see Gür (2004).

14. This shift coincides with a time when biological racist discourses of the 1930s were losing their relative force in history writing in Europe. However, the more specific dynamics that led to such a shift in Turkey needs further exploration.

15. Focusing on state and city as the two pillars of civilization is symptomatic of Eurocentrism in the postcolonial translations of the modes of nationalist history writing. These two dominant modes of organization, central to the nation-state, are still paradigmatic for the narratives of European history and influential in the subaltern practices of history writing. For a vigorous analysis of the relationship between Europe and history writing in the postcolonial nations, see Chakrabarty (2000) and Chatterjee (1993).

this discourse, the current Turkish state and the nation are constructed as the inheritors of the sedimented wisdom of the Anatolian civilizations that evolved from one another. The emergence of the "first" urban settlements, the "first" agriculture, and the "first" monetary system are conceptualized as indicative of a cultural essence imagined to originate from the Anatolian landscape that stimulated human progress.

The Anatolian Civilizations Discourse has inspired many representations and cultural products ranging from dance shows to construction of local histories in municipality annals. However, the discourse finds its institutional embodiment nowhere as much as in the Anatolian Civilizations Museum. To capture the basic tenets of the discourse, we will not turn to the dominant narrative of the museum and examine the spatial arrangements of the exhibition in detail.

Dominant Narrative of the Anatolian Civilizations Museum

The Anatolian Civilizations Museum (ACM) is a classical museum in the sense that its spatial organization resembles the discourse it represents. It imposes a single order on the visitors through the pedagogical orientation of its exhibition and the ways in which the objects are classified (Hetherington 1996, 160). The main organizing principle of the ACM's exhibition is chronology. As visitors follow the route imposed by the architectural design, they are called on to witness the reconstruction of Anatolian history through time. The feeling of time travel is rooted in a deterministic, unilinear, and evolutionary conception of history, which assumes a continuous development of humanity toward a singular and universal telos of civilization.

If museums are classifications of collective identity, ACM delineates the limits of the collective identity in Turkey by national borders. Given the larger nationalist discourse that shapes the exhibition, naming the collection "Anatolian" is not a simple reference to a geographical location. It signifies the articulation of the Turkish culture's territorialization and the discursive construction of the motherland. The museum tells the story of Anatolians: peoples in a chain of civilizations that share a cultural essence starting from the Paleolithic Age until the present. Museum booklets and tour guides define the mission of the museum as "collecting all civilizations of Anatolia under

one roof." Thus, the museum takes pride in having pieces from every civilization that established a city or a state in Anatolia.[16] The space chosen for the exhibition complements the story. The ruins of the central part of an Ottoman
bazaar *(bedesten)* near the Ankara Castle became the site of the exhibition after
thirty years of renovation. Details of the renovation and the history of the
building are included in the museum brochures. Consequently, the narrative
attributes a specific significance to the Ottoman bazaar by defining it as the
representative of Ottoman civilization in the chain of civilizations exhibited
in the museum. The halls, currently surrounding the inner courtyard, were
formed through the combination of the shops in the bazaar. The linear
arrangement of the shops makes them convenient for housing a chronological exhibit, since the microphysics of space structures the visitors' movements, keeping the routes in a straight line. Museum visitors usually follow the
route imposed on them, going through the halls surrounding the inner courtyard. They very rarely diverge from the designated chronological tour before
they make their way into the central hall.

The walking practice in the museum goes beyond just following the designated paths in a space; it develops into a bodily and cognitive performance.
The cognitive efforts to grasp the notion of time flowing in the exhibition's
narrative and the bodily motion manipulated by the microphysics of the
space, that is, the paths designated by the walls, arrows, and signs, invite visitors to imagine themselves situated in a particular history and geography. Visitors interacting with the museum narrative and space perceive their identity
and subjectivity against a background of history of civilizations in Anatolia
throughout the ages.

Museum representations that are based on a linear progressive understanding of history and culture usually have classical exhibitionary tactics, and
they maneuver their visitors through the chronological tour. In his Foucaultian analysis of modern museums, Tony Bennett calls this organized walking

---

16. In chronological order, the exhibit is composed of pieces from the caves inhabited in
the Paleolithic Age (Karain, Beldibi); findings from the Neolithic, Calcolithic, and Bronze Age
layers of the *höyük*s (Alacahöyük, Çatalhöyük, Hacılar, and Kültepe are particularly significant);
and artifacts dated to the Assyrian Trade Colonies, the Hittites, Phyrgians, Urartians, Lydians,
the late Hellenistic and Greco-Roman periods, the Byzantine Empire, and Seljuklus.

"an evolutionary practice" and emphasizes that the museum organizes not only the routes but also the mental and bodily performances of the visitors. Thus, classical museums embody and instantiate "ideologies of progress by enlisting their visitors as 'progressive subjects' in the sense of assigning them a place and an identity in relation to the assumed progress' ongoing advancement" (Bennett 1995, 179).

The place and identity ACM assigns its visitors is that of a privileged actor situated at the endpoint of the developmental flow of history. The exhibition of all Anatolian civilizations under one roof comprises the narrative that enlists the Turkish ACM visitors as the heroes traveling in time. Thus, it facilitates a mental performance where visitors construct contemporary Turkey as the achieved telos of a historical progress. Visitors are invited to read the story of the present and connect their identity with that of the former inhabitants of Anatolia. The visitor narratives of the museum show that most visitors internalize this privileged identity and respond positively to the hailing of the museum narrative.

In May 1998, I studied the practices of local visitors to the ACM, employing a participant observation method, and I collected museum narratives through interviews. After completing my own visit, I observed how my potential interviewees—any Turkish-speaking visitors—moved within the museum space, what kind of objects they paid attention to, and their interactions with each other. Then I asked for their permission for an interview.[17]

---

17. All interviews were conducted at the museum immediately after the visitors completed their tours. The duration of the interviews varied from thirty minutes to two hours. I interviewed the individuals as a group if they were visiting the museum together. After transcribing the fifteen narratives I collected at the end of these group interviews, I employed narrative analysis and came up with the central tropes, themes, and concepts. I classified parts of these narratives by examining how they engage with the dominant narrative of the museum. Each visitor's narrative combined various features of my classification scheme, and there were overlaps between categories. In other words readers should not assume that the unit of my analysis is the individual and each individual's narrative corresponds to one category only. In defining the dominant narrative of the museum, I examined the historical construction of the exhibition and the archeological discourses of the period, made use of the museum guidebooks, and interviewed the museum staff. I am particularly indebted to the museum director, İlhan Temizsoy, for our lengthy interview.

In the interviews, most visitors constructed stories about the distant past, present, and future in which they expressed affection for their "ancestors." These stories were usually embellished with depictions of Turkey's cultural wealth, the deep roots of "our civilization," and the pride they feel about these. I call the visitor narratives that evoke such themes, are organized around a progressive linear time pattern, and echo the dominant museum narrative, *territorial kinship narratives.*

Responding Positively to the Interpellation: Territorial Kinship Narratives

Erdoğan Baykal is a chemist who was visiting the museum with his family on the weekend.[18] His narrative not only illustrates the influence of the chronological arrangement of the exhibition on the visitors but also shows how a universalist narrative, such as that of the development of civilization, is translated into a particularistic national narrative. This interview also exemplifies the ways in which most of the visitors internalize the privileged identity construed through the subject effect of the exhibition.[19] During the interview, as he ex-

---

Considering the limited number of interviews and the fact that this research was conducted only in one archaeological museum, it is not possible to generate statements generalizable to all the people living in Turkey. It is my contention, however, that ethnographic data collected in detail and accompanied by in-depth interviews are invaluable in understanding the elusive meanings of notions like "Anatolia," "Anatolian-ness," "Turkish culture," and "homeland" in collective consciousness, which a survey method may easily fail to capture. The conclusion of such an ethnography of museum visiting is also a good starting point for thinking about culturally sensitive and well-contextualized survey questionnaires on the subject matter, if generalizability rather than in-depth interpretation is desired.

18. The names of the interlocutors mentioned in this essay are pseudonyms.

19. *Subject effect* means subjecting the self to the meanings, power, and regulation of a discourse by locating oneself in a position from which the discourse makes most sense (Hall 1997, 55–56). In the ACM case, this process takes place in the visitors' efforts to give meaning to the museum-visiting experience by taking the subject position of the "grandchildren of the forefathers" inheriting a cultural heritage or identifying themselves as "children of these lands" and as such sharing a cultural essence with the peoples who created or used the artifacts in the exhibition. Hence the visitors "enter" the story and "become" the subject of the narratives that are based on the assumptions comprising the Anatolian Civilizations Discourse. For a more de-

plained why museums and the history they represent are so significant for a society, we learn his definition of "shared national culture" and the ways in which he imagines himself in relation to it.

> It is hard to construct a future without knowing the past. I mean, what kind of a culture is he [pointing at his son] going to grow up with? Which culture is he going to defend? I was born in Turkey. Without knowing what belongs to Turkey, without the knowledge of Anatolian civilizations, I cannot know which culture I shall live in. Kids grow up in the family and take the culture of their family. They form their own consciousness, synthesize it with what they have learned, and Turkish culture is formed. Otherwise we create alienation in the society. Today, as an Anatolian, I have to teach my child what I have learned. Otherwise he becomes alienated and cannot know what to do.

Erdoğan identifies the museum as an institution that transmits a collective historical consciousness that has grown out of the Anatolian landscape. While arguing that the past has to set the tone of the future for the children of the country, he emphasizes the Turkishness of the Anatolian past. He defines a cultural essence transmitted from generation to generation by its unique relationship with the homeland. A Turk stands for this cultural essence, and he has to defend it, especially vis-à-vis the "outside." In Erdoğan's depiction, Turkish culture emerges as moral codes and norms into which Turkish children are socialized primarily through family and education. The child's spiritual growth is inextricably linked with the transmission of this cultural essence. Should these two processes, individual spiritual growth and cultural reproduction, diverge, according to Baykal, individuals could not forge an identity and recognize themselves as subjects. In such narratives, learning about the collective memory is a prerequisite of the construction of a self within the collectivity. In this respect, the museum is perceived as an institution that shapes the subjectivity of the Turkish youth through its ability to inculcate a particular cultural history. It is a pedagogically crucial institution to teach children the cultural

---

tailed treatment of the concept, see Foucault (1970), where he historically examines the subjectifying effects of the academic disciplines.

essence imbued through centuries, thus to show them "what they are made of."

After reading the retrospective narration of the present, most visitors identify with the subject position that the museum narrative invites them to occupy. The Anatolian Civilizations Discourse informs the ways in which culture, history, and geography are related in these visitor narratives. In defining themselves through their membership in a national community, visitors construct a narrative of the origins, present, and telos of a collective whose members are bonded through territorialized culture. A culture conceived as shared by breathing the same air, using the same water, and feeling the same wind constitutes the imagined common characteristic of the Turkish nation. According to most visitors, being brought up in Anatolia means being "the child of this homeland." In this way, they naturalize their membership in the imagined cultural community. For example, when Sibel Özdoğru, a housewife in her mid-forties who is visiting the museum with her daughter and husband, is asked which objects she liked most, she replies: "Actually I like those things from the Stone Age. How much labor must have gone into them! It is amazing how they managed without the tools. I was most surprised to see the jewelry. Women are women across all ages!"

Another informant, Hikmet Şen, feels similarly about the goddess figurines: "When you look at the people in Turkey, you really think that these kinds of things [referring to the artifacts] could come out of these people. The mother goddess figurines, for example, are very Turkish, very typical Turkish women! The relationship to the soil and the importance of fertility in the Mother goddess figurines [are still here]."

In their narratives, both Sibel and Hikmet imagine an invisible link between the inhabitants of Anatolia across the ages and express these imageries through the parallels drawn between anatomical features of women today and the plump bodies of the goddess figurines, or through common use of jewelry. Sometimes visitors establish similar links by invoking the resemblance between the mud brick houses in Anatolian villages today and the constructions excavated at Çatalhöyük.

In such narratives, which echo the museum's dominant narratives, the imagined cultural thread that ties visitors to their ancestors, whom they define as all the peoples who lived in their homeland in the past, expresses a certain affiliation and affection. I call this deeply felt affiliation with an imagined community of ancestors across the ages, anchored in a certain geographical space demarcated by the contemporary national boundaries, "territorial kinship." Territorial kinship narratives lie at the core of the process by which elitist top-down projects can become effective in the definition of self through imagining a collective "we" whose identity is expressed through an imagined common ancestry anchored in the landscape. This is the moment when a territory, a geopolitical unit, becomes a homeland for the visitor, enabling him or her to situate the self within the nationalist narrative.

Such a moment occurs in Hayriye Cankut's narrative. Hayriye is an elderly housewife visiting the museum with her grandchildren,, daughter, and son-in-law. In her narrative, she constructs a progressive link between contemporary and past inhabitants of Anatolia by establishing an evolutionary relation between the cauldrons she uses in her house today and the ones used in Anatolia thousands of years ago. Her narrative connects the signifiers of Anatolian culture to various objects she uses in everyday life that she assumes to be used in similar ways for similar purposes across the ages. Here we find a clear example of the role of the evolutionary walking practice in inducing an affinity for imagined territorial kin and anchoring larger social transformations in individual experiences.

> A: How do you think this museum and the past are related?
>
> Hayriye: I see it in steps. I mean, you see the steps, from the very beginning till today. Without the museum, seeing these steps would not be possible.
>
> A: Could you give an example of what you mean by steps?
>
> Hayriye: The kitchenware they used, for example. Their size changed, for one thing; you can imagine how they used to be. The illustrations and drawings help, too. You see how their life was. What we basically use today is a developed version of what they used. It got smaller and more developed. Actually one cannot know whether those huge cauldrons were used for the family or the whole village, but nevertheless it is a cauldron.

In many of the interviews, as in Hayriye's, the visitors establish imagined territorial kinship ties by making references to "common" everyday practices across the ages. The resemblance of the artifacts to contemporary utensils and their use-value increase the significance of the objects for the visitors. The fact that everyday practices constitute a discursive repertoire for the visitors, through which they make sense out of artifacts in the museum, has been noted in other museum studies as well (Bourdieu and Darbel 1990). However, in these studies, the importance of the conceptual work of immediate and mundane experiences in connecting larger political and social transformations with the everyday life of individuals is quite underappreciated.[20] The continuum between life and its representations in narratives that draw on everyday experiences opens a window to understanding how abstractions such as state and society across the ages gain meaning through these kinds of articulations. Analogies between life as the visitors know it today and the life as it is imagined to have been then constitute a basis for visitors' images of the nation, their ties to the polity, and the relation between the present and the past of the territory. Such narratives capture the moments in which Anatolia is imagined as a motherland under the roof of the museum, and the imagery of a geopolitical space crystallizes as a meaningful category in which the citizens have an emotional investment.

Anxiety about the Telos: Nostalgic Narratives

Museum narratives do not have a single meaning; visitors leave the museum with different perceptions and experiences. They attribute various multiple meanings to the museum stories, based on their own experiences and the discourses to which they were exposed through social institutions such as educa-

---

20. For example, in their study of the visitor narratives of the art museums in Europe, Bourdieu and Darbel (1990) divide the visitor narratives into two categories on the basis of the visitor's cultural capital. They call the narratives of the visitors with less cultural capital, that draw on "popular aesthetics," "naïve narratives." In these narratives visitors attribute meaning to art objects using their own everyday practices as reference points. For such visitors the value of an art object depends on its age, use-value, and relevance to everyday life. The visitors with "sophisticated narratives," on the other hand, judge the artifacts on the basis of pure Kantian aesthetics and usually draw on expert narratives. In Bourdieu and Darbel's analysis, "naïve narratives" mark a lower status habitus and are significant insofar as they are helpful in mapping the homologies among the different fields that constitute this habitus.

tion, media, and family. The territorial kinship narratives presented in this essay so far constructed Turkey as either an achieved telos or a country with a bright future implicated by the glorious past. Not all visitors, though, accepted and internalized the museum narrative and construed themselves as Turkish citizens who have inherited the sedimented wisdom of the thousands of years of Anatolian history. Some of the visitors approached the notions of modernity and civilization, and Turkey's location on the global map, critically, countering the museum's modernist, nationalist narrative with narratives of nostalgia for a time when Anatolian people were at the peak of human civilization. The problem articulated was not whether "we"—that is, humanity and the Turkish nation—should strive to be "modern" and "civilized," but rather whether we were on the right track to achieve those goals. These stories questioned the proximity of the Turkish nation to the promised telos of the developmentalist historical narrative, even though they still entertained a linear and deterministic conception of time. I call these *nostalgic narratives.*

The evolutionary walking practice within the museum evokes an anticipation of a good future because it draws on the unilinear, deterministic conception of history that anticipates a telos. In Turkish developmentalist discourse, the telos is defined Eurocentrically, and the purpose of the nation is to "catch up with the West" and be "modern." Visitors who are interpellated by this overarching public discourse but who also are aware of the acute problems in Turkey leave the exhibition disappointed. The expectations evoked by a walk within the three-dimensional story of the glorious past are contradicted by the larger social experience. The museum narrative manages to entice these visitors to connect themselves with the forefathers and locate their identity in the museum narrative, but it fails to evoke pride and contentment in the present. Instead, these visitors articulate shame for the present accompanied by a nostalgia for the distant territorial past. For example, Mehmet Altın, an accountant visiting the museum with his wife, criticizes contemporary architectural practices by comparing them with the museum building. Pointing to the Ottoman building that houses the exhibition, he says: "This building is magnificent! A couple of days ago I heard in the news that there was an old building used as military barracks, either in Erzurum or in Erzincan. Despite the fact that it was a second-degree historical building, they decided to demolish it. Although they used two tons of dynamite, they couldn't. See how the old buildings endure next to all these modern buildings that crumble into pieces when you touch them!"

The nostalgic narratives are saturated with complaints about pollution, political corruption, and the erosion of values inherited from our ancestors. The moral of the story usually is that instead of appreciating the Anatolian heritage and developing it further, Turkey is making no progress; thus, the sedimented wisdom of thousands of years is wearing away. Yasemin Göçmen, a secretary visiting the museum with her niece, argues that today is only a shadow of the glorious past, an embarrassing moment in our history. Then she sighs, pointing at the artifacts: "I think we do not deserve these. Compared to this civilization these people created, we are way behind them!"

In these narratives, the museum is a representation of a failure to be worthy of the past. This notion attributes an alternative meaning to the exhibition: it is a representation of the gaze of the ancestors, a moral reference for the present community. Nostalgic visitors situate the glorified historical heritage in a panoptic point.[21] Visitors, who share a notion that they should be worthy of their ancestors and history, imagine the past as a disciplining reference point for today's moral codes. They believe that the people in Turkey do not work hard enough to improve what they inherited and thus embarrass their ancestors by the contemporary problems they have created. These visitors cannot hold their heads up in the face of the high level of civilization the museum represents because contemporary Turkey is not a leading nation in the world, as would be expected from the archaeological evidence that constructs it as one of the oldest civilizations. The subject position in which nostalgic visitors place themselves is defined by their constant references to themselves as

21. Panopticism is a system of discipline embodied in an architectural design that renders the subject under surveillance completely visible at all times, while making the surveyor physically invisible to the surveyed. It is a concept that Foucault brought up in his discussion of the birth of the modern prison system in Europe (Foucault 1977, 197–200). Here I use Panopticon metaphorically, to delineate the pedestal on which the museum visitors place their imaginary ancestors. Just as in Panopticon, these imageries of the ancestors function as invisible surveyors that can see everything at all times.

the "grandchildren of (their) ancestors." Through the exhibit, these visitors imagine their ancestors looking at them and judging their lives. The gaze of the past disciplines their actions and oversees their moral development.

Prisms Fragmenting the Nation: Dissident Narratives

Museum visiting as a "Western" and urban practice has elitist connotations in Turkey. Going to a museum and being able to make sense out of this experience is taken as a sign of modernity. Binaries such as rural-urban and modern-traditional stand for the nation's social fault lines and are articulated through comments on visitors' levels of familiarity with the museum codes. In other words, the museum is a space in which visitors concurrently imagine a commonly shared national culture and fragment this culture by invoking the hierarchical network of relations constituting it. Hence, in some visitor narratives, which I call *dissident narratives,* instead of a reproduction of the tales on homogeneous culture and territorial being, the story line primarily rests on the coexistence of different lifestyles within the nation indicating loyalties to diverse groups engendering imageries of community that are alternative to the overarching nation. By mobilizing comparative imageries of the different segments in the country, museum exhibitions simultaneously unite and divide the nation.

Hikmet Şen is a twenty-four-year-old graduate student at the Middle East Technical University in Ankara. He compares contemporary peasants and the residents of Anatolia in prehistoric times, on the basis of material culture and norms. Hikmet projects the urban-rural distinctions he sees in contemporary Turkey onto a temporal distinction he makes between the peoples of the past and those of the present. He registers the differences in the lifestyles of urban and rural citizens on an axis of development.

A: What do you think ACM signifies? In other words, ACM is the museum of what?

Hikmet: It is the museum of the culture developed in these lands.

A: Could you expand upon that?

Hikmet: Okay, look, almost all artifacts exhibited here are found in Central Anatolia. To be more accurate, [they are] from inner lands, with no access to the sea. Ankara signifies deprivation from the sea, so it is just the right place. When you look at the people here, you really think that these kinds of things could come out of these people. . . . Actually what has been excavated is very rural.

A: What do you mean by rural?

Hikmet: The instruments, the agricultural instruments . . . weapons . . . idols. These are very peasant-ish! In the city things are different. For example, you do not see well-crafted statues in ACM. Perhaps this is because they belong to an earlier period, I cannot be quite sure about that, but they are by no means like Greek and Roman statues. In other words these are not pieces of art. These are instruments of everyday life! They are from peasant life! In the city, a statue is an ornament, whereas in the village you can imagine how it serves a religious function.

The identification of the modern peasant with the peoples of the past opens the door to a discourse of development, emphasizing the superiority of the urban over the rural, modern over the traditional, in terms of a constructed level of civilization. In Hikmet's narrative, the story of the peasants in Anatolia is separated from the story of the urban Anatolians. As such, the historical trajectories of different groups in the nation are isolated. Hikmet's narrative still adheres to the linear notion of history and speaks from a subject position—that of a privileged Turkish citizen inheriting the sedimented wisdom in which the museum narrative positions him. Nevertheless, Hikmet refuses to imagine the nation as a homogeneous whole. Therefore, despite its adherence to the parts of the dominant narrative, his narrative contests the fundamental tenets of the Anatolian Civilizations Discourse.

In dissident narratives, the stories about the backwardness of the peasants are interwoven with the stories of a "pristine, authentic Anatolian culture" located in the village. While defining themselves as "urban, modern, and cultivated," visitors telling dissident stories generate social distance from the "rest of the population," which they consider to be "rural, traditional, and uneducated." Such narratives indicate that the contradictions embedded in the nationalist discourses are reflected in the conceptual repertoires the visitors use to make sense of the museum. Thus, the rural-urban binaries embedded in the modernization discourse and the rhetoric of equality of all citizens embedded in the populism of the nationalist discourse continue to battle within the collective memory.

Visitors articulate the status differences they perceived among other visitors through the accounts of the relation between education and museum. My interlocutors expressed the differences they perceived between educated and noneducated with phrases such as "making sense of" or "not getting" the museum. They repeatedly stated, "Educated people understand the museum." When asked what they meant by this, they explained that a sophisticated *(kültürlü)* person would know where and when the artifacts were excavated and to which civilizations they belong. Such information is learned at school, but one learns to appreciate the importance of this kind of information in the family. Here, sophistication is equated with the correct upbringing. Thus, for my interlocutors, the major fault lines among Turkish citizens are primarily based on upbringing and education, and visiting a museum and appreciating the past and history signify high culture and status. Such visitor narratives show that museum visiting is a practice reproducing the differences within the nation, which official nationalist ideologies strive to define as homogeneous. They are reluctant to define culture on a national level, and as such they resist imagining the culture of different groups as shared and one.

The irony in the visitors' ability to produce stories of heterogeneity, hierarchy, and social distance out of a narrative of unity and homogeneity reminds us that the influence on a community of the official ideologies cannot properly be understood unless we pay attention to how the target audiences interpret the narratives state institutions produced. These audiences are not only capable of transforming the public representations and narratives beyond their intended meanings and purposes, but they also employ them in ways that destabilize the discursive reproduction of the national culture and the nation-state.

Museum Illiteracy as Dissidence

The regimes of self-expression, comprised of publicly available forms of storytelling, rhetorical techniques, and symbolic repertoires, play crucial roles in narrative construction. The level and substance of education and our interactions with media products mediate the ways in which we perceive and experience the world and how we narrate those experiences. Thus, incoherence and discontinuities in the visitor narratives can be accounted for by the variations in these factors. Nevertheless, the intended audience is also an important factor in determining the interaction between cultural products and their audience. We should particularly question to what degree the envisioned reader of a story at its moment of production corresponds to the actual reader and whether the discrepancies between these two have implications in terms of the coherence of the readers' narratives of the museums. This approach enables us to understand why some visitors' narratives seem more incoherent than others or why they attribute unexpected meanings to the museum. By paying attention to these narratives one can move away from the authoritative role attributed to the intended meaning of the museum and look at museum narratives from a more critical perspective.

The semiotic concept of model reader is helpful in accounting for the multiplicity of meanings in the visitor stories and going beyond a bipolar categorization of museum narratives, such as "coherent-incoherent." As Umberto Eco (1979) states, the moment of reading is not the final instance when the text finds its meaning. The intended reader is part of the process of meaning creation from the very beginning. The model reader of the text influences the author's narrative, not only as the author identifies for whom the story is being created but also as these choices delineate who is excluded from the pool of envisioned audiences. Therefore, we should look for the accounts of why there are multiple meanings, not only in the various interpretations of a text but also in the discrepancies between the readings of the model readers and the excluded readers.

When the ACM was formed as a state project to contribute to the dissemination of the official historical narrative, state officials projected a model visitor based on the "model citizen," the subject whom the nation-building projects aimed to create. When we also take into account the location of the museum and the characteristics of the exhibition, we can draw a profile of the model visitor as an educated, urban citizen who is familiar with Western European cultural codes and with the codes of modern public spaces. What happens if a Turkish citizen who does not match with the projections of the

Turkish elitist modernization project visits the museum? For example, some-one from rural Anatolia, who is illiterate and not familiar with the codes of the city?

During my fieldwork in the ACM, the most puzzling visiting practice I en-countered was that of two young soldiers. The two privates completed their visit of the museum in only fifteen minutes, unlike most other visitors, who usually took an hour and a half. With timid expressions on their faces, they walked quickly through the halls without paying much attention to the arti-facts or the explanations on the walls. They were about to rush to the exit when I stopped them and asked for an interview. Embarrassed but also inter-ested and flattered, they agreed.

Ali is from the Black Sea region, and Hasan is from eastern Turkey. Nei-ther of them had been to a big city before beginning their military service. This was Private Hasan's first and Private Ali's second year in Ankara. Since Ali had come to Ankara earlier, he knew more about the city than Hasan, and he was leading the museum visit. Hasan was very shy and uttered just a few words, and with the authority of having been in Ankara one year more than his friend, Ali spoke on his behalf, too. When asked why they chose to visit the museum in their free time, Ali said: "I come here to see people visiting, and my friend has not been to the museum before. You know, in the village there are no places like this. This is my second year in the service, and whenever we get out of the barracks, I bring the new ones here to see what people do in the city."

After defining the museum as one of the most interesting places in the city, Ali identified museum visiting as an urban practice, although he confessed that he could not make out what its use is. For him, the ACM is not a site of ed-ucation or a representation of the national past, as it is for most of the urban visitors. Rather, it is an exotic and wondrous display, like an amusement park or a circus. The ACM did not evoke any ideas or emotions in relation to national identity for these two voyeurs of the city life. They see it as a part of a lifestyle that is distant from their everyday life experiences and not accessible to them.[22]

22. At one point during the interview the two soldiers started asking questions about my project. Apparently to them what I was doing at the museum was as perplexing as the museum itself. By each question they posed, I felt the slow reversal of the ethnographic gaze blending

Hasan and Ali come from a social background where the modernist Kemalist messages do not reach, since these ideological messages are encoded in Western European codes of representation and institutional practices, and familiarity with these codes and institutions is presumed by the notion of a "modern Turkish citizen." Thus, the museum experience of the two soldiers consolidates the marginal status into which the Kemalist modernizing project has placed peasants and the people who remain outside the contemporary school system and delineates a subject position from which an alternative view of the early Kemalist cultural projects might emerge.

Through Ali's narrative we see how the mismatch between the envisioned visitor and the actual visitor destabilizes the dominant narrative and makes alternative interpretations possible. A visitor who does not know enough about the codes has the capacity to ignore the dominant narrative, undermining its hegemonic power over the act of reading. Ali's narrative is very similar to the dissident narratives in this respect, yet, unlike the visitors with such narratives, Ali speaks from a socially marginalized standpoint, and his identity is not enticed in any sense by the museum's story. This experience crystallizes a moment that renders the Turkish modernization project and the envisioned social function of the ACM problematic, since the discourses informing these projects fail to make a subject effect on these two young soldiers.

Conclusion

As Eric Hobsbawm once pointed out, nationalism becomes genuinely popular essentially when it is drunk as a cocktail (Hobsbawm 1995, 163). The ingredients of the cocktail, though, are contextual and historically specific. ACM visitors' narratives point out that when nationalist narratives are interpreted through the practices of everyday living in the context of nationalist museums, they reinforce the sense of belonging to the nation as they relate the familiar and immediate to the abstract and imagined. Nationalist sentiments

---

my subject position with the display of the museum. Later I was astounded with this realization during the transcription process, but I truly enjoyed the moment and thought I was a very good interlocutor for their "research."

thrive to the degree that hegemonic nationalist narratives are able to create spaces within which meanings of the everyday experiences of body, gender, class, and face-to-face relations in the street, the school, at home or at work are articulated and the contingencies of life and the sense of self are inscribed into the national linear story.

What kinds of experiences, practices, and narratives crosscut nationalist discourses, making the concept of nation meaningful and resonant? How do they interact with nationalist narratives? And what kinds of contexts facilitate such interaction? The ACM and its visitors give us a chance to see such cross-cutting meaning-making processes at work. The way in which ACM visitors respond to the Anatolian Civilizations Discourse, which hails them as Turkish citizens, reveals how the nationalist myth of linear destiny is negotiated and how everyday life practices, notions about womanhood, and urbanism, re-gardless of how variegated their meanings for the visitors, become the filters through which nationalism gains meaning, engenders personal allegiance to the abstract notion of nation, or leads people to challenge the ideological premises of that notion.

Most ACM visitors recognized themselves as the subject of the dominant museum narrative, which assigned them the role of the citizens of a heroic na-tion-state who are traveling back in their motherland's history. The land they were born in and the culture they grew up with defined their membership in the nation. As such, the subject position "citizen" was not constructed as a legal-rational category but rather as an emotionally charged identity, where the sense of belonging and identification was translated into willingness to serve and be governed by, connecting the people to the state at the most intimate level. The subject position was rooted in a notion of a shared national cultural essence that the Anatolian Civilizations narrative had anchored in the home-land. Thus, when the visitors narrated their experience of the museum and sit-uated themselves in the story the exhibition tells, they imagined a cultural homogeneity rooted in the territory, rather than in an ethnicity constructed through the metaphor of blood ties. They identified with their ancestors by creating links between their everyday practices and those of their imagined territorial kin. The ways in which such links were established, the kinds of af-fections expressed, and the narratives of territorial kinship that ensued from them when the institutionalized narratives interpellate the subjects, were crucial to understanding why most visitors accepted the basic tenets of the museum narrative and the subject effect of the Anatolian Civilizations Discourse.

Another group of visitors, although they too imagined territorial kinship ties and a historical linear trajectory delineated by the Anatolian Civilizations narrative, expressed nostalgia, rather than pride in the nation's past. The nostalgic visitors questioned the position the nation has come to occupy in the world order and were skeptical about the level of civilization it has achieved. Even though their narratives agreed with the territorial kinship narratives in terms of what the telos of the historical trajectory should be—that is, "Western modernity"—they contested the notion that the nation-state had already achieved it or even that the nation is on the right path leading to that telos. They inverted the museum narrative and reinterpreted it as a representation of failure, rather than success. The affection they held for their ancestors was tainted with shame, since they identified contemporary Turkey as an undeveloped country, unworthy of its glorious past.

For the visitors who challenged one of the most fundamental elements of the Anatolian Civilizations Discourse—the tenet that all Turkish citizens have a shared homogeneous culture—the relationship between culture and museum was crosscut by stories of habitus and nation simultaneously. For these visitors Turkey had to raise "modern individuals" in order to achieve modernity as a national condition. In other words, the agents of the nation's march toward modernity were first and foremost the citizens with a "sophisticated" and urban habitus. These visitors defined museum visiting as a ritual of the "modern subject" that draws a line between an urban, cultivated citizen and a rural, uncultivated one. When these hierarchies of taste were translated to a national level, the nation was imagined as divided by a fault line of dichotomized lifestyles, and the individual struggles for modernization overwhelmed the story of "Turkish nation on the road of progress" seen in the territorial kinship narratives. The rural populations were often relegated to categories denoted as backward, ignorant, and traditional, whereas urban identity was defined by the binary opposites of these adjectives. Thus, in the dissident narratives, the historical trajectories of these two dichotomized groups were seen as separate, and in the language of these narratives heterogeneity, fragmentation, and hierarchy replaced national homogeneity, union, and harmony.[23]

While studying representations and narratives of the "nation" embodied in institutions, paying attention to the intended audience is important because audiences that fall outside the scope of the profile are potentially capable of subverting the intended messages by reading unexpected meanings into them. In this essay, the narrative of the two soldiers who interpreted the museum as an urban amusement park unrelated to an Anatolian-based national identity signaled that there are visitors who do not respond to the hailing of the nationalist discourse of the museum. The two soldiers' concepts of urbanity and modernity did not crosscut an imagined Anatolian nation, which was the inalienable subject of the historical narratives in both dissident and territorial kinship narratives. The museum narrative was not able to create any commensurability between their sense of self and their conceptions of nation. ACM, in failing to represent to these visitors the odyssey of the heroic nation marching toward an imagined state of modernity in linear time, did not have the power to pivot their imagery of the nation and interpellate them as citizens. Their alternative interpretation reminds us that experiencing the public institutions that embody official ideologies does not necessarily mean internalizing those ideologies. The work of interpretation and the combination of official ideologies with other processes of meaning making—such as various ways in which people narrate and give meaning to their own subjectivity and their everyday life—are crucial in how people form their imageries of nation. In this respect, to understand how hegemonic narratives circulate and stay powerful, it is not sufficient to ask whether citizens read nationalist textbooks, at-

23. Ethnographies of the practice of not going to the museums are warranted as much as the ethnographies of museum visiting to fully understand how people interact with the nationalist and modernist discourses embodied in the museums. In my study I focused on the museum visitors to examine more closely the mechanisms and moments of interpellation by these institutions as an empirical question, and to highlight the necessity to explore the power of these institutions to socialize people into certain subject positions. Given more time and other resources, museum studies that inquire why people do not go to museums and what kinds of narratives they generate on this subject will be invaluable to understand how and why people do not interact with these institutions and decline their hailing. Such studies will no doubt shed more light on alternative narrations of museums and their relation to the nationalist narratives.

tend state ceremonies, or are compelled to go to museums that present nationalist narratives. It is vital to examine how people represent these cultural products in the stories they tell and rewrite official narratives filtering them through the prism of their own life experiences.

In locating ourselves in social narratives to articulate our experiences, we come to recognize ourselves by the social categories of that narrative, construct identities, and occupy subject positions in a collectively imagined community.[24] In this regard, the links visitors established between the physical attributes of the Turkish women's bodies and that of the mother goddesses, the designation of Urartian cauldrons as the prototypes of today's saucepans, or the constructions of a primordial authentic Anatolian culture through allusions to the continuous use of mud brick houses in Anatolia throughout the ages, create a commensurability between the public narrative of Anatolian Civilizations within which the story of Turkish nation-building is inscribed and the immediate, personally meaningful experiences of everyday life. Without studying such minute processes of creating commensurabilities between everyday practices and macro social processes and the sites that enable such conceptual work, it is hard to grasp in this globalizing and fragmenting world how nationalist narratives can continue to meaningfully articulate "nation," "state," and "homeland" with one another, hailing people as "citizens," and, more importantly, why people answer to this interpellation with feelings of belonging, commitment, and loyalty to the nation.

Ethnography of the interpretive labor of imagining the nation also enables us to see the cracks in the field of influence of the dominant narratives claiming hegemony over the interpretation of history. In the people's narratives, the moments and spaces that crystallize the relative positions of margin and center in the discursive field where public narratives and their critical alternatives struggle to gain hegemony over the symbolic representation and spatial embodiment of the national identity construction, become traceable.

24. See Bertaux (1981); Bertaux and Kohli (1984); Linde (1986); and Somers and Gibson (1994) for discussions of the ways in which life stories are embedded in public narratives.

4

Remembering a Nine-Thousand-Year-Old Site

Presenting Çatalhöyük

Ayfer Bartu Candan

Consider the following portrayals:

M. is from Küçükköy, the closest village to Çatalhöyük, a nine-thousand-year-old archaeological site in Central Anatolia. He was born in the village and has been living there with his wife and two children and his mother, brother, and sister. They are among the poorest families in the village. They do not own any land, and until M. and his brother and sister started working at Çatalhöyük, their primary sources of income had been through animal husbandry, selling produce grown on the land they rent each year and working in the fields as seasonal laborers. Now, M. is employed through the local office of the Ministry of Culture as one of the guards at Çatalhöyük. His sister has been employed by the Çatalhöyük research project during the excavation season since 1994, first to work as part of a group that sorted heavy residue and more recently as one of the kitchen staff in the dig house. M.'s brother has also been working at Çatalhöyük, first as a laborer hired from the village to work at the excavation and more recently as a guard.

Z. is the mayor of Çumra, the closest town to Çatalhöyük. He is from the

The research for this project is based on fieldwork conducted between 1998 and 2003 in Turkey (Çatalhöyük, Istanbul, Ankara), Britain, and the United States. I would like to thank especially the members of the Çatalhöyük research project who so willingly accepted me as part of their team and all the people who shared their Çatalhöyük stories with me. I owe special thanks to Can Candan for his encouragement and support and to Esra Özyürek for her patience and insightful comments on an earlier version of this paper.

ultranationalist conservative political party, MHP (Nationalist Action Party), which has been the most popular party in this region for many years. He often visits Çatalhöyük and provides help to the excavation project through the resources of the municipality.

A. owns a carpet business with his brother in Konya, the closest city to Çatalhöyük. He has been in the carpet business for many years and lives in Konya with his family. A.'s brother is mainly in charge of the store in Konya, whereas A. runs the international part of the business. He has Western European partners and clients. Along with his German business partner, A. has been interested in designing kilims using images from Çatalhöyük wall paintings.

B. is a well-known fashion designer in Istanbul. Her office is located in one of the upscale neighborhoods in the city. Although she is based in Istanbul, she travels widely for work. She recently opened a shop in France. Her main interests are natural dyes and fabrics. In 1997 she publicly presented her Çatalhöyük collection in Istanbul in a fashion show she named "Women of Another Time," where the models walked out of a reconstructed Çatalhöyük house with images from Çatalhöyük flashing in the background.

D. is a performance and visual artist who lives in the San Francisco Bay Area in California. Since 1982 she has been involved in various performance art events and has been traveling widely to different parts of the world, including Turkey, for these performances. She belongs to a nongovernmental organization called the International Center for Celebration that was formed by an international group of artists and architects. D. has also been affiliated with a women's group in Istanbul called Anakültür (Mother Culture) that is interested in designing projects to empower the "ancient wisdom and knowledge" of women. D. visited Çatalhöyük a couple of times and performed what she calls the "Mother Goddess Dance" on the mound.

T. is an archaeologist from England. She has been part of the Çatalhöyük research team since 1998. Like other archaeologists at the site, she stays at the dig house for two months every summer. Although she has worked at other prehistoric sites in Turkey, her dream has been to excavate at Çatalhöyük, which she claims to be one of the most important archaeological sites in the world.

These people belong to diverse groups who are involved with Çatalhöyük. Archaeologists, Goddess groups, local and central bureacrats, artists, and nearby villagers constitute the present publics of a nine-thousand-year-old past. In recent years, there has been a growing awareness of and interest in the publics of the past, specifically the archaeological past: groups of people claiming rights over the remnants of the archaeological sites (LaRoche and Blakey 1997); archaeologists, journalists, and writers who produce scientific and popular knowledge about these sites (Abu el-Haj 2001; Hodder 1999; Meskell 1998); and descendants or groups of people who claim to be the descendants of some ancient populations who inhabited the sites (Castaneda 1996). What happens when a nine-thousand-year-old site such as Çatalhöyük, with no apparent links to any current ethnic, racial, or religious group, is "remembered" today? What are the entanglements of its prehistoric past with the present?[1] When I joined Çatalhöyük research project in 1997 as a social anthropologist, I started exploring the claims different groups make and the links they forge with this prehistoric site.[2] In the "multi-sited ethnography" (Marcus 1995), I have been participating in and observing the activities of these groups and interviewing them in an attempt to examine the production and consumption of different kinds of knowledge about Çatalhöyük.

In this essay I examine encounters between the various publics of Çatalhöyük with the site and with one another, explore the ways in which these encounters are entangled with the local, national, global, social, cultural, and political contexts, and demonstrate the ways in which the public memory of Çatalhöyük is shaped by these encounters and entanglements.

Encounters with Çatalhöyük

Archaeologists

In terms of legal ownership, Çatalhöyük is owned by the Turkish state. When it was discovered and excavated in the 1960s by the British archaeologist James

---

1. The use of the term "entanglement" is inspired by the use of the term "entangled objects" in Nicholas Thomas (1991); he discusses the entanglements of material culture, social life, and colonialism in the Pacific context.

2. See Hamilton (2000) and Shankland (1996, 2000) for other kinds of anthropological work on Çatalhöyük.

Mellaart, this archaeological site became part of the national heritage. A reconstructed Çatalhöyük house and various finds from the Mellaart excavations became part of the display in the Anatolian Civilizations Museum in Ankara (see chap. 3). As is true for all archaeological sites in the country, it is guarded and controlled by the Ministry of Culture and its local offices, and any intervention at the site, including any archaeological excavation, has to go through the permission procedures of the Ministry of Culture, Directorate of Museums and Monuments. Even with a valid research permit, a government representative has to be present at the site for any kind of excavation.

Çatalhöyük is considered to be one of the most significant archaeological sites in the world. With its well-preserved mud brick architectural features and elaborate symbolism and the scale and density of the settlement, it has attracted significant attention from archaeological circles. When Ian Hodder, one of the leading figures in postprocessual archaeology, started excavating at Çatalhöyük in 1993, the scientific community had already claimed it as one of the most noteworthy sites, with the potential of providing important clues as to the origins of human settlement in the Mediterranean and the Near East. Besides its importance for understanding the Neolithic world, with the renewed excavations headed by Ian Hodder Çatalhöyük has also become a testing ground for new methodologies in archaeology. Hodder describes the major components of the current project as field research that involves excavation, environmental reconstruction, and regional survey; conservation and restoration; and heritage management that involves covering parts of the site, constructing a visitor center, and devising other ways to make the site an informative and attractive place to visit (Hodder 1997). The current project has become a highly visible case study for reflexive archaeological practice and innovative fieldwork methods (Bartu 1999b; Hamilakis 1999; Hassan 1997; Hodder 1997, 1999, 2000). Already, several volumes of books and series of articles about the site have been produced.

Visitors

Compared to some of the other archaeological sites both in the region and elsewhere in Turkey, Çatalhöyük attracts few visitors. Although there are no official visitor statistics for Çatalhöyük, a visitor survey I conducted between

1998 and 2001 suggests that in a year the site attracts approximately 5,000 to 7,000 visitors, compared to 1.2 million visitors to Mevlana Museum in Konya and 225,000 visitors to the Ephesus museum in İzmir (Shankland, Bezmen, and Bunbury 1995). Results of the visitor survey point to the following profile of the visitors to Çatalhöyük: 30.7 percent of the visitors are from Western European countries, 27.3 percent are from North America, and the ones from Central Anatolia region (including Çumra and Konya vicinity) constitute 26.1 percent. Almost half of the visitors (44.5 percent) are forty-one years of age and above, and the majority (72.5 percent) are college or university graduates.

The visitors are mostly interested in the age of the site and the archaeological process itself. Although most of them express a sense of disappointment due to the absence of visually attractive monuments, different groups of visitors relate to and experience the site in diverse ways. In the following examples, visitors to Çatalhöyük, who are from different national, social, cultural backgrounds, articulate the reasons for their visits, their experiences of the site, and the ways in which they make sense of the site.[3]

N., from Istanbul, is thirty-six years old and the owner of a small shop. He was born and raised in one of the neighboring villages. He came to visit the site with his wife and six-year-old daughter:

> It was my conscience *(vicdanım)* that brought me here. I was born in a village that is three kilometers away from Çatalhöyük. I lived in that village until I finished high school but had never been to Çatalhöyük. Recently I read about Çatalhöyük and the ongoing excavations here in one of the newspapers. I was angry at myself and was ashamed of the fact that I had never been there although this is where I am from. People come all the way from America and England to work here because they are curious about this site, but I have never been here. When we came here to visit my family in the village, I thought I should see Çatalhöyük. It was really my conscience that brought me here.[4]

3. These examples are based on the visitor survey I conducted between 1998 and 2001, the guest book at the visitor center, and interviews I conducted with the visitors and tourists at the site.

4. This and further references and descriptions come from my interviews and field notes unless indicated otherwise.

Although many visitors, especially those from the nearby villages and towns, share N.'s sentiments of guilt and shame for not having visited Çatal-höyük before, they also express a sense of local and national pride for having such an internationally well-known site in their region. Others express frustration with the government, state offices, and Turkish sponsors for not showing enough interest in the site and not appreciating its commercial value. Nationalist sentiments are also widespread among visitors from different regions of Turkey. They express a sense of disappointment that the site is being excavated by an international group of archaeologists with few participants from Turkey. One of these visitors put it in the following terms: "The major disappointment for me is to see foreigners excavating this site rather than Turkish archaeologists. But I am not sure who to blame for this—the government that doesn't invest in things like archaeology, disinterest of the Turkish archaeologists, or what?" Such nationalist sentiments point to the construction of a genealogy of the site that links it with a particular land and territory defined by the boundaries of the nation-state.

An Australian writer in her fifties, however, constructs a very different genealogy of the site. While she sits on the mound watching the fields and the mountains, she describes what she makes of Çatalhöyük and why she came to the site:

I am from Australia. I am a writer. I have been in Turkey for three days only and just arrived here today. Until I came here I was suffering a certain amount of culture shock with the difference in language, not being able to communicate with people, offending them all the time because I don't know the customs. But I sit down here in the grass and look around and I could be in Australia. I feel awfully at home in the physical landscape here. And that's because two hundred years ago the Europeans brought the species that were domesticated on this site to the Australian continent and began a process of land degradation that we are trying to recover from now. My family as farmers had been part of that land degradation. But more than that, they have been part of a disposition of Australia's indigenous people, which is a great burden that all Australian writers feel one way or another that I especially feel because of my pastoral background. One of the things that interests me in Çatalhöyük is the perceived continuity between people who lived here nine thousand years ago and people who are farming today. I mean perhaps that is more imaginary than real. But in my country, in Australia, there has been a major discontinuity, and those indigenous people have been massacred and dispossessed totally. And they are a living, breathing population of people who are suffering the burdens of this agricultural colonization. In there somewhere is an explanation for why I came here.

In her genealogy of the site, the Australian writer draws a link between her ancestors, the origins of agricultural colonization, and Çatalhöyük that makes her feel very much at home at this site although she has been suffering from culture shock in different parts of the country. It is through the links she makes between different parts of the world across a wide time span that she constructs the present memory of Çatalhöyük.

Another example of visitor encounters with Çatalhöyük, that of the "Goddess" groups, points to a different kind of genealogy, one based on spiritual links formed with the site. These groups claim that the site is the origin of the Mother Goddess worship. Although these types of visitors are few at Çatalhöyük, they are part of a larger and growing network of Goddess feminist groups (Rountree 2001). Despite their common interests, there is a diversity within these groups ranging from ecofeminists, to Goddess worshippers, to women simply interested in the role of women in early times. Some visit the site as part of Goddess tours that they describe as pilgrimages, and others visit in smaller groups. These tours, which cost three to five thousand dollars per person, cater primarily to women, most of whom are from North America. The itinerary usually includes Goddess sites in southern Europe, Greece, Malta, and Turkey. Çatalhöyük is usually the culmination of these journeys. During their visits to Çatalhöyük, each group engages in some form of a ritual on the mound to "communicate with the Goddess," to "feel her positive energy," as they put it. But the nature of these rituals also varies from one group to another. These spiritual encounters with the site are usually described in an embodied way and include, most commonly, words like empowerment, awe, and transformation.[5] D.'s description of her experience during a dance she performed on the mound at Çatalhöyük is a revealing example:

5. See Rountree (2002) for her discussion of similar experiences at other Goddess sites.

I felt my spinal column connecting with the earth and prayed also to the [goddess] Magna Dea to fill me, and to reveal HERSELF through me as SHE had the previous year. My body became electric, an empty vessel moving in timelessness. I entered a Samadhi, state of absorption into Oneness, and slowly, gradually, almost imperceptibly SHE began to wake up, rattling and crumbling her paper lair exploring her surroundings. SHE found an opening to HER enclosure, and SHE felt the afternoon air, space. SHE cupped it in HER hand and withdrew, safe inside HER membrane. Yet the sensation was curious, SHE stretched both arms out and, after a while, HER entire body. SHE breathed in oxygen, air, and space. SHE touched the earth and rubbed it on HER arms and face, pulled wild grasses and poured them on HER head and tasted the earth. Sensing vastness, finding the sky, SHE stood up, a link between the sky and earth. SHE saw distance, mountains, hills, plains surrounding HER. SHE began to move in the circle inscribing them, extending out into creation, out along the earth, out in the sky and wind and light. Touching HERSELF, SHE saw others similar to HER surrounding HER. SHE looked into the eyes of each person, SHE rang her Tibetian Singing Bowl and flew HER wings of liberation.[6]

As the above accounts illustrate, there is multiplicity in the types of visitor encounters at Çatalhöyük. As are many other tourist spaces (Edensor 1998; Urry 1995), Çatalhöyük is diversely experienced and represented by different groups of people. These encounters are shaped by and entangled with personal, social, national, and spiritual identities. The visitors construct diverse genealogies of the site through the nation-state, the origins of agricultural colonization, and the origins of Mother Goddess worship. It is through these genealogies that they relate to the site in the present.

Mayors

The following series of encounters draw attention to the ways in which different local groups capitalize on archaeology as a means to achieve local objec-

---

6. This is an excerpt from a text written by D. after her performance at Çatalhöyük on June 27, 1998. It is in her personal collection.

tives. Çumra and its town government have been forging links with Çatal-höyük in various ways. Since the excavations resumed at the site in 1993, many places in Çumra have adopted the Çatalhöyük name: the annual agricultural festival has been named the Çatalhöyük Çumra Agricultural Festival; the sports club in town is now named after Çatalhöyük; the bus terminal carries the sign "Welcome to Çatalhöyük city Çumra." The current mayor has been very open about his naming strategy. As he put it in an interview in his office, "We want to be associated with Çatalhöyük, and the easiest way to do that is to use the Çatalhöyük name in as many places as we can and make Çumra a Çatal-höyük city."

In the summer of 2001, the mayor opened a new center called Çatalhöyük Çumra Arts and Crafts Center to produce souvenirs and kilims based on Çatalhöyük imagery (see illus. 1). Given his interest in using every opportunity to affiliate Çatalhöyük with Çumra, he has been adamant about establishing a local museum in Çumra where artifacts from Çatalhöyük excavations would be displayed. Despite the reluctance of central government officials in Ankara to issue a permit to open such a museum in Çumra, the mayor has already designated a building in town for the museum and asked his staff to start working on the interior design.

1. Souvenir plate designed and produced by the Çumra municipality. Photograph by Can Candan. Courtesy of the photographer.

The symposium the mayor organized in the summer of 2000, "Çumra—from Çatalhöyük to the Present," is another example of the town's claim to an affiliation with and "ownership" of Çatalhöyük. For this symposium the mayor invited scholars from Selçuk University, the local university in Konya, and various members of the Çatalhöyük research team. Scholars were asked to present papers on the current findings at Çatalhöyük, on the history of Çumra, and on the current pressing problems of the town and the region. The proceedings of the symposium and another book on the recent findings at Çatalhöyük were to be published by the Çumra local government after the symposium. It is important to note that everyone in the region, including the current mayor, knows and agrees with the fact that the town of Çumra was founded in 1926 to settle the Turkish migrant population from the Balkans (Karabayır 2001). Thus, the name of the symposium did not necessarily imply or claim an ethnic continuity of the population with the Neolithic residents but rather a present ownership of the site.

But this symposium also pointed to another way in which Çatalhöyük is entangled with the present claims and demands especially of the farmers in the region. The timing of this symposium overlapped with the visit of the minister of agriculture and village affairs to the region. At the end of this symposium the minister was to have a meeting with a group of farmers to discuss the current problems in the region and the agricultural policies of the government. One of the key issues in the agricultural sector has been the negotiation between the government and the International Monetary Fund regarding a decrease in state subsidies. This meeting with the minister was crucial for the farmers to sort out their anxieties about the subsidies. Farmers started coming into the symposium room and waiting impatiently for the presentations to end. It was clear that they were more interested in meeting with the minister than in hearing the presentations on the recent findings from Çatalhöyük. But Çatalhöyük seemed important in the farmers' attempts to reclaim the significance of agriculture in this region. There were several banners in the symposium room that read, "Agriculture Is Nine Thousand Years Old in Çumra." One of the farmers waiting for the minister explained these banners on the wall in the following way: "We know that agriculture started in this region a long time ago. They say Çatalhöyük is nine thousand years old. So it started a long time ago. We are still involved in it, and we want to continue with it. But it is impossible to do that without the subsidy of the government." In this context, the presence of Çatalhöyük in the region became a means to forge links to the origins of agriculture in the area.

Villagers

The town of Çumra and its municipality are not the only local actors appropriating and claiming Çatalhöyük. Over the years, a growing number of villagers from Küçükköy, some of whom are hired at the site, have started to develop an affiliation with Çatalhöyük. With their smaller financial and political resources, the villagers have been trying to appropriate Çatalhöyük by using different mechanisms, strategies, and alliances.

A majority of the villagers perceive Çatalhöyük primarily as a tourist site, with the potential to generate revenues from tourism if developed properly. Çumra municipality's efforts to affiliate Çumra with Çatalhöyük is seen as a source of competition over the potential material benefits from the site. Although much of tourism research demonstrates the asymmetrical power relationship in host-guest interactions, it is time to go beyond the portrayal of hosts as passive agents. As Stronza suggests, it is misleading to depict locals as "passive, unable to influence events, as if they themselves were somehow physically locked in the tourist gaze. Missing in these analyses is the possibility that locals can, and often do, play a role in determining what happens in their encounters with tourists" (Stronza 2001, 272). In the context of Çatalhöyük, although there are other actors in the tourism scene, such as the Ministry of Tourism and Culture and travel agencies, villagers in Küçükköy and Çumra municipality are also active agents in their attempts to shape the nature of touristic development and the beneficiaries of this development in the region. Conflicts and tensions between Çumra and Küçükköy and the encounters between the visitors and tourists and the local population point to such attempts.

One of the major sources of conflict between Çumra and Küçükköy has been the road to Çatalhöyük. From Konya to Çatalhöyük there are two possible routes, one through Çumra and the other through Küçükköy. Although the road through Küçükköy is shorter, the Çumra road is in better condition and is thus preferred by visitors. When discussing the touristic opportunities Çatalhöyük presents, one of the villagers from Küçükköy, who has been working at Çatalhöyük for several years, expressed a sentiment shared by most of the workers at the site: "The other day when the mayor came to visit Çatalhöyük, we asked him about the Küçükköy road, and he explicitly told us that he has no intention of fixing it. He knows and we know why he will not do that. He wants tourists to go through Çumra, and we know what that means. That means spending money there rather than our village." Another villager joined in the conversation: "They also make sure they use the Çatalhöyük name everywhere in Çumra, so now whenever the Çatalhöyük name is heard, people and especially tourists will associate this name with Çumra. The other day I suggested to my friends in the village that maybe we should change the name of our village to Çatalhöyük. We cannot let Çumra benefit from this name that is supposed to be ours. This is a struggle we have to put up with."

The tensions between the villagers and Çumra municipality are over the potential benefits and opportunities provided by the touristic development of the region. But conflicts between the villagers and some of the visitor groups point to the limits and constraints of this kind of development and draw attention to the agency of the villagers in shaping the nature of tourism in the region. The following example regarding a project initiated by a Goddess group in Küçükköy demonstrates this point. It was the winter of 1997 when a woman's group in Istanbul, Anakültür, bought an old house in the village to convert it into an international research center called HerInn. In a meeting with the coordinator of this group in her Istanbul office, the coordinator described the aim of this organization as follows:

> We want to advance the status and role of women in the development process. Our activities focus on educational and cultural activities for awareness raising, capacity building for girls and women in rural areas, and lobbying nationally and internationally. We want to work at the grassroots level for various empowerment projects for the women by using centuries-old indigenous knowledge, wisdom, and culture that women possess. We want to call these centers HerInn, and of course the one in Küçükköy is especially important since it is so close to Çatalhöyük. This center has the potential to attract many researchers from all over the world who are interested in women's issues in different historical periods. In Küçükköy, we want to be able to work with local women and bring in all those people interested in doing this kind of research.

The house was partially renovated during the following summer, and the coordinator of the group organized a visit to Çatalhöyük with participants from Istanbul and North America. Their visit also included an opening ceremony at HerInn and a gathering in the courtyard with a group of women invited from the village. In the winter of 1998, for reasons that are still unclear, the house was burned down. Although it is still difficult to untangle the reasons for the incident, my interviews with different groups in the village point to tensions in the village. At first villagers claimed that it was an accident. It was an old house, and the problems with the electrical system in the house caused the fire. But further conversations indicated that a group of villagers, mostly men, were disturbed by the sale of this house to what they called "foreigners"—meaning people coming from outside of their region. They were also disturbed by the involvement of their female relatives in the opening ceremony of HerInn, the content of which they were not so sure. The tone of the conversations pointed to the possibility of arson rather than an accident, and this can be interpreted as a sign that the presence of the Goddess groups in the village was not welcomed.

The ongoing excavations at Çatalhöyük are also entangled with the local micropolitics. The presence of such a high-profile project so close to the village becomes a means to achieve various local objectives and to manipulate and contest local power relations. In a way, archaeology becomes one of the "weapons of the weak" (Scott, 1985). One example of such a process is the way in which the current *muhtar* (village head) of Küçükköy has been trying to form alliances around the excavation project. One of his primary aims has been to persuade the governor of Konya to start the construction of a school building in the village that would accommodate more children from different age groups.[7] The *muhtar* had been unsuccessfully lobbying the governor's office for several months regarding the problem. In the summer of 2001, he decided to use another strategy for his efforts—getting the archaeologists involved in the process. When we were discussing the schooling problem of the village, he declared his new strategy:

7. The change from five-year to eight-year mandatory education in 1998 made the old school building that was already in appalling condition structurally dangerous and totally insufficient to accommodate all the school-age children in the village.

I have been going to the governor's office so many times to raise the issue of a need for a proper school building in the village, the need for a proper road, and the need to build a new well that will help with the water problem we have. It will be much more effective if Ian Hodder comes along with me to one of these meetings. You are more powerful people in many ways. You are more educated. Your word will carry more weight than mine. I go and tell the governor all I can tell. He just nods his head and sends me away, and nothing gets done. He will treat you differently, he will take you more seriously.

The *muhtar* was actually correct in his assessment of social hierarchies and local power relations. A meeting attended by the *muhtar,* Ian Hodder, and myself took place in Konya in the governor's office in the summer of 2001 where the governor agreed to apply to the Ministry of Education for funds to start the construction of a new school building in Küçükköy.

Another example of the ways in which archaeology has been capitalized on and used as a "weapon of the weak" comes from a project implemented in the summer of 1998. This project consisted of organizing slide shows in Küçükköy as a way of informing villagers about the kind of work done at Çatalhöyük, and sharing the kind of archaeological knowledge produced about the site. The idea was received enthusiastically by the workers at the site, but it was actually the women who expressed more interest in it. In a series of discussions regarding the timing and logistics of the shows, the women revealed the main reason for their eagerness. They were extremely concerned about rumors in the village, for example, that they were taking their head scarves off around foreign men and that they were just sitting around all day long with the foreigners. The women insisted that I use as many slides as possible showing the kind of work they do and highlight the importance of this for the project. So the slide shows would serve several purposes for the women workers. They would provide visual evidence of what women actually do and wear at the site, thus dispelling the rumors. The emphasis on the importance of their work for the archaeological project would also grant them social prestige in the village.

Relatively speaking Küçükköy is a prosperous village relying mainly on agriculture and animal husbandry. The villagers hired at the site are in many ways the economically and socially marginal men and women of the village.

They are among the poorest families in the village; one of them is a divorced woman with one child who came back to the village after her divorce to live with her mother and brother's family. It is only the ones who do not own any land who are interested in the seasonal labor provided at the excavation site. Although that has been changing in recent years, especially in the early years of the excavation, working at the site was seen as a sign and acknowledgment of poverty and desperateness for work. Given this, it was important to them to capitalize on their roles at Çatalhöyük as a means to achieve social prestige.

Goddess Groups

Goddess communities relate to Çatalhöyük in different ways than the nearby villagers. Although they are few in number, they constitute one of the most visible publics of Çatalhöyük. They are part of a larger network and are very active in promoting alternative tours to Goddess sites. Even though they are not a homogenous group, they do share similar interests and relate to Çatalhöyük in similar ways. Çatalhöyük Web sites developed by New Age or Goddess groups promote a particular interpretation of the site. On the Sacred Journeys Travel Tours Web site, maintained by a U.S.-based group that organizes Goddess tours to Turkey, the tours are referred to as "Celebrating Goddess—a Sacred Journey" and described in the following way:

> A sacred journey takes us to the heart of the Goddess in cultures around the world. We celebrate Her as She was known in ancient times and places, and we celebrate Her continuing presence. Together, we create rituals of gratitude and healing to honor and connect with Her transforming spirit. . . . I travel because I want to learn first-hand, from Mother Earth herself, about the many cultures, the many people who have found spirit in the animals, in the trees, and the grain, in the rivers and oceans, and in the land, as well as in themselves. She is everywhere—in all things. I find Her in my travels, and I carry Her with me—for She is within me as She is within you. Our ancestors say it has been so since the beginning. Archaeologists have found small figurines of female figures, round with child and with full, heavy breasts. These figurines portray the miracles of reproduction and the ability of the mother

to feed her young from her own body. The expression of these miraculous facts of life would seem to indicate a desire to acknowledge their absolute necessity. Without the mother, the newborn cannot survive—nor can the people. The mother, therefore, is sacred. (www.wordweb.org/sacredjo)

Such a description of Çatalhöyük relies heavily on James Mellaart's interpretations of the figurines from the site (Mellaart 1967) and on Marija Gimbutas's claims about an ideal world in prehistory when the Mother Goddess ruled (Gimbutas 1991).[8] Sacred Journeys Travel Tours depicts Çatalhöyük as a representation of the prehistoric Golden Age symbolized through the rule of the Great Goddess of Anatolia where "people lived in a balanced matrilineal social structure." The tour organizers argue that the wall paintings found at the site are part of this worship, and they give special meaning to the red ocher used in some of these paintings: "The color of blood, the regenerative blood of the womb, with its promise of fertility, signifies the belief that life returns, that death is a journey back to the source of life." The depiction of the female figure that has become the symbol of the site is also in line with these interpretations: "Seated upon her throne, with each hand resting on the back of a lioness, she gives birth, regenerating all life on Earth, and connecting human and animal in her 'great cultural cycle' " (www.wordweb.org/sacredjo). The tour organizers, like many other Goddess groups, suggest that gynocentric cultures such as Çatalhöyük made sure that people lived in peace and harmony and that is the main reason why we do not see any type of fortification around the site.

In addition to their interest in the site itself, some of the Goddess groups also interact or engage with the current project members and are very eager to be informed about the recent findings. For example, the late Anita Louise, who was also the tour coordinator of Sacred Journeys, had started a correspondence by e-mail with Ian Hodder that is posted on the Çatalhöyük research project Web site.

8. It was primarily the archeologist Marija Gimbutes and her work on prehistoric European sites who popularized the idea of the "Mother Goddess." Although she passed away in 1994, she is still considered to be one of the icons of the Goddess movement.

Some other groups, however, show less interest in the ongoing research at the site. Their visits are a way of reinforcing their beliefs about the Mother Goddess and are mostly dominated by the rituals they perform on the mound. One example of such a group is the one that visited Çatalhöyük in May 2000 on a tour called "In Her Footsteps: A Journey of Renewal in the Land of the Mothers of Anatolia," part of Sacred Journeys tours. The itinerary of this all-women tour included visits to Istanbul, the Anatolian Civilizations Museum in Ankara, Hattusas (a Hittite site, referred to as the Hittite Goddess site), Cappodocia (referred to as the site of ancient Goddess temples), and Çatalhöyük (referred to as the archaeological site of a Neolithic city where a culture of the Goddess dwelled in peace for two thousand years), and ended up at Tohum (Seed) Living Earth Center, a New Age resort in southern Turkey. The highlight of this tour was the visit to Çatalhöyük. Although their visit was during the off-excavation season, I was at the site to help the tour guides. When I offered to give a tour of the site and inform them about the ongoing excavations, the tour guides warned me that this group was not really interested in those things but was very impatient to go up to the mound and start performing their rituals. They were eager to be on the mound and "feel the positive energy of the Goddess." They were not only uninterested but were also highly critical of the ongoing excavations and the interpretations offered by the current team. This group especially took offense at the fact that the archaeologists are questioning and reevaluating the concept of the Goddess and shrines. As a California artist from this group put it: "What Ian Hodder is doing is actually just reproducing the patriarchal interpretation of the site by questioning these concepts. He is trying to take away the sacred qualities of this site, and therefore I believe that he should not be digging here. You need to be able to relate to the sacred qualities of this site, and only those kinds of people should be digging this site."

Another Goddess group that visited Çatalhöyük shared similar sentiments about the current project. This visit was part of an international symposium called "Earth Shaped by Woman, Woman Shaped by Earth: Woman in Prehistory, Today and Tomorrow." The symposium was organized by a women's group in Istanbul affiliated with Goddess groups in Europe and the United States—the group that had bought the old house in the village with the aim of turning it into a research center that was later burned down. The symposium took place in Istanbul in June 1998. Participants consisted of archaeomythologists, archaeologists mainly interested in Marija Gimbutas' work and Goddess issues, artists, activists, and several members of the Çatalhöyük excavation team. The one-day trip to Çatalhöyük at the end of the symposium was the highlight of the event. The visit included a performance or ritual on the mound and an excursion to Küçükköy where the group visited the burned-down house with the aim of "turning the negative energies in the house to positive ones." The head of the women's group from Istanbul expressed her sentiments in the following way:

> It is very important that we claim this site through our positive energies, and I definitely believe that Mother Goddess will help us in that way. I can feel her energy here. We cannot just leave this site to the villagers or to the archaeologists. We have to put the Goddess issue on the research agenda. That's why I really wanted to establish this HerInn as a research center where we would host researchers working particularly on these issues. I am sure the villagers did not like this idea, especially the men, because they are worried that we will contaminate their women. But we will not give up even if they burn down every single house we buy here.

Goddess groups' depictions of Çatalhöyük and their encounters with the other publics of this site raise a series of questions regarding the politics of remembering Çatalhöyük. Although archaeologists, nearby villagers, and Goddess groups all appropriate the site for their present agendas, various tensions arise in their encounters with one another. Groups of archaeologists, including the ones from Çatalhöyük, have been highly critical of Goddess feminism. One argument has been that this movement undermined and did harm to the agendas of feminist archaeologists by creating orthodoxy through the construction of a Golden Age (Conkey and Tringham 1995). Another critique has been that Goddess groups appropriate the past for their current political agendas based on unscientific evidence (Meskell 1995). But there is also a group of archaeologists that takes a different view of the Goddess groups.[9] The con-

9. Also see Rountree (2001) for a comparative analysis of Goddess groups' and archeologists' appropriations of prehistoric sites.

versation I had with a British archaeologist after the visit of a Goddess group at Çatalhöyük summarizes such a view. This archaeologist, who has been working at Çatalhöyük for seven years, expressed her thoughts in the following way: "What we do is no different than these Goddess groups. We come and dig here. We go back and write articles about it, so in a way we appropriate the site in this way, for our agendas. We do it through science; they do it through rituals and their belief system. We also have to accept that it is partly through the efforts of the Goddess groups that gender issues have stayed on the research agenda of many archaeological projects."

It can be argued, as this archaeologist does, that Goddess groups, archaeologists, or any other group are not that different in the sense that they all appropriate Çatalhöyük for their present agendas. But it is also essential to recognize the structural inequalities and the unequal power relationships that are part of this process. The nature of encounters between the nearby villagers, Goddess groups, and archaeologists demonstrates this point. The arson incident does suggest that the villagers are active agents in shaping the nature of their interactions with the Goddess groups. But the Goddess groups still maintain their privileged positions vis-à-vis the villagers in terms of the resources to which they have access. The cost of the Goddess tours, for example, is nearly equal to the annual income of some of the families in Küçükköy. Goddess groups can also publicize their interpretations and experiences of Çatalhöyük through the Internet, whereas the villagers do not have access to such a resource.

Similar issues are also pertinent in the encounters between archaeologists and nearby villagers. It is true that archaeologists at Çatalhöyük and villagers from Küçükköy form alliances for the immediate needs of the village, such as the construction of the school building and a water reservoir, and finding solutions to environmental problems that affect both the village and the archaeological site. It is also true that the members of the current project are interested in getting the wider public involved in both the interpretation and public presentation of the site. To this end they devised various mechanisms such as an interactive visitors' center, community exhibits, and discussion groups on the Internet to engage in a dialogue with various interest groups and to represent the multivocality in the public presentation of the site (Bartu 2000). The villagers, especially the ones working at the site, have also been part of this process, that is, they were involved in the community exhibit where they expressed their perceptions of the site; they participated in the discussion sessions with the archaeologists where they interpreted the recent findings from the site; and their interpretations are part of the forthcoming publications of the research team. Given these efforts, the following questions still remain: Who is in charge of the orchestration of these multiple voices? What are the implications of such an orchestration and which voices are heard more than others in this process? It can be argued that the voices of the villagers are heard through the filter of the archaeologists, that is, through the archaeologists' selections of "relevant" comments to appear in a particular form of representation either as part of an exhibit or academic publishing—a process that points to the structural inequalities and the unequal power relationships that are part of the politics of remembering Çatalhöyük.

Artists

Local and international artists, including kilim designers, painters, fashion designers, installation artists, composers, and jewelry designers constitute another public of Çatalhöyük. The imagery from the site takes various forms in the contemporary art world.

One set of artwork comes from a group of painters and designers who are inspired by the symbolism from Çatalhöyük. An Istanbul-based non-governmental organization, Friends of Çatalhöyük, organized an exhibit in Istanbul in March 2003 where they brought together the work of a group of Turkish artists and designers. Various of the artists who participated in the opening ceremony of the exhibit expressed that their work had been inspired by the "naïveté," "purity," "authenticity," or "simplicity" of the forms and symbolism of prehistoric art. As one put it: "The forms in prehistoric art are so genuine, so simple and pure. In the contemporary world we are bombarded with images, forms, and information. In my work I search and yearn for the genuineness, authenticity of the prehistoric world." Many of the artists expressed nostalgia for what they believed to be "uncontaminated" prehistoric times.

A similar search for authenticity and purity in prehistory is apparent in the work of Bahar Korçan, an internationally recognized fashion designer who based the designs for her 1997 collection on Çatalhöyük themes. Fascinated by the idea of the Goddess and interested in the role of women at Çatalhöyük, she called her fashion show "Women of Another Time" (see illus. 2). She suggested that she imagined the women of Çatalhöyük wrapped in natural fabrics and therefore she wanted her show to express the "naturalness and purity" of that time. To enhance this sense of purity and authenticity, the models wore no shoes or accessories, and the clothes were of natural silk without any metal fasteners or buttons. Ian Hodder introduced the fashion show; the catwalk was constructed in front of a full-sized model of a Çatalhöyük house with images from the site projected in the background. In the examples of the art exhibit and the fashion show, the prehistoric past is encoded in contemporary

2. Scene from the fashion show "Women of Another Time." Courtesy of Çatalhöyük Research Project.

paintings, sculptures, and dresses—a process through which another time that is believed to be more authentic, genuine, and pure is reconstructed.

Another kind of search for authenticity comes from the interest of the local and international carpet and kilim groups in the imagery of Çatalhöyük. Their interest is derived mainly from the claims that the origins of designs found in contemporary kilims can be traced back to the art at Çatalhöyük (e.g., Mellaart et al. 1989). Their search for authenticity is, however, entangled with the politics of the contemporary carpet market rather than nostalgia for the prehistoric past. An example of this is the recent proposal made by a group of people in the kilim business to the Çatalhöyük research project. The suggestion is to produce handmade kilims using designs from Çatalhöyük wall paintings and to introduce them to the market with accompanying certificates or booklets produced by the project. The certificates will contain information about the history and significance of the site and be signed by Ian Hodder to ensure the authenticity of the product.[10] In one of the meetings he had with Ian Hodder at Çatalhöyük, the owner of the carpet business clarified his intentions for his proposal as follows: "In the carpet business, we need to introduce an original product into an increasingly competitive market. There needs to be something that distinguishes our product from others. There has to be an authentic component to it." In this case, handmade production and association with the Çatalhöyük project will ensure the uniqueness and authenticity of the product. Images from a nine-thousand-year-old past resurface within the politics of the contemporary carpet and kilim market where the criteria of authenticity is constantly negotiated between the producers, dealers, and the consumers.

The artwork of Adrienne Momi, an installation/landscape artist from California, raises another set of issues regarding the past in the present. Momi produced an installation art at Çatalhöyük during the 2001 season that she called *Turning Through Time: Communication with the Distant Past at Çatalhöyük*. Her work constituted a big spiral on the ground made out of white and brown paper, with Çatalhöyük images printed on handmade paper placed on white and brown paper. In addition to her interest in tracing the continuities of the

10. This proposal is still under negotiation between the kilim producers and Ian Hodder as to whether there will be such cooperation between the two.

ancient past in the present, Momi describes her work as an attempt to question and blur the boundaries between art and science, drawing attention to novel ways of using both artistic and scientific depictions in narrating the past: "We just have to accept that there are certain things that we can learn and know through science and scientific methods. But there are certain areas such as human experience, emotions, or relationships that are better understood through the use of art. What I am trying to do is actually to marry art methods with scientific methods to learn about the human condition. I use installation art as a method of inquiry."

During my interview with her, Momi challenges the contemporary methods of archaeology through her method of inquiry—installation art. "There has been enough digging at this site," she says. "I want to cover it up, give the images that have been dug out back to the site." Placing papers with Çatalhöyük imagery on the mound is her way of "giving back" the symbolism of the site. The installation art is also her means of communicating with the prehistoric past.

Concluding Remarks

Çatalhöyük is a nine-thousand-year-old archaeological site with no apparent links to any contemporary ethnic or racial group or religion. But perhaps it is precisely this aspect of Çatalhöyük that renders the multiple readings, interpretations, appropriations, and claims described above. It is presented and re-presented by various groups ranging from bureaucrats to archaeologists, from New Age groups to kilim designers, from local villagers to fashion designers. The appropriation and contestation of the past and the resulting tensions and shifting alliances between various groups bring into focus the complex meanings the word "heritage" acquires. As Raphael Samuel suggests, " 'Heritage' is a nomadic term that travels easily . . . a term capricious enough to accommodate widely discrepant meanings" (1994, 205). Çatalhöyük is a heritage site in this sense. For the Turkish state it is part of the national heritage that should be protected and controlled. For the archaeologists it is an extremely significant site that can provide scientific clues as to the origins of human settlement in the Mediterrenean and Near East. For the local communities it is a means for social and economic development, a medium through which the nature of the "local" is (re)formulated and (re)confirmed, and the existing power structures and hierarchies are (re)worked. For the New Age and Goddess groups, it is a spiritual and sacred site. For the artists and fashion and kilim designers, it is a source of inspiration and a marketable product.

It is through the encounters of these publics of Çatalhöyük that the public memory of the site is constructed. Series of alliances and identifications are formed among these groups that cross-cut, complement, and trouble one another. Archaeologists interact with the local and central government officials in various ways, such as acquiring research permits, participating in local symposiums and festivals, and getting help in the day-to-day running of the excavation. They work with the nearby villagers in interpreting the findings at the site, but they also deal with improvements in the infrastructure of the area. Local bureaucrats use every opportunity to claim and "own" Çatalhöyük and compete with the local villagers over the "ownership" of the site. Although the villagers are interested in archaeological tourism as a means for development, in their interactions with Goddess groups they reevaluate the nature of this development. It is through these encounters and the practices of claiming the site that Çatalhöyük is presented and remembered as an archaeological site, a touristic site, a sacred site, an inspirational site, and a national site.

Such varied and discrepant uses and interpretations of Çatalhöyük do not necessarily imply that each of these groups has equal power in the production and consumption of the public memory of this site nor are their interpretations all equally valid or tenable. Multiple and discrepant representations of the past are not free-floating representations but are embedded within the existing power relationships and are used to either reinforce or challenge them. Any representation, as Stuart Hall notes, "is always positioned in a discourse. It comes from a place, out of a specific history, out of a specific set of power relationships. Discourse, in that sense, is always placed" (Hall 1991, 36). The challenge is to understand in what sense all of these discrepant accounts of Çatalhöyük are valid. It is vital to examine the different historical contexts that give rise to the diverse narratives and situate them within existing power relations and practices. It is only through situating the politics of heritage in specific locales with particular historical, political, and social trajectories that we can deal with questions of who gets to tell which story about the past, and to whom, and under which circumstances, and through what means; and which histories are invoked for what ends, and how these are contested and reworked.

5

An Endless Death and an Eternal Mourning

November 10 in Turkey

Nazlı Ökten

The shrill sound of sirens heard all over the country every November 10 at 9:05 A.M. refreshes collective memory in Turkey, signaling the presumed moment when Mustafa Kemal Atatürk, founder of the Turkish Republic, died in 1938. It is difficult to find an educated Turkish person who has not memorized the poem beginning, "My Ata closed his eyes in Dolmabahçe at five past nine, and the whole world cried," or has not recited the line "My Ata, my Ata, wake up! I will lie down in your place."[1] Declaring allegiance to him and memorizing tales about his childhood and adult life are common practices for primary school children. His portraits are ubiquitous, covering the walls of government offices as well as homes. Since the 1990s, his image appears even in pop music video clips and advertisements.

Atatürk is the most important hero as well as a controversial figure on the Turkish political scene. In his authoritative biography, Andrew Mango (1999) reveals conflicts in the historical events attributed to Atatürk as a way to understand the contradictions involved in the process of nation formation. Although Turkish citizens unanimously agree on his role as savior of the country, commander-in-chief of the national liberation army, and founder of the republic, they debate the appropriateness of his reform policies that replaced Islam with a secular-nationalist doctrine. Especially after the coup d'é-

---

1. *Atam* literally means "my ancestor" and *Atatürk* means "the ancestor of Turks." Many times it is translated as "the father of Turks" in English, but since father is *baba,* this phrase fails to give a full sense of the cult of ancestors prevalent in Turkish culture.

tat of 1980, admiration for Atatürk evolved to veneration and reached its peak in the 1990s as a reaction to the rise of political Islam. Following depoliticization measures in the 1980s, the only legitimate ideology was Atatürkism.[2] Atatürk was also the only remaining symbol by which to declare support for a secular-modern way of life. The emergence of Atatürk as a cult figure can also be interpreted as a statement against the fundamentalists (Saktanber 1997). A dramatic increase in the building of Atatürk monuments and statues was accompanied by acts of vandalism against them. This is not a simple polarization between Islam and secularism, however, because the Islamist party has also begun to appropriate the image of Atatürk (see chap. 6).

Islamists' use of Atatürk's image to project legitimacy in the public sphere is the most suspect among many so-called fake-Atatürkist acts. Using the dominant paradigm to gain easy access to a limited public sphere in this case leads to the malformation of a public ground for mutual consent since its terms and conditions of participation are not clearly and openly debated. Secularists fear that Islamists are doing *takiyye,* that is, they are hiding their real intention, which is to attain an Islamic state. Islamists similarly suspect the secularists of having a hidden agenda to preserve the existing status quo at all costs. According to the Islamist party, secularists misinterpret Atatürk's aims and goals for Turkey. Islamist appropriation of Atatürk as an icon comes after a long period of rejection. It can be seen as an effort to use the hegemonic iconography in order to conceal the existing conflict with the secularists and to move on to more crucial issues for their electorate. As a result both groups express their commitment to common national goals by venerating Atatürk. The most important part of this veneration is organized around the leader's death. Both Islamists and secularists utilize November 10 memorials as an opportunity to express their contemporary political agenda.

Ceremonies and rituals constitute an important part of the political dramaturgy in every modern society. They contain and transfer information (Abélès 1990) and at the same time dramatize power relations in society (Balandier 1971). Hence, political culture consists of values, codes, and symbols

2. In that period, even the word *ideology* had a negative connotation. The official ideology of the state, once known as Kemalism, was renamed Atatürkçülük (Atatürkism) in order to remove any ideological connotations.

that mediate between affectivity and rationality. Reverence for and admiration of national heroes and nation builders are shared characteristics of nation-states. Succeeding generations of citizens reevaluate the historical role and career of their leaders. Atatürk is one such symbol, which determines political affectivity. Every verbal or physical act relating itself symbolically to Atatürk gives us important clues about Turkish political culture. The different symbolic forms that venerate Atatürk intertwine the sacred with the profane, the public with the private. Appropriation of Atatürk's imagery helps political groups to achieve distinct identities. Furthermore, his images provide the means to achieve legitimacy in the eyes of the public.

The main premise of this essay is that the rites and acts relating to Atatürk's death play a crucial role in the formation of a certain type of political habitus that Pierre Bourdieu defines as "systems of durable, transposable dispositions, structured structures predisposed to function as structuring structures" (1977, 72).[3] The first section of the essay discusses how various actors in the public sphere utilize Atatürk as a key symbol in Turkish political culture. In the second section, narratives of senior citizens who witnessed the day Atatürk died are analyzed in order to understand how this past is reconstructed today.

Mourning: Sacred or Profane?

Since December 26, 1938, when the Republican People's Party Congress named Atatürk the "immortal leader," commemorating Atatürk's death has been central to organizing the symbolic forms of respect for the nation builder. Today bars and clubs are no longer closed down for the national day of mourning, but it is possible to observe people stopping and getting out of their cars and sometimes even warning others who do not when sirens wail at five past nine. Like other rites, November 10 is constantly reinvented in the sacred and profane realms through continuous production of consent or obligation. What sorts of processes lead to this kind of reinvention? Partha Chatterjee (2000) reevaluates the debate on the Westernization of mourning

---

3. According to Pierre Bourdieu, habitus also involves interiorization of social practices, such as the manners of making, of seeing, and of feeling.

practices in the late nineteenth century in India through Jurgen Habermas' definition of a new personhood, where the private and intimate is reoriented toward the public. An Indian poet who protests the Western style of commemorating death, on the basis that it is showy, argues that rejecting traditional mourning practices causes an artificial ambiance. The problem that the poet faces is the struggle between different types of public expressions. A comparable debate took place in Turkey a few years ago over the commemoration of Atatürk's death. Some Islamic groups proposed to recite *Mevlid* and prayers on November 10, instead of engaging in Western ceremonies that are accompanied by flowers and a moment of silence.[4] They asked, "If he was a Muslim, why don't we pray for him?" The question is full of allusion. There are two ways of stating the issue: One group of Muslims believes that Atatürk was the leader and the savior of a Muslim nation. Others believe that Atatürk was an enemy of religion. The first group—a rather small one—searches for a way to relate the leader to their mystical beliefs. In 2000, a group of people calling themselves the Mevlana Lovers Association published a CD entitled "Declaration of Love: Hymns and Mevlevi Service for the Memory of the Great Leader" (İlan-ı Aşk: Büyük Önder'in Anısına İlahiler ve Mevlevi Ayini).[5] In some hymns Atatürk is called "the shadow of God and the sword of the prophet Ali," and many other mystical characteristics are still attributed to him.[6] Such attributions are quite disturbing for other religious groups.

Mevlid ceremonies reveal the possibility of overlapping of religious and secular types of publicity. National television channels broadcast *Mevlid* recitations from important mosques on religious holidays. In the final part of the ceremony the reciter prays in Turkish for the well-being and peace of the nation. He also recites a prayer for the memory of the nation's saviors and heroes and specifically for Mustafa Kemal Atatürk. When they lose a loved one, ur-

4. In Arabic and Turkish literature, long poems written as a eulogy to the life of Prophet Mohammed are called *Mevlid.* These poems are recited along with other prayers during special occasions such as birth or death ceremonies.

5. Mevlana was a fifteenth-century Muslim mystic and spiritual leader of the whirling dervishes.

6. Ali is the spiritual leader of the Shiite sect. Turkish Shiites known as Alevis have a heterodox view of Islam and are supportive of the secular principles of the Turkish Republic.

banites pay religious professionals to recite the *Mevlid* at their home or elsewhere and at the end ask them to pray for Atatürk as well. The scope and content of the last prayer vary. However, this practice is a reminder to each family member of Atatürk's death. His death continues with every other death in Turkey. Like the national commemoration of Atatürk's death on November 10, *Mevlid* prayers increase the sense of loss and underline the continuity of it. Volkan and Itzkowitz (1984) call this an "unfinished work of mourning." Within the same framework, they also consider the fact that Atatürk's body was not buried for fifteen years, until his mausoleum was completed. Unfinished mourning for Atatürk's death and the simultaneous rejection of it are revealed in sentences that begin with "If he were alive. . ." This trend reaches its peak when people make him tell what he would do in a given situation. One of the most striking examples of this phenomenon is revealed on a billboard next to the military barracks near the O-2 highway in Istanbul, which can be seen by passersby.[7] The text next to a picture of Atatürk reads: "They destroyed my bust. They insulted me. My fault was to have saved the country. It was not enough! They said, 'If he were alive, he would be one of us.' Nothing could have offended me more."

Anyone familiar with the political context can easily guess that this statement is a response to Necmettin Erbakan, the former leader of the Islamist Welfare Party, who said that if Atatürk were alive he would be a member of his party. This event is revealing for both sides. The Islamist party tries to accommodate Atatürk instead of rejecting him, while his most fervent defenders do not refrain from making him speak sixty years after his death.

Anıtkabir: The Public Space of Absence

Norbert Elias (1991) argues that power relations standardize the means of communication and at the same time have emotional implications. Political rituals are often related to psychological processes such as idealization and projection. Mausoleums built by the state, guarded by honor guards, and visited in

---

7. The commander Çevik Bir ordered the placement of the billboard in Hasdal military barracks near the O-2 highway in May 2000.

silence, turn the connections between life and death into political obligation (Cohen 1979). Major national political gatherings and monuments to the dead are also sites of political legitimization. Anıtkabir, Atatürk's mausoleum, is no exception.

In her work on the Pantheon in Paris, Mona Ozouf (1984) discusses the characteristics of individuals worthy of remembering: the heroes and the great men of the republic.[8] She defines the hero as the fighter endowed with miraculous forces, and the great man as the founder-legislator with rational projects. The latter is a product of the Enlightenment and takes his power from his human potential rather than possessing sacred powers. As a public figure, Mustafa Kemal Atatürk was endowed with both kinds of powers. As the savior of the country and the liberator of the nation, he was protected by miraculous powers. The story of his pocket watch, which protected his heart from a bullet, is widely known by the Turkish public. At the same time, he is seen as the one whose far-sighted projects carried the nation toward a modern future. In his personality, private and public interests overlap the sacred and profane spheres. The relation between the nation and its savior is emotional and durable: the nation shall be worthy of him because "he dedicated his life to the nation." The theme of citizens being worthy of the founding father can be observed in different domains of life ranging from boats to novels. In 1999, a poster decorating the commuter boats in Istanbul read, "Be a citizen worthy of Atatürk. Do not spit!" This statement defines Atatürk in not only the political but also the physical habitus. Another example of not being worthy of Atatürk comes from a novel by a well-known woman author, Adalet Ağaoğlu (1990). After cheating on her husband, the university professor Aysel wakes up in the middle of the night and looks at the lights of Anıtkabir with a guilty conscience. She thinks that she is unworthy of Atatürk, the superego.

Anıtkabir is also the site of multiple political expressions of national unity as well as conflict. Anıtkabir turned into a wailing wall especially after the march for secularism in 1994 following the Islamist Welfare Party's success in

8. Ozouf (1984) characterizes the Pantheon, where the great men of France are buried, as the Ecole Normale of the dead—a reference to one of the most important colleges where almost all presidents of France received degrees.

municipal elections. Since 1997, a specific kind of protester with Islamist tendencies, called *meczub* (possessed) in the mass media, has haunted the November 10 ceremonies. Calling the protestors *meczub* insinuates that such individuals are irrational dropouts rather than conscientious citizens, for in order to be against Atatürk one has to have lost his mind. Such protesters can hardly utter a word against the ceremony before they are caught with their Qur'ans in hand. In 1999 the police revealed plans for an airplane attack on Anıtkabir by Hizbullah, a terrorist organization with radical Islamist tendencies. This event carried the symbolic importance of Anıtkabir to an even higher level.[9]

To the extent that channels of political expression are obstructed either because of corruption or the structural problems of Turkish democracy, "complaining to Atatürk" has become an increasingly legitimate medium of articulation. Examples of this phenomenon are abundant. On June 9, 1995, students from the Hürriyet Elementary School in Ankara and their parents marched from their school to Anıtkabir to perform a moment of silence. Their aim was to protest the closing of their school. They held banners saying, "Atam, they favor money over schooling." Although their demands should have been oriented toward the Ministry of Education, parents and students were well aware that voicing their protest toward Atatürk would be a more efficient way of gaining publicity.

On June 24, 2000, a convoy of 80 buses traveled from Istanbul to Ankara. The passengers included the current and former employees of Türkbank, a well-known national bank. At the same time 120 buses of Türkbank employees from other regions of Turkey were also moving toward Ankara. That day more than ten thousand employees gathered in Tandoğan Square in Ankara. Their objective was to protest the merging of Türkbank with eight other banks, which would lead to the dissolution of their bank and their dismissal. The report of the event in the newsletter of the Banking and Insurance Workers Union read: "At 3:00 P.M. 10,000 members of the Türkbank family visited

9. One should also remember that the infamous events of September 6–7, 1955, when Christian minorities of Istanbul were attacked, started with a rumor that Atatürk's house in Salonica had been bombed.

Atatürk in order to pay respect with a moment of silence, in a manner worthy of their institutional culture."

The newsletter was covered with pictures of their march to Anıtkabir with Turkish flags in hand and of the moment of silence they observed. The headline of the newsletter over a picture of Anıtkabir read, "Ankara, Ankara, hear our voice." [10] The article emphasized that the mentality that was trying to close Türkbank was embarrassing for "Atatürk's Turkey." On this occasion, too, we see that a legitimate address to the national political will requires a reference to Atatürk.

Similarly, on June 28, 2000, a father who had lost his young daughter in a car accident began to march from Istanbul to Ankara, aiming for Anıtkabir to demand an efficient traffic code. The media supported him during his walk, and the authorities allowed him to sign the formal guest book in Anıtkabir. His access to the guest book demonstrates that officials recognized his demand as legitimate. The use of Atatürk as recourse for public demands, complaints, and wishes has become routine. Atatürk's mausoleum has become the refuge for unfulfilled expectations.

Meanwhile, citizens not only make demands and complaints to Atatürk but also avow their feelings of indebtedness and gratitude. The first Turk elected to the American National Academy of Sciences, geologist Celal Şengör, told a Turkish journalist following his election: "I am happy to see that we are on the right path. By the way, I am thinking of going to Anıtkabir in order to thank Atatürk. We could not be where we are without him. That is why I will go to Anıtkabir and say to Atatürk, 'Paşam, we executed this part of the mission.'" *Paşam* is a form of address used by Atatürk's contemporaries and colleagues. By addressing him this way, Şengör might be implying that he was a colleague of Atatürk struggling for an unfinished project. As an accomplished scientist, Şengör is responsible and grateful to one person: Atatürk. He does not see his success as a personal one but as the result of the republic's modernization project. On this particular occasion, Celal Şengör represented the Turkish elite who identified themselves with Atatürk.

---

10. Ankara is the capital of Turkey.

The Private Space of Absence: Individual Memory

You and Us

How do citizens who witnessed the death of the savior and founder of the nation remember and reconstruct his death and his immortality? In order to see how individual memories reconstruct and are reconstructed by collective memory, I conducted more than thirty interviews during November 1999 and June 2000 mostly with middle-class men and women over seventy years old. I asked them to tell me about their personal reactions, as well as those of their relatives and friends, when they learned that Atatürk was deceased. I informed them about my questions a few days in advance in order to give them time to rethink and remember their experiences. I asked them if they remembered where they were that day; what they were doing when they heard the news; how they felt; when the first time was that they saw Atatürk's image; and how they define the characteristics of his charismatic leadership. They also talked about their life experiences and worldviews. My aim was to understand how moments of personal history overlap with national ones. Every interviewee expressed anxiety over not being able to remember and not having adequate knowledge. It was interesting for them to try to find those points of intersection between private and public histories (between the ego and the other), but it was also tiring. My first interviewee was especially noteworthy. Nivert was a ninety-seven-year-old Armenian lady who had been living alone for twenty-two years. As a minority, a woman, and a senior citizen, her ties with the external world were loose, but her past was as precious as her mind. She was in good health, even capable of doing housework. Nivert's ultimate fear was losing her memory. She told me the story of the friend of a friend, who rang his neighbor's door six times in an hour in order to give information that he had already given. She thought this was a nightmare, and she prayed to God to let her die before he took her memory and consciousness away. Nivert separated herself from others in another way: "Let me tell you something. I remember Atatürk very well. Men used to wear the fez [a nineteenth-century Ottoman male head cover]. I was in Paris. I had been there to see my brother for a few months. When I came back I saw that men were wearing hats. That was great.

And then you used to write from right to the left, you know. At the time we were not learning Turkish at school. I learned it myself by speaking. And then Atatürk wanted to have a new alphabet for the Turkish, too, didn't he?"

Nivert then started to speak about two well-chosen memories. The first one was about the role of Agop Martayan, an Armenian linguist and encyclopedia writer, in the preparation of the new Turkish alphabet with Latin letters. The second one was about the piano tuner who tuned her piano. The tuner told her that he also used to tune the piano at Dolmabahçe Palace, where he met Atatürk. At first he was afraid. She said, "Of course, he was not used to being in the presence of great men." But then Atatürk conversed with him about his skill. As an Armenian intellectual who had taken an active part in the development of the republic, Agop Martayan was binding her to the nation-state, and the tuner was connecting her to the founder of the nation through her piano.

During her lifetime, Nivert was distanced from the public sphere both as a woman and as a minority. During the interview, however, she presented me with two stories that connected her to the national history. From the first moment in the interview, she put herself at a distance from me without hesitation by referring to "you" as "Turks" and to "us" as "Armenians." Nivert had not stepped out of her apartment for decades. Her already limited participation in public life was at minimum. In a sense, Nivert had anticipated my perception of her and easily put religious and cultural categories in their places. Speaking French, citing Goethe, playing the piano—she was cultivated.

Atatürk impressed her because he asked the piano tuner where he learned how to tune. Atatürk was so intelligent and perceptive that he thought about such details: "What can we say about a man of such scale? Who are we to talk about him?" Others shared her confusion. They found it difficult to understand why somebody would be interested in their memories and ideas about Atatürk. Like the piano tuner who was unaccustomed to the presence of great men, as ordinary individuals they could not grasp why I asked them questions about a great man. Most of the time they saw our interviews as a useless confirmation of what was already evident. They thought of our conversations as performing their duty toward Atatürk rather than providing useful information.

Whatever their reasons for agreeing to talk to me, they all found themselves related to the public life through small details. Although details differ sharply, the symbolic patterns were similar. They thought that they were not worthy of attention when compared with Atatürk and that what they had experienced did not matter. But they all had kept even small details of their memories about Atatürk in their minds. For it is such details that make them feel a part of the larger history of the nation.

Common Man in the Presence of a Great Man

The division between the ordinary citizen and the great man reinforces the perception of Atatürk as "unquestionable." The name Atatürk combines the miraculous achievements of the hero with the enlightened projections of the great man. This synthesis creates a protective halo that renders him untouchable. When I asked Kenan, another contemporary of Atatürk, what he thought when he saw Atatürk's image for the first time, he answered: "As if he were a transcendent being, like a supreme being, different from everyone— you know the mind of a child. . . . But as I learned more about him I saw that he was even greater, really superior. . . . But, you know, we imagined that he was omnipotent, capable of frightening the entire world and our enemies. We were told that no harm could touch us while he was alive and so we believed."

Even though Kenan defined his perception as coming from the mind of a child, he regards Atatürk as "really superior." What he learned and what he believes converge even if they are on different levels of understanding. What he meant by the mind of a child was not insignificant. It is a mind that perceives its own limits in front of the superior one. Atatürk, the omnipotent figure, the one who scares everyone, symbolizes the unified power of the nation. Not only politicians, leaders, and peoples were afraid of him: entire countries were. The image of a trusted father who is able to protect his children revealed itself in a conflict with Italy. Rumors have spread that when Atatürk was angry with Mussolini, he said, "They should not force me to wear the boot"—referring to Italy's geographic shape. Kenan added:

> What I would like to tell about Atatürk is that whatever is said [about him] is useless. What makes him great is the fact that he dedicated himself to the Turkish nation. A magnificent man, there is nothing to say about him. [Al-

most shouting] Nobody can do anything about it. In 1928, Atatürk made a speech in Dolmabahçe: İsmet Paşa had been saying that we must give three years for the alphabet revolution [changing from Arabic to Latin script].[11] Atatürk responded to him, "Paşa, Paşa, we will do it in three months, not in three years." As a matter of fact, Atatürk did a lot in three months in order to put his nation into shape.[12] I was in primary school at the time. For three months every one of our teachers studied day and night. At the end of the three months they really learned a lot and finished it as Atatürk said. Quite an endeavor!

Fikret is a retired banker and the recipient of a research prize given by a daily newspaper in 1981, on the one-hundredth anniversary of Atatürk's birthday in 1981. During the interview he insisted on glancing at his study. When I told him that I was interested in his experiences, he laughed as though they were unworthy of attention. I encountered the same laugh when I asked Fikret to evaluate Atatürk's accomplishments. He and I were inadequate to judge his worth, his grandeur.

The difference between the ordinary man and the great man is also projected onto Atatürk's relationship with İsmet İnönü. While anything was possible for the great leader (as can be seen in the matter of alphabet reform), İnönü was a common man who needed to be realistic. An eighty-two-year-old retired merchant from İstanbul made the same comparison between Atatürk and İnönü in relation to Turkey's neutrality during World War II: "If Atatürk were alive he would have gone to war. The worst mistake of İsmet Paşa was to let the twelve islands go from our hands. Atatürk would have taken them. How can one let go such an occasion? İsmet Paşa was good, but he was too cautious. In İnönü's place, Atatürk would have gone to war [laughing]. I think of this possibility. His grandeur is beyond explanation. You know the circumstances today. He would not allow this: this [political] party, that [Islamist Welfare] party."

11. İsmet İnönü was the second president of the Turkish Republic, replacing Atatürk. He also carried the title of *milli Şef* (national chief). He took the secular reforms further and held an authoritarian position against both leftist and rightist attempts at political formation.

12. The term used here is *adam etmek*. It means making someone a man so that he becomes useful to society. This phrase is reminiscent of a father teaching his son how to be a man.

For Fikret, what was appropriate for Atatürk was not appropriate for İnönü, and vice versa. İnönü did the right thing by keeping Turkey neutral during World War II. Atatürk would not have done the same, but that would ultimately have been the right thing to do as well. Great men have their own secret ways that we, ordinary people, cannot understand. It was easy to see from Fikret's smile and his euphoria that he saw in Atatürk the energy of an unmanageable little boy. This was the key to Atatürk's revolutionary power. He could challenge the status quo.

Fikret described seeing Atatürk:

—The first time I saw Atatürk was when he came to Ordu. He was received with a remarkable ceremony. At that time he had not taken the name Atatürk yet. He was Gazi Mustafa Kemal Paşa. My mother, may she rest in peace, took me to see Atatürk. She was veiled at that time. She told me that she saw Atatürk, but personally I do not remember.

People loved him. [They] would like to see him everywhere but he was hard to see in that time's conditions. I saw him in person just once. But I do not remember the exact date right now. There were villas in Mecidiyeköy at the time. I saw him in person, on the horse.

—What did you feel?

—I got excited. All the people of Mecidiyeköy came by and waited for hours in order to see him.

In fact I was so young at the time, when we went from Sivas to Kayseri (Central Anatolia), that I did not even know that he was Atatürk himself. They said Paşa is coming, and we went out. My grandfather, my father, they were all excited, for Paşa was coming, but I did not know who the Paşa was; I was skipping a rope.

Mecidiyeköy in Istanbul, in Ordu, or in Sivas, wherever he went Atatürk magnetized people. His slightest glance, his smallest gesture carried the myths about him further. His contemporaries say he could remember any person he glimpsed just once, that his magic passed to everyone who was in some way or another related with him. But at the same time he was humble and showed interest in people, asked questions, and gave advice. He had every reason to be inaccessible and distant, but still he was approachable and receptive: unexpectedly accessible. On the one hand, he incorporated republican values and kept an equal distance from every citizen. On the other, being a miraculous hero, he could come surprisingly close. A retired banker, İsmet, recounted Atatürk's visit to his high school at the time. His grandson was smiling ironically while the banker told me that Atatürk caressed his hair during the visit; that made me think that not all the details might be accurate. True or not, the desire for the magic touch seems obvious. As İsmet recalled the event,

> I was in Elazığ when Atatürk came in after taking Hatay [on the Syrian border]. All the teachers were called to People's Houses *(halkevleri)*.[13] We were waiting outside. He came out with a group of people. We did not even hear his voice. Later they said that he was ill at the time. But he looked at everybody one by one. He nodded to everyone; he was so intelligent that I am sure he would recognize everyone if he met them elsewhere. I wanted to go near him, but my husband would not let me. We saw Atatürk and then we left. But, of course, we regretted his death very much. After I saw him, I held his hand in my dream. I said to myself: If this hand does not get smaller he will get well. But it got smaller.

Even in dreams, Atatürk's touch could be seen as possessing the power to foretell the future. Lale, another of Atatürk's contemporaries, hides the frustration of seeing him as more vulnerable than she had imagined by stating that he could remember everybody. Still, his hand became smaller in her dream. The sight of vanishing power becomes a portent of the inevitable end.

The themes of seeing and being seen by Atatürk arise frequently in Turkey. Like a superego watching the ego to keep it under control, Atatürk keeps his eyes on the Turkish nation to see if it does well on the way of

---

13. A nationwide system of "People's Houses" functioned as community centers, town halls, and venues for cultural activities for children and adults in the early days of the republic. In the memory of the leftists they constituted a massive contribution to mass education, graduate studies, and cultural renaissance in Turkey, while for the right-wing they inculcated communist and atheist ideology in Turkey. The People's Houses were closed by the September 12, 1980, military coup d'état.

progress.[14] In response, Turkish people see his image everywhere and not only as effigies. There are a number of natural events and places identified with Atatürk's image. The picture of a pile of clouds looking like Atatürk's eyes, originally published by a national newspaper, now decorates many walls in private and public places. At least two places are called Atatürk cliffs because of rock formations that resemble his profile.

According to Walter Benjamin (1969), gaze expects a response from where it is oriented. To sense the halo around an object is to give it the possibility to look back at us. It is not surprising that the Turkish people want Atatürk to look back at them since his image is omnipresent in Turkey in both public and private places. When the picture looks back at us, it seems as if he is looking from his death.

Very few of the interviewees replied to my question about whether they had heard anything negative about Atatürk. Most of the answers were about criticisms of his drinking habits and his negative attitude toward religion. They repeated the accusations with the fear of being misunderstood. An interviewee remembering the rumors he had heard about Atatürk just after his death said the following while looking at his picture in a newspaper: "People used to talk about him, but they will stay just like this, like kittens. It is Atatürk who made a man out of them. The greatest man of the twentieth century is Atatürk. Nobody else. . . . No need to doubt, after seeing his face. . . . I have four pictures of him at my house."

The people who remain as kittens in his presence wanted to hear and know everything about him. One person said: "We heard that he was having long dinners in his private life. But his policies were for the people's sake, for sure." Another one said: "My aunt told me what it seems that her father had told her before: Atatürk and Latife Hanım [his then wife] used to quarrel. Latife Hanım peeled an apple, stuck it on a knife, and gave it to Atatürk in order to make peace." And another interview declared, "I don't remember the exact date, but when he said to Mussolini, 'They shouldn't force me to wear the boot,' everybody talked about it for days."

14. A 1997 book written by Bedri Baykam, a famous Turkish painter and an ardent Kemalist, is named *Gözleri Üzerimizde* (His Eyes Are Over Us).

Whether it concerned his relationship with his wife or Turkey's relations with Italy, every word Atatürk uttered, every move he made, mattered. He lived completely in the presence of people. So also did he die.

Finding Out about His Death

Before his death, Atatürk was ill for a long time; almost everybody knew that he was on his deathbed. For this reason, no surprises preceded the grief. Almost all interviewees remembered the details of the ceremonies that followed Atatürk's death quite well. His corpse was taken from Dolmabahçe Palace to Sarayburnu, where it was transferred to a battleship that took it to a train heading to Ankara. In Ankara, the corpse stayed in the Ethnography Museum until the construction of Anıtkabir in 1953. Many of the interviewees recounted those details before they were asked about them. His death was the beginning of a journey that was closely followed by newspapers. The fact that the corpse was not buried for years must have had an effect on the people.

> We were in Bursa on November 10. I was at primary school. When we heard the news, the classes stopped. The teacher informed us of the death, and they organized a quick ceremony. Everybody was sad; my sister cried. She was fourteen years old. All the week was sad. There was no television yet, so it was the radio that informed us live about the ceremonies. We did not have a radio. We bought one in 1940. Everybody gathered in the garden café in Setbaşı in order to listen to the radio. It took five or six days to transfer the corpse; the radio and newspapers gave all the details. We used to read *Cumhuriyet*.[15] I can still picture the catafalque taken to the battleship. We followed everything.

The fact that means of information did not exist in individual homes but only in public spaces might be seen as rendering remembrance difficult. We accept Benedict Anderson's (1983) argument that the means of communication are also the means for constructing a nation. Yet, the scarcity of those means may have led to a different kind of sociability. Sharing the news with

15. *Cumhuriyet* functioned as a quasi-official newspaper of the young Turkish Republic.

others may have further enhanced social ties. Feelings of a shared destiny intensified in coffeehouses, tea gardens, and schools: "We were high school students at the time. We used to walk from Mecidiyeköy to Şişli. There was a kiosk at Şişli where newspapers were displayed. We used to read the front pages because we couldn't afford to buy [the paper]. Or we used to go to coffeehouses and tea gardens in order to listen to the radio."

Among the photographs taken on November 10, 1938, one can see women of all ages crying. Many women recall Atatürk's lifetime as a golden age. Women who lived outside Istanbul, especially in Anatolian cities, yearn for those days as they utter sentences such as "His most important achievement was to open men and women to humanity." The same woman said: "I lived in Elazığ [eastern Anatolia] for at least fifteen years; my son was five years old. There was real liberty. I could come in and go out without fear. My daughter used to go to high school in Diyarbakır [another eastern city] without being mistreated. I saw all this."

When the same woman was asked about the ceremonies for Atatürk's death, her answer gave a more accurate idea about women's limited participation in public life. "There was more liberty in Elazığ than in Kayseri, but I couldn't go by myself. I don't remember if they did [a ceremony]."

There was "liberty"[16] but to participate in a ceremony by herself was still inconceivable in a provincial city. Besides, Atatürk's loss raised new concerns. A period of abundance and affluence came to an end with his loss. After the death of the founding hero, there was a vacuum filled with anxiety: "Turkey trusted him so much. . . . It was feared that nobody could replace him, the country would be damaged. . . . Happily, İsmet İnönü, the closest friend of Atatürk, was elected as the president. Then people got peace of mind."

Even if citizens believed that the golden age had come to an end with his loss, they admitted that change was inevitable. When I asked if Atatürk was feared, an elderly man replied: "The people paid him an endless respect, rather than fear. Love and respect all together. People were not as cultivated as today. Now there is more liberty. . . . We say democracy, human rights. . . . Those were not the concerns of that time. In the poverty of the time after the liberation war, it was a huge blessing to have such a leader."

---

16. The word most commonly used is not *freedom (hürriyet* or *özgürlük*), but rather *liberty (serbestlik)*.

This gentleman told me about how respect and fear were intertwined at that time. He said that the kinds of relations fathers and sons, teachers and students have today used to be unimaginable. It is significant that he recounted the transformation of his relationship to authority by showing a parallel with school and family. Like many of the interviewees he was able to question the sources of legitimacy and authority by surpassing an enchanted attachment to the charismatic leader while keeping an affective relationship with his person.

Final Remarks: Will He Find Peace at Last?

Atatürk's figure as *the* political leitmotif of the 1990s shaped the grammar of the public sphere both as an object of transference—to borrow from psychoanalytic terminology—and as an instrument of legitimization. It is an object of transference in the sense that it stands for another. The lack of commonly accepted principles of social and political ethics and the incapacity to produce a sound symbolism of secularity, modernity, or democracy pave the way for a public space that makes reference to Atatürk almost obligatory in order to gain legitimacy. For the cultural elite, Atatürk is a common point of reference that guarantees identification with the masses. As for the masses, who are deprived of the means of efficient participation in the public sphere, it is an intermediary medium. Yet since the real terms and conditions of this medium are not freely debated, fears and suspicions about the authenticity and sincerity of commitments to Atatürk make different sides of the debate distrustful of each other. The scope of significations contained in the persona of Atatürk is in constant evolution within the social sphere, while in the political arena the multiplicity of the significations is not debated. Imposing ideology not by resorting to open debate but by calling on the forces of the collective subconscious, appropriation, legitimization, and manipulation of the image are the main impediments in the way of a democratic political communication.

Talking as if Atatürk is still alive, speaking from his mouth, presenting him as the only figure of legitimacy, points to a constantly reinvented mourning that goes beyond what Volkan and Itzkowitz (1984) call the unfinished work of grief. The symbolic continuation of this mourning in different and renewed forms may be an impediment to the formation of a ground for mutual consent and debate. Each moment of public crisis adds new layers to the halo that surrounds the founding father. Each layer hides within itself unsettled conflicts. The image of Atatürk, which sees and is seen by every Turkish citizen, stands at the heart of the Turkish political and social sphere like an overburdened focal point. His image is a model of political habitus and subjectivity for millions of Turkish citizens. Sixty-five years after his death, the ground of his legitimacy is unquestionable. His image intertwines the durability of efficient charismatic leadership and ideological manipulations of the leader as a symbol of legitimacy. The changing qualities of his veneration argue for more information about the evolution of Turkish political culture.

6

Public Memory as Political Battleground

Islamist Subversions of Republican Nostalgia

Esra Özyürek

On October 29, 1998, the seventy-fifth anniversary of the Turkish Republic, national newspapers were covered with full-page pictures of Mustafa Kemal Atatürk, the founding father of Turkey. *Sabah* published a picture of him sitting on a wall in golf pants with his adopted daughter Sabiha Gökçen, the first woman aviation pilot in the world and thus a potent symbol of modern Turkey.[1] *Milliyet* had a smiling picture of the leader in a three-piece black suit surrounded by young Turkish women in European clothes and hats. *Cumhuriyet* and *Yeni Yüzyıl* selected pictures of him in fashionable hats, elegant coats, and wooden walking sticks, demonstrating the new kind of clothes Atatürk required Turkish citizens to wear.[2] Front-page placement of pictures of the founding leader, a Republic Day tradition of almost eighty years, carries Atatürk to the immediacy of the present day. In 1998, it seemed, newspapers paid particular attention to displaying Atatürk in the modern and secular context he aimed to create for his citizens, rather than printing his isolated portraits.[3]

On the same day, the Islamist daily *Akit* also followed the tradition, but it published a unique photograph of Atatürk. This one has never appeared in

---

1. For the symbolic importance of Sabiha Gökçen in Turkish nationalism, see Altınay (2000).

2. Of these newspapers, *Sabah, Yeni Yüzyıl,* and *Milliyet* have mainstream, liberal, nationalist, and secularist outlooks. *Cumhuriyet* is a left-wing Kemalist daily.

3. For a detailed discussion of the changing image of Atatürk, see Özyürek (2004a).

114

school textbooks, Atatürk documentaries on the official television channels, or Republic Day sections of mainstream newspapers. In this photograph, taken on October 29, 1923, following the public declaration of the new regime as a republic, Atatürk appears among a group of men on the balcony of the National Assembly building. To readers the most striking feature of the photograph is that a religious leader with a white turban stands next to Atatürk. Moreover, everyone in the group, including Atatürk, is saying a prayer with their chest-level palms turned upward. Undoubtedly when they finished their prayer, they rubbed their palms to their faces, said "Amen," and asked God to accept their prayer and protect the new regime.

Akit's editors conflated the extraordinary picture of Atatürk with another equally striking but more familiar one on the same page: a policewoman covering the mouth of a veiled university student. Just as mainstream newspapers placed Atatürk next to images of young women and students, *Akit* also put a

3. Cover page of the daily *Akit,* October 29, 1998. The larger headline reads, "It started like this," and the smaller subhead on the next line reads, "And it became like that." Courtesy of Raip Arpacik.

picture of a young Turkish student next to that of the leader. The female student that appears as Atatürk's ideal, however, wore a flowery pink veil rather than a Western hat or a miniskirt. The picture was taken during the ongoing nationwide protests on university campuses organized by veiled university students after they learned that they would not be allowed to register at universities for the new academic year unless they took off their headdresses.[4] Hence, by using this picture *Akit* indicated that it was the present secularist Turkish government, not the religious people, that was opposing Atatürk's founding principles, which they defined as Islamic. They were reminding the secularist state officials of the earlier alliance Atatürk had made with religious leaders in the country, an alliance that has been forgotten in nationalist history writing and public memory.

During the seventy-fifth anniversary of the Turkish Republic, the memories of the founding years became a way for Islamist and secularist politicians to define their political position and cultural identity. These memories have been deployed, mediated, and managed at an especially charged moment, when the Islamist Welfare Party, after having received the most number of votes in the 1995 general elections, was outlawed in 1997 on the grounds of working against the laicism principle of the Turkish Republic.[5] The officials and supporters of the Virtue Party, which replaced the Welfare Party, attempted to challenge the foundational myths of the Turkish Republic, and more importantly tried to inscribe themselves into the politically legitimate center by revisiting the public memory of the early years. By choosing memory as a site of their political struggle, Islamist activists demonstrate that public memory is not only a ground of cultural reproduction but also a source of resistance to it. The Virtue Party's failure to alter the nature of what is considered as the legitimate public sphere in Turkey, however, points to the limits of memory in transforming present politics.

4. For information on the veiled-student movements in Turkey, see Göle (1996).

5. For an analysis of the constitutional court cases that banned the Islamist Welfare Party and the pro-Kurdish People's Labor Party, see Koğacıoğlu (2003).

Structural Nostalgia

The competing versions of public memory for the foundational years—and more specifically the way they are expressed in public media such as newspapers, political speeches, posters, and banners—point to the fact that nostalgia is not a purely personal emotion. Neither is it merely a romantic moment of recollection. Rather, it can be a politically motivated representation of the past that serves the present. Both Islamist and secularist activists who had access to the media utilized the prevailing disappointment about the present situation in Turkey to depict the foundational years as a time when there was perfect harmony and unity between the state and its citizens. The nature of that unity was, however, hotly contested. Whereas the Virtue Party activists saw religion as the basis of this unity, for secularists it was the desire to be part of the "civilized world." Both camps claimed that their own interpretation of the past should determine the nature of legitimate politics in contemporary Turkey. In other words, as both camps used a nostalgic representation of the past as a blueprint to transform the present, representation of the past became a battleground for struggle over political legitimacy and domination.

Different groups in society often turn to identical moments in the past in order to make competing claims for the present. Based on his study of Greek mountain villages, Michael Herzfeld (1997) argues that a shared vision of the past allows two parties with conflicting interests to interact with each other in a mutually understandable framework. For example, in Crete both state officials and lawless citizens who engage in animal theft share nostalgia for a time when the relations between state and society were perfectly balanced. Herzfeld calls this shared representation of an unspoiled past "structural nostalgia."

Anthropologist Lisa Rofel also demonstrates that in postreform China, different generations remember the socialist regime fondly, but in divergent ways. Older-generation workers who are now marginalized remember Mao's era nostalgically in order to legitimate themselves as heroes of socialism. Contemporary factory managers, on the other hand, have nostalgia for the pre-Cultural Revolution days when workers were obedient, dedicated, and afraid to speak out. Thus, Rofel argues, nostalgia is not only a sentiment but also a "strategy of representation" that individuals employ in order to create a political space or legitimacy for themselves (1999, 35).

Nostalgia can become a political battleground for people with conflicting interests. What is most interesting for our purpose is that structural nostalgia shared by different groups in society can be a resource for the marginalized. By creating alternative representations of an already glorified past, they can make a claim for themselves in the present. It is this kind of a presentist negotiation that the Virtue Party administration sought by redefining the foundational past and more importantly by establishing an exclusive relation to it. The Virtue Party, which invoked an alternative memory of the past, did not necessarily transform the present political sphere. Rather, memory of this authoritative moment moved the party from the margins of the political system to its center.

The Seventy-Fifth Anniversary of the Turkish Republic

The seventy-fifth anniversary of the Turkish Republic was celebrated in a unique political context where politicians, intellectuals, and citizens debated the past, present, and future of their country. Although not traditionally a significant number, the seventy-fifth anniversary became the most widely and enthusiastically celebrated anniversary in the history of the Turkish Republic. In the late 1990s Islamist, Kurdish, and liberal intellectuals in Turkey, political advisers in Europe, and funding agencies in the United States criticized the Turkish state for being oppressive and limiting political, social, and economic freedoms. Turkish state officials and army leaders most often interpreted these criticisms as challenges to the founding principles of the Turkish Republic as a secular, homogenous, and independent state. The central state and its supporters used the anniversary to counter these challenges and demonstrate the voluntary support of citizens for the past and present policies of their state. The main target of the activities was, however, curbing political Islam, which had gained unprecedented support during the mid-1990s and challenged the strictly secular principles of the Turkish Republic.

Both international and local factors have contributed to the rise of political Islam in Turkey. Turkish (and Kurdish) Islamists have been influenced by the growth of a larger, worldwide Islamist movement (Roy 1994; Kepel 1994).

Moreover, as Turkey's integration with world capitalism accelerated in the 1980s and the 1990s, owners of small industries in Anatolia, who were mostly religious, grew economically and politically stronger (Gülalp 1999, 2001). The Turkish Islamist movement also benefited from the fact that the 1980 military coup promoted a Turkish-Islamic synthesis as a social glue to hold together the nation, divided along political lines (Sakallıoğlu 1996), and suppressed the leftist movement that was effective in the 1970s (Tuğal 2002). As a result, although living conditions have become increasingly more difficult for the lower classes in the last two decades, only the Welfare Party has emphasized the importance of economic justice. Most importantly, the Welfare Party organized a very effective political campaign in the early 1990s that mobilized local women and built on the already existing relations of trust in the neighborhoods (White 2002). In its political campaign the Welfare Party promised a "just order" *(adil düzen)* that would redistribute wealth morally and support small businessmen (Buğra 2002). In the local elections of 1994 and the national elections of 1995, the Welfare Party won the largest number of the votes and became the leading party in the Parliament, and the party leader, Necmettin Erbakan, became the prime minister.

Even though the conditions were ripe for Islamists to come to power, the Welfare Party's electoral success came as an alarming surprise to many Kemalist citizens (Bartu 1999a, Navaro-Yashin 2002) and army officials. The army, judiciary, and secular nongovernmental organizations quickly organized to conduct an effective campaign against the party (Erdoğan 2000). On February 28, 1997, the army issued a declaration that emphasized the urgent need to protect the laicism principle of the Turkish Republic. When Welfare Party officials received the message, they immediately resigned from government. Other parties in the Parliament formed a new coalition government and implemented a series of policies, named the February 28 measures, that would inhibit political Islam from regaining power. Such measures included banning the Welfare Party and its leader, Erbakan, from politics.

Attempting to rally people against political Islam, the government worked with a nongovernmental organization and planned a mass celebration. Because the new government had come to power after the Welfare Party was banned, the new parties in the coalition were not legitimized by electoral support. If celebrated enthusiastically and without the involvement of the government, the Republic Day celebration would be a proof of popular support for the new government in power and the anti-Islamist measures. Thus, the Economic and Social History Foundation, founded in 1991 by a group of two hundred academics in order to "develop and spread historical consciousness in Turkey," was funded by the prime ministry to organize the celebration (Monceau 2000; Özyürek 2004b).

İlhan Tekeli, the chair of the foundation, stated that the main motivation for a participatory celebration was to make a statement against political Islam. "When the Welfare Party came to power in 1996," he said to me during an interview in the summer of 2001, "as enlightened Turks *(Türk aydınları olarak)* we felt responsible for the Republic and wanted to do something against the religious uprising." In the report he prepared about the celebration, Tekeli argued that the social situation in Turkey required a change in the nature of the celebrations: "Recent threats against the Turkish Republic, in terms of its unity [i.e., the Kurdish movement] and modernization [i.e., the Islamist movement], added significance to the celebration of the Republic" (Tekeli 1998, 21). The new celebrations, Tekeli suggested, would be likened to a festival *(şenlik)* and be organized around three concepts: mass participation *(kitlesel katılım)*, spontaneity *(spontanlık)*, and enthusiasm *(coşku)*. Through such a conceptual reorganization, the celebration would allow citizens to express freely their support for the Turkish state. More importantly, by framing their voice as unrestricted and spontaneous, it would give the supporters of the Turkish state legitimacy against opposition groups.

As secularist officials and intellectuals were attempting to monopolize the legitimate grounds of politics as well as its celebration, Islamist politicians engaged in creative methods to include themselves in the political center from which they were excluded. The banned Welfare Party was reopened with a new name (Virtue Party) and a new leader (Recai Kutan). Even though the party organization and membership were practically the same, Recai Kutan drew a conciliatory portrait and adopted a moderate political discourse. He abandoned the earlier Islamist, anti-Western, and countercapitalist platform in favor of a conservative, center-right one. One interesting strategy the new party embraced was to celebrate the seventy-fifth anniversary of the republic wholeheartedly. This was a novel approach since earlier Welfare Party officials were notorious for not participating in the national celebrations, not singing the national anthem, and not visiting Atatürk's mausoleum. When they celebrated Republic Day, the Virtue Party leadership contested the earlier depictions of the early republic as strictly secular and redefined it as Islamic. By doing so, partisans were able to critique the contemporary secularist officials as departing from the foundational principles and thus wrongly marginalizing Islamists both from the past and the present of the Turkish Republic.

Islamic Representation of the Early Republic

Prior to the seventy-fifth anniversary celebrations in 1998, prominent Islamists had been more interested in commemorating the Ottoman past than the republican regime that had erased the imperial legacy as well as its memory (Houston 2001b). Promoters of neo-Ottomanism had a rather flattened sense of the seven-hundred-year-long rule of the Ottomans and saw the empire as proof of the superior achievements of a "Turkish" state that accepted Islam as its official religion. Ottomanism became especially popular among the newly rising Islamist elite whose members began to use consumerism to mark their political identity as well as their class position (Navaro-Yashin 2002; White 2002). Neo-Ottomanism found nonconsumerist political expressions among the public as well. When the Welfare Party won the local elections in Istanbul, the municipality organized mass celebrations for the previously unpopular anniversary of the conquest of Constantinople on May 29 by the Ottoman sultan Mehmed IV in 1453 (Bora 1999; Çınar 2001). Alternative Islamic commemorations for Istanbul Day, Alev Çınar argues, "serve to construct an alternative national identity that is Ottoman and Islamic, evoking a civilization centered in the city of Istanbul, as opposed to the secular, modern Turkish Republic centered in the capital city of Ankara" (Çınar 2001, 365).

In 1998, after the Welfare Party was banned and reincarnated as the Virtue Party, it adopted a new political strategy in relation to history-based identity. Party activists publicly embraced the memory of the republic without letting go of their Ottomanism. Unlike Kemalist officials and activists who see the rise of political Islam as a fundamental threat to the secular principles of the republic, the Virtue Party officials and some like-minded Islamist intellectuals emphasized the religious origins of the republic. They argued that the current hardships faced by political Islam and religious Muslims contradict the original intent. By resurrecting forgotten aspects of republican history, the Virtue Party countered the contemporary pressures exerted on them by the secular government, which defines the founding principles as strictly secular. More importantly, they aimed to create a legitimate space for themselves in the political center that is defined through commitment to the foundational principles of the Turkish Republic.

A close look at the early years of the republic provided Virtue Party activists with numerous images and sayings of Mustafa Kemal Atatürk in favor of Islam. Even though Atatürk became decreasingly tolerant of religion in the 1930s, during the early 1920s he worked with some religious leaders and mobilized them for the national uprising between 1919 and 1922 (Zürcher 1998, 158–59). During this era he uttered many speeches in favor of Islam, the caliphate, and veiling that are contradicted by his later speeches. In this period, Atatürk also formed alliances with some Kurdish tribes in the southeastern region of the country (Zürcher 1998, 176–80). Once he established the Turkish Republic, consolidated the single-party regime, and defeated his political rivals, Mustafa Kemal delivered a marathon speech to Parliament in 1927 in order to leave behind an official narrative of the foundation of the new regime (Parla 1991). In this narrative he denounced the great majority of his earlier alliances. It is the later approaches and attitudes of the leader that have defined the predominant public memory about the early republic as uniformly secular and nationalist.

After the Turkish Republic was founded in 1923, the single-party regime increasingly became more oppressive toward any public expression of Islam (Berkes 1988; Toprak 1981; Davison 1998) as well as non-Turkish identities (Yıldız 2001). The first major attack on Islamic institutions occurred in 1924, when the six-month-old General Assembly abolished the caliphate, the symbol of Islamic leadership. A year later dervish orders were dissolved and tombs of saints closed down. In 1926, the calendar was changed from the Islamic lunar calendar to the Western solar Gregorian one, and Islamic law was abolished and replaced by the Swiss Civil Code, Italian Penal Code, and German and Italian Commercial Codes. In 1928, the Latin script replaced the Arabic script. During this process, many influential religious leaders, including Muslim sheikhs and clerics, lost their jobs and positions in society; scholars became illiterate overnight. Moreover, they were forced to take off their religious outfits and wear Western hats in accordance with the hat reform of 1925. Although there was no law against veiling, women who veiled faced public pressure and even violent opposition. Many of the witnesses of the early republican era I interviewed told of times when youth gangs would rip veils off women.

The memory of religious oppression is vivid among many religious groups in contemporary Turkey. There is no doubt that not all religious groups have a fond memory of the early republican policies. There are Islamist Web sites that condemn Mustafa Kemal for being a drunk, a womanizer, and an enemy of Muslims.[6] Other Islamist intellectuals, such as Ahmet Kabaklı, recognize him as a great military leader who saved the country from foreign powers, but argue that he is only one of the many military heroes in Turkish and Islamic history and should be treated accordingly (Kabaklı 1998). Thus it would be erroneous to generalize the nostalgic claims of the Virtue Party and affiliated intellectuals toward the foundational years and Mustafa Kemal to the heterogenous Islamist movement in Turkey.[7] It is also important to recognize that some religious groups were only loosely connected with the Welfare and Virtue Parties, and some others support different center-right political parties. The unusual history campaign led by the Virtue Party during the seventy-fifth anniversary celebration was a well-planned rhetorical strategy intended to neutralize past and present pressures against the Islamists and clear a space for Islam in the politically legitimate center.

The Islamist Subversion of the Republican Past

In her contribution to this volume, Nazlı Ökten argues that Atatürk is the central focus of the political sphere in Turkey. Constant referrals to the leader, she claims, serve both the political elite and the masses. For the former, Atatürk is "a common point of reference that guarantees identification with the

---

6. Because of the Turkish law against insulting Atatürk, anti-Kemalist individuals and groups use cyber space to disseminate their ideas. For an example of such a site, founded by Turkish citizens living in Germany, see www.mustafakemal.de.

7. For an account of the ideological-, class-, and ethnicity-based diversity of the Islamist movement in Turkey, see Houston (2001b).

masses," and for the latter "who are deprived of the means of efficient participation in the public sphere, it is an intermediary medium." The political elite often utilize Atatürk to delineate the boundaries of legitimacy, regardless of what the masses desire. In the hegemonic Turkish political sphere, Atatürk stands for the state, the nation, and the public and determines the boundaries of legitimacy.[8] For example, prosecutors of the court case against the Welfare Party in 1998 made frequent reference to sayings of Atatürk critical of Islam in order to prove that the party contradicts the state's foundational principles (Koğacıoğlu 2003). In such a tightly demarcated arena of political legitimacy, Virtue Party activists utilized the medium of Atatürk to have access to the legitimate public sphere from which they were banned.

On Republic Day the headline of *Akit,* located just above the picture of Atatürk praying, reads, "It started like this." Another smaller headline next to the picture of the arrested veiled student contrasts, "And it became like that." In his analysis of newspaper photographs in Egypt, Gregory Starrett suggests that "newspaper stories increasingly act as elaborate captions for their photographic coverage. Descriptions of events provide directions for the reading of the visual images they accompany" (Starrett 2003, 407). By carefully selecting and conflating two powerful pictures, the editors made sure that the photographs told a story on their own. Yet, they also added subtitles to stress further the divergence between the foundational years and the present: "Seventy-five years ago, when Mustafa Kemal Atatürk established the Republic, there were religious leaders in their turbans next to him. And they were praying all together." And "Seventy-five years later this picture is a proof against the claims that the Republic brought freedom." Even though the pictures and their sub-

---

8. Such a close association of political legitimacy with the legacy of a deceased leader contradicts Claude Lefort's definition of modern power. He argues that unlike the premodern world, where authority is invested in the sacralized body of the king, in the modern world political power is disembodied. He argues that in modern society "people experience a fundamental indeterminacy as to the basis of power, law, and knowledge" (Lefort 1988, 19). In the Turkish case, the locus of legitimate power, law, and knowledge ceases to be under the monopoly of a certain individual or group, particularly because it is represented and haunted by the deceased body of Atatürk. A discussion of the reasons and consequences of such a conceptualization warrants a separate essay.

titles made a strong statement, *Akit* provided a more elaborate Islamic interpretation of the republic's foundational years in an editorial:

> The Republic, founded seventy-five years ago following the War of Liberation, was fought by the whole nation, which included the veiled, the bearded, and the baggy-panted.[9] It was declared with prayers and affirmation of the greatness of God. Seventy-five years ago on this day, the enemies were kicked out of the country, the French soldiers who tried to unveil our women were killed by those like Sütçü İmam; the Greek army had to leave the way it came. And seventy-five years ago today, Atatürk declared the Republic next to turbaned religious leaders. And again seventy-five years ago [the Constitution] declared that "the religion of the Turkish state is Islam" in accordance with the beliefs of the people. In those days, there was no such concept as "secularism" used as a tool of oppression. The Republic that was established by blood is celebrated today with whiskey. . . . It was declared that with the Republic, people would be freer. But today, the grandchildren of the people who established the Republic are not allowed in the universities; their right to education is taken away from them.

The above narrative depicts a peculiar portrait of the foundational moment and defines it as Islamic. By doing so, it turns the tables, casting Islamists as the true republicans and secularists as people who diverge from the original aims of the republic. The editors of the newspaper claim that it is the religious Muslims who saved the country from the Allies and the Greeks and allowed a new republic to be born. In those days, they argue, Islam was central to the newly founded state, but today, oppressive state officials have diverged from the foundational spirit. After redefining the foundational intent, *Akit* accuses the Turkish officials of being "counter-Republican" because by banning veiling in the universities, they disrespect the religious principles of those who sacrificed their lives for the republic.

9. Veils, beards, and "baggy pants" are the visible signs of religious Muslims and those of rural background.

On the anniversary of Atatürk's death the same year (Nov. 10, 1998), *Milli Gazete,* another Islamist daily closely associated with the Virtue Party, printed a similarly nostalgic approach to Mustafa Kemal and his era, which they defined as Islamic. That day, their headline read, "We Wish You Had Lived" *(Keşke Yaşasaydın).* Under this call was a picture of him with his then-wife, Latife Hanım, in her black veil, to whom Atatürk had been breifly married in 1924, before he launched his secularization reforms. Even though the French-educated Latife Hanım wore Western garb and let her hair show at other times, she wore a black veil when she accompanied her husband through Anatolia. The section under the veiled picture of the First Lady next to her husband read as follows:

> Mustafa Kemal, the founder of the Republic, on the seventy-fifth anniversary of your creation and on the sixtieth anniversary of your death, we are faced with a group that tortures our nation. This group does not consider the villagers, whom you called the masters of the nation, as humans. They betray you by calling anyone who resists their torture enemies of Atatürk. This group, which is responsible for fulfilling the goals you showed [us], created the following scene: the literacy rate is below the rate in the rest of the world, the per capita income is painful. . . . On the anniversary of your death we recall your sayings about veiling to those who could not learn them during the past seventy-five years: "It is not an issue for us to make changes in how women dress. We are not obliged to teach our nation new things on this issue. As individuals, we can use all kinds of dress according to our taste, our desire, and our education and economic level," and "The veil recommended by our religion suits both life and *virtue* well. Those who imitate European women in their dress should consider that every nation has its own traditions and national particularities. No nation should be an imitator of another." (From a speech delivered by Atatürk on Mar. 21, 1923; emphasis added)

Here *Milli Gazete* adopted the secularist strategy of talking and complaining to Atatürk especially on the anniversary of his death as if he were alive and contemplating the state of his country. The Islamist editors blamed government officials for not being respectful of the traditions of the Anatolian people, whom Atatürk labeled "masters of the nation" *(köylü milletin efendisidir).* They claimed that when government officials denied veiled students the right to an education and work in government offices, they degraded traditional values and even called people who observe them "enemies of Atatürk" *(Atatürk düşmanları).* They also accused officials of misinterpreting Atatürk by abolishing veiling in his name. By publishing Atatürk's words in favor of veiling uttered in 1923, several months before he declared the new regime, *Milli Gazete* tried to demonstrate that contemporary officials were acting against the leader's teachings. Because they were so far away from the foundational intents and principles of the great leader, editors argued, present government officials are even incapable of administering the country properly.

During the 1999 election campaign, six months after the seventy-fifth anniversary, the Virtue Party administration once again emphasized their exclusive connection to the foundational intent. The party activists covered practically every single corner in Istanbul with a simple banner that bore one short sentence: "The republic is virtue" *(Cumhuriyet Fazilettir),* followed by Atatürk's familiar signature. Atatürk had pronounced this sentence during the initial years of the republic while telling people how good a regime a republic is. By choosing this saying as a slogan for their party, the Islamist politicians from the Virtue Party declared themselves both loyal followers of Atatürk and the only true republicans to whom the leader had bequeathed the nation. Through this slogan, they once more challenged secularists who accused them of being Atatürk's enemies and wanted to exclude them from politics.

During the same election campaign, the Virtue Party reemphasized its appreciation of Atatürk and his reverence for religion with a powerful poster. In the background is a black-and-white picture of Atatürk's mother, Zübeyde Hanım, and her adopted son, Abdurrahim Tunçak.[10] In the picture Zübeyde Hanım sits on a chair, her hair loosely covered with a white head scarf. Abdurrahim Tunçak, his face only partly exposed, is respectfully bowing down to

---

10. In later stages of his life Abdurrahim Tunçak declared that he was Atatürk's illegitimate child and that is why Zübeyde Hanım raised him. Although Sabiha Gökçen, one of Atatürk's adopted daughters, denied this statement, the similarity of Abdurrahim Tunçak's features with those of Atatürk are striking.

4. An election poster for the Virtue Party. The caption reads: "The Republic was born in the hands of mothers and will grow up in their hands." Courtesy of Mehmet Bekaroğlu.

kiss her hand, which she keeps at the level of her chin as she proudly looks at the camera.[11] In the poster Abdurrahim Tunçak looks just like Atatürk.[12]

Any Turkish citizen who finished elementary school would have learned

11. For Atatürk's biography, see Kinross (1965), Volkan and Itzkowitz (1984), and Mango (1999). In their famous biography of Atatürk, Volkan and Itzkowitz used the same picture, but

that Zübeyde Hanım was a religious woman. First graders learn that Atatürk was born in a pink house in Salonika to Zübeyde Hanım and Ali Rıza Bey. They also learn that at age seven his parents had an argument about what kind of school little Mustafa should attend. Zübeyde Hanım wanted to send him to a religious school in the neighborhood, but his father wanted to send him to a European-style school. In the end, Mustafa went to the religious school for one year, but because he did not like it there, his father switched him to the progressive one the following year. Soon after the incident Mustafa's father died and his mother raised him, but she was not able to have further influence on his education. It was not even necessary to know these historical references in order to receive the poster's message. The poster appears to show that Mustafa Kemal Atatürk used to bow down in front of his mother in her head scarf. It also reminds viewers that the person who gave birth to and raised the father of the Turkish Republic was a religious woman.

The second image in the poster is also a powerful and carefully chosen one. A smaller color picture visible in the lower right corner of the poster portrays a woman holding a small child in her arms. Like Zübeyde Hanım, this woman also wears a white head scarf. Her loose head cover and simple flowery dress indicate that she is a peasant or a squatter, a recent immigrant to a city. The slogan on the poster reads: "The Republic was born to [veiled] mothers and is growing up in their hands." The poster narrates continuity from Zübeyde Hanım and Atatürk to contemporary veiled religious mothers and their babies. By doing so, it includes veiling, the most potent symbol of a religious lifestyle, in the nationalist symbolism.

The choice of these two head-scarfed women in this poster involves another strategic political move. The secularist army and judicial authorities often argue that political Islam introduced a novel, foreign-inspired, and politically motivated practice of veiling (Özyürek 2000). The kind of veiling that is associated mostly with university students or other young urbanites involves wrapping a wide head scarf around the head in a particular way and attaching

---

the note under the picture says: "A grateful nation pays homage to Atatürk's mother. An unidentified Turk kisses Zübeyde Hanim's hand" (1984, 16).

12. I asked ten or so Turks who the man and woman were in this picture. They all identified the man as Mustafa Kemal and the woman as Zübeyde Hanım, his mother.

it with pins.[13] The fact that Zübeyde Hanım and the peasant women also have head scarves highlights the fact that veiling has historical and traditional roots in Turkey and is a nonpolitical practice that is part of everyday life.

In addition to creating a new representation of the Kemalist past as Islamic, some Islamist intellectuals also subverted the common accusations that they are reactionary *(irticacı)*. This is an old concept used since the nineteenth century by modernist Ottoman and Turkish intellectuals in order to accuse religious people of hindering Turkey from its intended unilinear path toward progress and Westernization. In 1998, during the political campaign in which the Virtue Party attempted to associate itself with the republic and rescue it from the monopoly of the secularists, they turned the "reactionary" accusation around and used it against the secularists who were becoming increasingly nostalgic for the foundational years. Two weeks before Republic Day, the editor of *Milli Gazete* accused the secularists of being "backward":

> Ten to fifteen years ago, covered women who worked in the fields were accused of being reactionary because they were reluctant to send their daughters to school. Now, the same women face political accusations because their daughters go to school with their head scarves. The leftists, who are a continuation of the "single-party" ideology, cannot realize that in real Republican systems, it is the people that count. . . . Does the Republic mean the people, or does it mean Ecevit and Baykal? These men, who are trying to bring back the darkness of the 1940s, will not be able to gain anything by pointing to the nation who founded the Republic as the enemies of the Republic.

Here the editor made a subversive move by saddling the very people who accused Islamists of being backward with the same label. He argued that Islamists are not reactionary but rather progressive, even by the secularists' own criteria. They want to send their daughters to school, but the reactionary secular state officials prohibit them by not allowing veiled students to enroll. He accused the two leaders of the center-left secularist parties, Bülent Ecevit of the Democratic Left Party and Deniz Baykal of Atatürk's Republican People's

---

13. About the politics of wrapping the head scarf in different ways, see Özdalga (1998) and White (1999, 2002).

Party, of wanting to return the country to the dark days of the single-party regime, when people's demands were not taken seriously. Even the choice of the adjective "dark" to define those days subverts the secularist association of religious people with "darkness" and modernization with "enlightenment."

In this piece, the editor clearly named only the 1940s as the "dark ages of the single-party regime," excluding the 1920s and 1930s. By doing so, he disassociated Atatürk, who died in 1938, from the oppression of the single-party regime and held only İsmet İnönü, who succeeded the leader after his death and ruled the country until 1950, responsible for the severe measures against Islam.[14] Although many anti-Islamic measures were taken during Atatürk's time, the editor strategically found an Islamic basis for the foundational intent of Atatürk. This enabled him to go along with the familiar nostalgic narrative of deterioration since Atatürk's death.

The novel turn of the Virtue Party toward the foundational past had particular demands on the present. As secularist intellectuals were organizing an anti-Islamist Republic Day celebration in 1998, the Kemalist judiciary was discussing the possibility of banning the Virtue Party as well. The opponents argued that the Virtue Party was a direct continuation of the Welfare Party and thus a threat against the fundamental principles of the Turkish Republic. By redefining the foundational past as Islamic, the Virtue Party officials emphasized their respect for the founding principles of the republic as well as its founding leader. Rather, they claimed, it was the secularist parties in coalition that diverge from Mustafa Kemal's teachings. Thus, they attempted to demonstrate to voters from diverse sections of society that they are the most appropriate party for ruling the country.

An Alternative Public Gathering of Holding Hands

The public memory of the foundational history was not the only political site the Virtue Party challenged to make it inclusive of Islam. The other symbolically powerful site they chose was the Republic Day celebrations in 1998. During the seventy-fifth-anniversary celebration, Virtue Party supporters organized an alternative gathering that subverted the official messages of

14. For İsmet İnönü's era, see Heper (1998), Koçak (1986), and Aydemir (1966).

national unity. In order to understand the symbolism utilized during the alternative gathering, it is necessary to describe the official anniversary advertisements prepared by the Economic and Social History Foundation.

The Republic Day advertisements published in major newspapers and broadcast on national television channels elaborated the theme of civilian and national unity around secular Republican values. Their main theme was a display of Turkish citizens from all walks of life, including urbanites, peasants, students, and elderly, holding hands. The headline of all the ads read, "We Meet in the Republic" *(Cumhuriyet'te Buluşuyoruz),* indicating that all the citizens come together in republican ideology. Although the main purpose of the ad was to show that Turkish citizens from all walks of life are together, hand in hand, for the Turkish Republic, religious people were excluded in these pictures. All of the hundreds of women, except for four, were bareheaded, mostly wearing suits. Discerning eyes could see the few women in the background wearing head scarves in a mountain village. These women stood for

5. A nationwide "Hand in Hand" demonstration in which veiled protesters in more than twenty cities formed human chains. Courtesy of Raip Arpacik.

peasants, and their head scarves were part of their traditional outfits rather than political statements. Their physical location in the photograph matches their temporal positioning in secularist ideology as belonging to the past. In other words, veiling represents the kind of practice that is supposed to be disappearing as Turkey progresses on its unilinear path toward modernization. Women in the foreground, who would carry Turkey toward its new future, were bare headed and looked like secular urbanites. By depicting only certain kinds of people, the advertisement conveyed the message that only middle— and upper-middle-class and secular people were devoted to republican principles. Moreover, it pointed out that only such people had the duty and privilege of protecting the republic, not only from external threats but also from internal challenges posed by the religious groups.

On October 11, almost three weeks before Republic Day, Virtue Party officials organized a nationwide gathering that challenged the Republic Day advertisement. The initial aim of the gathering was to protest increasing pressures against Islamists in general and veiled university students in particular. Following the banning of the Welfare Party on February 28, 1997, university administrators were ordered to keep veiled students off the campuses for the 1998–99 school year. The protest against the new policies, named "Hand in Hand: A Human Chain for Humanistic Respect and Freedom of Thought," took place simultaneously in more than twenty cities. In each city protestors formed kilometers-long human chains, holding hands, or holding the ends of ribbons to prevent unmarried men and women from holding hands.

Following the Islamist gathering of holding hands, Islamist intellectuals and politicians argued that people in the Republic Day advertisements do not represent the "real" Turkish people. They claimed only the ones who joined the alternative gathering do. Moreover, they asserted, "Hand in Hand" was the only true Republic Day celebration since the chain included all the groups of society without excluding the religious. A day after the protest, İhsan Karahasanoğlu, a columnist for the Islamist daily *Akit* argued that the meeting united the people who had been marginalized by the secular state:

> Television channels broadcast an advertisement for the seventy-fifth anniversary. . . . In the advertisement young and old people from all kinds of backgrounds hold hands. The only missing people are the ones with head

scarves and beards. What we see as the people are only the bare-headed ones. In the advertisement, holding hands symbolizes the celebration of the seventy-fifth anniversary. On October 11 [during the human chain] people with and without beards, with and without head scarves were holding hands. Although the message of the advertisement talks about equality, it does not take an important section of the people into consideration. On October 11, people were in the streets just like the way it was originally intended in the advertisement. But when the real people *(gerçek halk)* held hands, some claimed that they were resisting the Republic. If the Republic brought equality, peace, and freedom, why are people who hold hands on October 11 not equal to other citizens?

It was not only the Islamist intellectuals who were challenging the Republic Day advertisements. As Republic Day was approaching, the Virtue Party printed an alternative poster to the Republic Day advertisements. The poster was very similar to the Republic Day advertisement in showing large groups of people standing next to each other, but this time, instead of the crowd being composed of secular urbanites, it was dominated by veiled and bearded individuals. Above the picture, the slogan "They met in virtue" replaced the original phrase "They met in the republic." By printing this advertisement, the Virtue Party officials declared their commitment to a republican public sphere while at the same time signaling their intention of redefining it as for and populated by religious people.

Despite their opposition toward the exclusionary nature of the secularist definition of republican principles, Islamic intellectuals shared their understanding of civilian participation in politics. Like secularist officials, they believe that there is a single unitary will of the Turkish nation and only one group can represent it. For example, Sadık Albayrak wrote the following in the daily *Milli Gazete:* "The first thing to do on the seventy-fifth anniversary is to find out where the national will that founded the Republic lies. After that, we need to discuss the principles that will be claimed by the whole nation, that will bring together the nation on every single issue."

Albayrak, similar to other Islamist as well as secular intellectuals, believed that the Turkish nation is a holistic entity, one that can come together on every issue. In negating the differences and conflicting interests, Albayrak painted a corporatist picture of society, similar to the one promoted by the single-party regime in the 1930s. This ideology took shape under the influence of the Durkhemian concept of organic society and contemporary authoritarian regimes (Parla 1985). Kemalist corporatism assumed that Turkish society was exempt from interest conflicts and that status differences helped it to function like a harmonious machine working to realize the nationally shared goals. Instead of emphasizing the legitimacy of their different yet marginalized interests in the political public sphere, post-1997 Islamic intellectuals affiliated with the Virtue Party chose to redefine a unitary national will as Islamic.

Conclusion

The changing temporal orientation for constructing utopias had profound effects on the way dominant and oppositional groups represented themselves at the end of the twentieth century (Boym 2001). In late-1990s Turkey, both Kemalist and Islamist politicians located their utopias in the past rather than the future. As opposed to Kemalists, who yearned for the 1930s, Islamists took an alternative approach to memory-based identity and idealized the Ottoman period when Islam was the official religion of the state. Yet, when the February 28 measures against political Islam limited the legitimate boundaries of politics in Turkey in 1997, officials of the new Islamic party (Virtue Party) turned toward the republican past. By highlighting the Islamic aspects of the foundational moment, they tried to include themselves in the politically legitimate sphere.

A question that follows the above observation regards the consequence of the political move the Virtue Party made toward the political center by introducing a novel memory of the founding moment. Has the Virtue Party been successful in transforming the nature and limits of what is considered as the legitimate political sphere in Turkey? Was it able to create an alternative political sphere? Or has the party transformed and adapted itself to the rules of the dominant public sphere?

In his recent work "Publics and Counterpublics" (2002), Michael Warner questions the relationship between the dominant and alternative public spheres. His analysis builds on the earlier critiques of a Habermasian concept of the public sphere—a discursive arena where citizens are free to discuss political matters important to them rationally and critically (Habermas 1991). Agreeing with scholars who demonstrated that the European and American public spheres were not open to all but rather were closed to women (Fraser 1999; Ryan 1999), the working class (Eley 1999), and nonwhites, Warner aims to understand the transformative capacities of counterpublics formed by such excluded groups.[15] He defines dominant publics as those "that can take their discourse pragmatics and their lifeworlds for granted, misrecognizing the indefinite scope of their expansive address as universality or normalcy." Counterpublics on the other hand "are spaces of circulation in which it is hoped that the poesis of scene making will be transformative, not replicative merely" (Warner 2002, 88).

According to Warner's definition, we can consider the secular public sphere in Turkey as the dominant public, in the sense that it takes its life world as granted and normal, and imagines all Turkish citizens as its natural addressees. The Islamic public—or at least those who support an Islamic party—can be defined as a counterpublic, since it addresses a subgroup with particular needs and interests. By accepting the key symbolisms of the dominant public sphere, however, the Virtue Party replicated the codes of the dominant public sphere rather than transforming them. In the late 1990s the Virtue Party activists made reference to the authoritative nature of the foundational history in determining present politics in contemporary Turkey. Yet, rather than recognizing it as a multifaceted process shaped by different groups with sometimes contradictory interests, the Islamist politicians also defined the founding moment with a singular aim. They challenged the secularist monopoly over this moment, but embraced a similarly narrow definition and argued that Mustafa Kemal and his friends had aimed to create a country infused with Islamic principles.

Even if many partisans did not embrace the memory of the founding leader in their private lives, invoking the memory of the founding moment indicated the center-right direction the Islamist party was heading toward. This trend was more apparent in the alternative celebration of the Republic Day

---

15. Earlier Nancy Fraser (1999) also wrote about the effects of subaltern publics in expanding the limits of democracy. Michael Warner (2002) criticizes her approach by arguing that Fraser does not define how such publics would be able to transform the dominant one.

"Hand in Hand" gathering that made a reference to the central nationalist symbol of "the people." In their evaluation of the event, Virtue Party-affiliated intellectuals reproduced the dominant image of a homogenous—and exclusively Islamic—nation, undivided along lines of class, ethnicity, and religiosity. Instead of introducing the multiplicity of religious beliefs and political positions as a means of legitimacy—which would have a transformative impact on the political sphere—they reproduced the symbolism of the dominant public, which imagines a uniform public and perceives a singular representation as sufficient. In the end, the attempts of the Virtue Party in revoking an alternative memory of the founding moment were more effective in transforming the party from its marginal position toward center right and less effective in challenging the limits of the legitimate public sphere in Turkey. Despite its attempts at moving toward the center, the Virtue Party was also eventually banned from politics on the basis of being a direct continuation of the Welfare Party. Yet, as this essay is being written, the Justice and Development Party, which is an offshoot of the Virtue Party, is in government and implements a center-right, pro-European Union and pro-International Monetary Fund political agenda with an increasingly less religious discourse.

7

Memories of Violence, Memoirs of Nation

The 1915 Massacres and the Construction of Armenian Identity

Cihan Tuğal

How does memory shape the construction of national identity?[1] What is the place of the remembrance of violence in this construction? Social scientists have often emphasized that nations are "imagined communities" (B. Anderson 1983). The "constructivist" literature of the last twenty years has in fact established the idea that nations are constructed (Brubaker 1996; Gellner 1983; Hobsbawm 1995), but it has not informed us sufficiently about the form in which they are imagined by their individual members. Indeed, as the critics of this literature have argued, its prominent figures have mostly focused on the elite's understanding of the nation, ignoring the passions and nonrational cravings of the larger society (Nairn 1997; Smith 1986). Although this essay adopts the constructivist position, taking the nation as a linguistic and ethnic community that is politically brought together as a result of deliberate strategy and contingent events, it also incorporates nonrational motivations in its account of the making of the nation. In this context, the essay shows how the act of remembering, which we are inclined to think of in its individual dimension, has consolidated the formation of an imagined group. While the hypotheses developed here are based on an analysis of the imagination of the

1. I would like to thank Ann Stoler, whose questions have laid the bases for many of the arguments developed in this essay, to Esra Özyürek, whose comments were very useful in revising it, and to Aynur Sadet-Tuğal, whose help rescued this piece in a difficult moment.

138

Armenian nation, they can be tested in other cases to reach a deeper understanding of the construction of nationhood.

Under the influence of national discourse, scholars generally conceptualize the relations between Turks and Armenians during the demise of the Ottoman Empire as interactions between already existing national units. This perception contradicts the social and political practice of the Ottoman Empire, which divided its subjects into *millet*s, or communities based on religion (Braude and Lewis 1982). Armenians were distinguished from Turks and Kurds not on ethnic or national bases, but on religious grounds. Although nationalism had started to spread throughout the empire by the end of the nineteenth century, people still conducted their relations with others in religious (and, to a narrower extent, ethnic) terms. The fact that the Muslim and Christian populations were divided further into several sects made it harder to think of the Turks, the Kurds, or the Armenians as unified nations.

Lately, social scientists have shown that Turkish identity became consequential only in the final decades of the empire and that the deportation of Armenians was crucial for this transformation (Akçam 2004). Yet, scholars have not sufficiently questioned the assumption that Armenian-ness constituted a meaningful identity on its own before the Armenian people suffered severe violence. Indeed, most scholars have taken Armenian-ness as a given (Hovannisian 1998; Melson 1992) and have paid scant attention to its construction through time. Looking at the Armenian issue from the perspective of memory studies enhances our understanding of the making of Armenian identity. Although scholars have recently explored the role of memories and literature in unifying and empowering Armenians, they utilized neither recent theoretical contributions to memory studies nor the constructivist understanding of nationalism in their analyses (Miller and Miller 1993; Peroomian 2003). Drawing on these two alternative ways of looking at national identity, it can be seen that the massacres of 1915, and especially their construction in memory, played a vital role in the making of the Armenian identity. Nevertheless, there are drawbacks to treating memory in exclusively political and instrumental ways. Consequently, this essay also discusses the ties, exchanges, and tensions between memory and history in order to free memory studies from this instrumentalism.

The arguments in this essay are supported by the published memoirs of men and women who lived in Anatolia during the 1915 massacres. The publication dates of the memoirs span a long period of time. Whereas there are memoirs published as early as 1916, immediately after the massacres, some of them were published as much as fifty or even sixty years later. In addition to the memoirs of Armenians who have migrated to the United States, other texts are studied in order to compare techniques that authors deploy to make claims to truth. Such a comparison is crucial to analyzing the relationship between official memoirs or history and the memoirs of ordinary people. Most of the memoirs analyzed here were written for an English-speaking public. They are politically important because they are used as evidence in the diplomatic, academic, and popular discussions on the existence or absence of genocide. Having been written in the United States, they also involve psychological and cultural-political implications. New World myths and a certain reading of the American dream by the survivors have immense effects on the narrative of Armenian nationalism, or rather on the popular reception of this narrative.

This essay explores memory and history as two different forms of constructing the past, by analyzing the interactions between memories of massacres and historiography. Even though memory, like history, is situated in national discourse, its mode of working displays the horizon of national discourse in a way that history cannot. Memory and history work together in the imagination of the Armenian nation. However, memory has a peculiar relation to the *nonsignifiable*—to that portion of human experience that cannot be expressed lucidly in language. Due to this relation, memory disrupts the construction of meaning that is vital for the formation of identity.

Memories of Massacres

The massacres are intricately related to the historical context in which they unfolded, the most prominent characteristics of which were the demise of the Ottoman Empire, Westernization throughout the Ottoman lands, and the subsequent rise of nationalism. The Ottoman Empire turned decisively toward the West in 1839, through a set of legal reforms known as the Tanzimat. From then on, until the demise of the empire in 1923, the rulers of the empire made several changes that led first to Western control of internal affairs, then, at each step, to the intensification of this control.[2] Both the introduction of nationalist ideas that resulted from this control and the active (financial, diplomatic, and logistic) incitement of nationalism by Western powers (Hovannisian 1967) led to the birth of nationalism in various parts of the empire, followed in time by the separation of several countries, including Greece and Bulgaria (Jelavich 1983; Dadrian 2003). Even though the Armenians were also affected by this tide of nationalism, the fact that they constituted the minority in most of the lands on which they lived made it harder for them to organize a strong national movement, that is, one strong enough to fight against the forces of the empire.[3]

The Turkish and the Armenian sides interpret the massacres, which developed in response to Armenian nationalism, quite differently.[4] The first active manifestation of Armenian nationalism was in the form of resistance to Sultan Abdulhamid's decision to standardize tax policy throughout the empire. In Sasoun, which had had the privilege of paying lower taxes, Armenians, joined even by some non-Armenian elements, refused to pay taxes (Suny 2001). According to the Turkish thesis, this resistance was what incited the first tide of massacres, lasting from 1894 to 1896. The Armenian thesis, however, claims that the resistance was only an excuse and that the real reason for

2. Ottoman reform movements date back to the eighteenth century. The role of the West in inciting and shaping changes in the Ottoman system is widely discussed by Bernard Lewis (1968) and Eric Zürcher (1998).

3. The debate about the exact numbers and proportions of Armenians living in different parts of Anatolia has remained inconclusive to this day. See Justin McCarthy (2001) for a recent account.

4. When talking about "sides" in this essay, I am referring not to national essences but to certain theses. The thesis of one side can be defended by someone who does not belong to that nation (Güney 1984). Of course, these theses are not absolute, either. As the main theses can themselves change over time, certain historians can occupy intermediate positions that fit neither of the theses. For example, Bernard Lewis (1968) uses the term *genocide,* which is a taboo for the Turkish side, and holds the Armenians responsible for their own suffering. Furthermore, Müge Göçek (2003) points out that postnational "sides" are emerging, the accounts of which in the future might constitute alternatives to official and national positions that are now dominant.

the violence was Abdulhamid's attempts to thwart the upward social mobility of Armenians, which had gained pace after Westernizing reforms and the partial liberalization of the Ottoman economy were set into place (Melson 1992). Indeed, by 1891 the sultan had begun organizing Kurdish tribes as paramilitary units that would fight against the Armenians when necessary. From this point on, the Kurds, who were much more numerous than the Turks in the regions, were going to become key actors in clashes among civilians.[5] The sultan's anti-Armenian policies, including the 1894–96 massacres, did not sever all relations between Turks and Armenians because Abdulhamid targeted not only Armenians but also any group that challenged the government. Indeed, this shared victimization built both a political alliance and an effective tie between Armenian nationalists and the constitutionalist Turkish nationalists, namely, the Young Turks (Suny 2001).

The autocratic regime of Abdulhamid was overthrown by the CUP (Committee of Union and Progress) in 1908, a political move that led to a constitutional monarchy that was enthusiastically welcomed by Armenians, who found in the Western-educated Young Turks true allies and hoped that the new regime would bring freedom and equality to Christian subjects.[6] Ironically, the year 1909 was marked by another series of massacres in which the involvement of the Young Turks is questionable. These events occurred right after the March 31 uprising, when religious groups supported by Sultan Abdulhamid rebelled against secularist and nationalist Young Turk rule. This temporal overlap between the uprising and the massacres focused the attention on Abdulhamid (Zürcher 1998). However, some Armenians suspected that CUP sympathizers were also involved in the killings. The good relations between Armenians (specifically, the main nationalist party, the Dashnaks)

---

5. To the degree that Turkish accounts accept that Armenians were massacred throughout the crises, they lay all the blame on these Kurdish tribes. The Armenian accounts, however, underline civil and official Turkish as well as Kurdish involvement in the massacres.

6. The more nationalist and authoritarian wing of the Young Turks (Ottoman intellectuals who had received Western education and defended far-reaching Westernizing reforms) were organized in the Committee of Union and Progress, which was to stay in power between 1908 and 1918.

and the CUP members were not harmed;[7] this situation continued more or less without tension until 1915, despite increasing pressure from some Kurdish tribes on the Armenians and the intensifying authoritarianism of the CUP. Significantly, the Dashnaks supported the Ottoman state during the conscriptions for the world war in 1914 (Suny 2001).

Even though the Armenian and Turkish narratives regarding 1908–9 are not utterly different, those concerning the attitudes and actions of the Ottomans and the Dashnaks immediately before and during World War I are sharply at odds. The Turkish thesis claims that the Armenian support during 1913 and 1914 was a façade and the Armenians' real intention was to obtain Ottoman weapons and join the Russian army (Shaw and Shaw 1977).[8] According to this thesis, the Ottoman state, which was then controlled by the Young Turks, was forced to deport the Armenian population, which had the potential of backing up the Dashnaks, in order to prevent large-scale rebellions and secession (Lewis 1968, 356). In response, the Armenian side asserts that the Dashnak demanded only autonomy, that it did not carry out any activities in favor of independence, and that the 1914–15 rebellions attributed to the Armenian people never took place (Melson 1992).

Who ordered the massacres, and for what purpose, remains unclear. There is a major diplomatic controversy between the Turkish and Armenian governments about the degree to which the Ottoman state (its high officials, its secret service, its ministers, and its ruling party) was directly responsible for the massacres. Also, it is still hotly contested whether the massacres were intended to exterminate or simply relocate the Armenian population who inhabited the lands of the empire. Likewise, the estimates concerning the

7. By the time of the major massacres of 1915, the Dashnaks were the primary political organization within the Armenian population. They had replaced in efficacy first the local societies that were influential until the 1870s and 1880s (Halaçoğlu 2002; Hovannisian 1967), and then the socialist-oriented Hnchaks that were popular in the 1890s. In 1914, groups such as Hnchaks, Hunchakak Vergazmiyal, and Ramgavar Committees were still operating, though only under the shadow of the powerful Dashnaks.

8. This part of the Turkish thesis has become an official position, as attested by the proclamation of the Speaker of the Turkish Parliament that the Dashnaks had openly sided with the Russians as soon as the latter declared war on the Ottoman Empire (İzgi 2001).

number of people killed during the events ranges from two hundred thousand in official Turkish accounts to one and a half million in some Armenian accounts.

Claims of Authenticity

In a field loaded with so much controversy, memoirs written by survivors gain immense political significance. The proponents of the Armenian thesis resort to survivor memoirs to fill in the gaps in historiography or to consolidate its credibility.[9] Moreover, the memoirs are held up as proofs equivalent to archives, trials, and historiography (Melson 1992, 150). For example, the introduction to a series of survivor memoirs compiled by the Zoryan Institute for Contemporary Armenian Research and Documentation presents the memoirs as "experiences by Armenians who witnessed the Genocide" (Yervant 1988, iv).[10] Introductions to other memoirs make the same claim. The aim of the analyses below is neither to discredit nor to substantiate these memoirs and claims but rather to show the techniques and processes of memory construction.

The emphasis on authenticity has a direct political meaning, since the memoirs give hints about the organization of the massacres. In order to establish that the massacres were genocide, the Armenian thesis must demonstrate that people unrelated in time suffered the same experiences. This would prove that the violence was coordinated centrally and that central Ottoman institutions and officials had a direct responsibility. In most of the memoirs, there is a fixed sequence that starts with the forced conscription of males,[11] followed by their disarmament and consequent murder, then the murder of the remain-

9. Participant and survivor accounts have been used in similar fashion in the reconstruction of most other traumatic events (wars, the Holocaust, revolutions, etc.).

10. The Zoryan Institute is "devoted to the documentation, study, and dissemination of material related to the life of the Armenian people" (www.zoryaninstitute.org).

11. This claim contradicts historical writings showing that the party with the most influence over Armenians, the Dashnaks, supported and encouraged conscription into the Ottoman army (Suny 2001). It also casts doubt on the rest of the memoirs and increases the likelihood that some of the recollections that are repeated in various memoirs are outcomes of collective reconstruction.

ing males, and finally the deportations of women and children, with journeys on foot characterized by theft, rape, and murder. Most important for the Armenian thesis is that this unchanging sequence is encountered not only in the written memoirs analyzed here but also in oral history studies (Miller and Miller 1993).[12] Armenian historiographers use these accounts as solid proof that the massacres were highly coordinated.

Publishers use different techniques to reinforce a sense of authenticity. In most of the introductions or prefaces, the authenticity associated with the word "experience" is reinforced through reference to the innocence of childhood. For instance, the preface to *The Urchin*—a memoir taken to be an important source by Armenians in America—makes implicit reference to the widely held belief about the purity of children by arguing that the "detachment" of a little boy makes "objectivity" possible. This does not mean that the events a person experiences as an adult are ruled out from this discursive space. When an adult memoir is in question, the person or institution who presents the memoir attempts to make its claim to truth stronger by pointing out that the memories of an adult are not subject to the same kind of distortion and suggestibility to which memories of childhood are prone (Sakayan 1997, xix).[13] Still, the innocence attributed to childhood is in sharp contrast to, for example, the accounts coming from statesmen. The latter constitute an important portion of the material put on the table by the Turkish side. The reader is inclined to read these accounts with a suspension of belief without necessarily being aware of it. This contrast is intensified as childhood memoirs put emphasis on vivid recollections of everyday details and on sensory material. These all together make the memoirs more natural and everyday.

In academic and diplomatic fields, memoirs of the 1915 massacres are

12. The greatest methodological problem here is the relation between history and memory: the production of memory can be understood only when its relation with the production of history (with which it is in constant interaction) is taken into account. The unchanging sequence seen in the memoirs under analysis is also put into circulation by Armenian historiography. Hence, the unfailing repetition of the event sequence in every written memoir might not be as straightforward a proof as it might seem.

13. Suggestibility is an issue that creates problems not only in the remembrance of macropolitical violence but also in the recall of individual cases such as forced incest. See Ceci and Loftus (1994); and Lindsay and Read (1994).

likewise reduced to function as the raw material for a political struggle based on claims to truth. The memoirs are read either as documents expressing the truth or as fabricated stories. Instead of trying to untie this knot and prove in a positive manner which of the remembrances are real and which made up, this essay examines the acts of remembering and the memoirs they create from an interpretive angle. Without rejecting the political and ethical importance of the debate about the truth of the Armenian genocide and the indispensable place of memoirs in this struggle, it must be emphasized that memoirs are not only factual documents; they also construct meaning. The remainder of this essay analyzes the ways in which memoirs construct Armenian nationality.

Utopia, Nostalgia, and Violence

What is the cultural-political and cultural-psychological meaning of remembering? Why do victims of violence insist on remembering moments that are so painful for them? What are the cultural results of such remembering? Analysts of the Armenian massacres have already pointed out the importance remembering has for psychological survival since it settles accounts with the past and maintains the social unity of the survivors (Hovannisian 1998; Shirinian 1998). Others (Miller and Miller 1993, 161) emphasize how remembrance saves Armenian culture from disintegrating. All these authors assume that an Armenian nation meaningful in its totality already existed before the massacres and that memoirs simply reproduce this already existing unit. The next section examines the validity of this assumption.

Violence as Destructive of Lost Community

The way in which life before violence is nostalgically remembered gives some idea about how memory shapes national identity. Survivors remember the way of life before the violence in a very favorable light. There was peace and the land was fertile, everything was natural and spontaneous, people were united, and hard working (Ketchian 1988, 6). Individual details enrich this portrayal further. For example, a female survivor remembers the Easter just before one of the massacres, and her prospect of going to a European school (Mardiganian 1990, 8–9). Memory is doubled in its effect by the introduction of history: Tarsus and Urfa, cities with thousands of years of a history rich in philosophy and art, were home to Armenians (Yernazian 1990, 20–21, 35–39).

The remembrance of a place one has left usually involves memories of relations, plenitude, and authenticity (pertaining to that place). Scholars argue that all of the above are the constructs of nostalgia as afflicted and imaginative memory (Robertson 1991, 13–37; Casey 1987). The same kind of remembering is at work in the memoirs analyzed here. What is specific to survivor memoirs is that the authors desert their place of origin because of mass violence. The time and place of perfection are disturbed, indeed, forever destroyed by violence. Even before the violence itself arrives, the news of it, coming from neighboring villages and towns, shatters the picture of happiness. James Sutherland, one of the survivors, remembers the day when the first news of violence reached them: "This was the end. Not only the end of the school year, but it was the end of the school and *everything*. The school [from] which I had never missed a day . . . was closed forever. . . . The memory of the beautiful city, the *taste* of the water and *smell* of the fresh air will never leave my memory as long as I live" (Sutherland 1964, 109–10; emphasis added).

The use of intense sensory memory refers readers to a previolent state of affairs in all its regularity and comprehensibility. During the deportations, the known world disappears altogether, and the elements generally excluded from the recognized flow of daily life—such as death and excretion—become the order of the day. People start to live side by side with corpses and human waste, sometimes degrading themselves to the degree of searching for money in the bowels of dead people or in the bodily waste surrounding them (Bedoukian 1978, 14, 19, 29). For example, a mother gets so frantic about the gold her son has lost, which they were going to use for finding food, that she cares no longer for the life of her beloved son who faces death at that moment (24–25). In short, during the massacres the world turns upside down, a diabolical carnival reverses the states of life and death.

Violence as Constitutive of Community

Taking such drastic massacres and their painful memories as factors that have played into constituting the Armenian nation might seem a little awkward at first sight. Yet, Gyan Pandey (1998, 44) has shown that while violence disturbs the known world of the victim and a particular sense of being in the world, at another level violence forms the previolence universe and defines community.[14] The previolence condition of Armenians illustrates how this is also the case with Armenian national identity. The Armenians of the empire did not comprise a single and united community. Even though they had some sense of affiliation due to a shared language, the lives of the Armenians of the capital and those of the provinces were unrelated. While some Armenians were ordinary peasants, others were prominent merchants, artisans, traders, and interpreters (Hovannisian 1967). Furthermore, this Christian population was marked by the prominence of sects that sometimes tended to separate themselves behind thick walls. By the end of the nineteenth century, Armenians were divided into four churches (Halaçoğlu 2002).

Despite these differences, it is only in one instance within hundreds of pages of memoirs that we get a feeling that any significant tensions existed among Armenians. However, the one instance is poignant and informative: a Protestant male remembers that when he was a child, he and others used to fight Catholic Armenians of their city with stones and sticks. In one of these fights, in which even the bishops participated, the narrator risked death (Sutherland 1964, 33). Yet, this past full of tension and division is rarely mentioned. The outsiders' violence, and the memory of that violence, unites the Armenian people, dispersed by class, location, and sect, into a nation.

The constitutive functions of violence (and the remembrance of violence) are best demonstrated in the collective signification of individual memories. Remembering the massacres becomes central in the affirmation and reproduction of individual identity as Armenian. For example, in one of the memoirs, the mother of an Armenian boy tells him that if he forgets what was done to his father (assassination by torture), he will lose himself—that is, his true self as an Armenian (Aved 1979, 104). In other words, forgetting the massacres implies opting out of his Armenian identity and, when considered at the collective level, would mean the annihilation of Armenian-ness altogether. In sum, as Pandey (2001) asserts, violence constitutes community, or, as

14. Pandey has developed this thesis in his work on the remembrance of violence experienced during Muslim-Hindu clashes in India.

demonstrated in this essay, the remembrance of violence forms the imagined community of Armenians in the American diaspora.

America as Future Utopia

In memoirs written by Armenians who have settled in the United States, the process of coming to and settling in the New World occupies a central place. Survivors remember America as being the aspiration of all those Armenians who found themselves in the midst of the massacres.[15] America is almost never represented as a contingent destination to which the narrator is drawn under the pressure of events. Survivors also picture America as a stainless whole.

In addition to being a haven of freedom, America was also the cure for pain. For example, a survivor relates how, once he had disembarked from the ship and stepped on American soil, the lice he had been carrying around since the days of terror were extinguished for good (Sutherland 1964, 220). America is remembered also as the promise of peace and happiness that kept the victims psychologically alive during the days of violence (Mardiganian 1990, 91). Tenacious, persevering men of the community naturally ended up in America, which was imagined as the land of money and work (Sutherland 1964, 45).

When we keep in mind that these memoirs are being written in English for an American audience and are distributed by institutions dedicated to the Armenian cause, we could think that reproducing the American dream in a literally ornamented way is nothing but a strategy for getting the support of Americans. In this case, we would be led to read the memory of the imagination of America as a flat, purposive memory that has nothing to do with the past. Although this purpose might have incited the grandiose and exaggerated portrayal of the United States (and the hopes invested in it even before having arrived on the new continent), a focused study of the depiction of America conveys another dimension of utopian-nostalgic memory. When things are

15. Only in Bertha Ketchian's memoir is America realistically portrayed, as a safe place where the survivor's father is and also as a natural endpoint when it is no longer possible to return home. Unlike others, the new country is not romanticized (Ketchian 1988, 89–90, 137).

going well for the narrators, neither the nostalgic Armenia nor the utopian America is mentioned. For instance, a male survivor who describes in his memoir his successful post-1915 life in Istanbul talks about neither the lost heaven nor the promised heaven (Aved 1979). Both come into his story at points where there is a lot of pain and violence, or the threat of violence. In these instances, the senses of the past and the future are so enlarged that they swallow the present. Then, because of the impossibility of returning to the past (of even imagining the return to it), all the positive aspects of the past utopia are displaced onto the future utopia. A similar displacement is frequently seen in the memoirs of Armenians who have settled in the United States. For example, Leon Surmelian tells how, after all his lonely days in the United States, he found "home" again while staying with and working for an American family: "For the first time in America, I did not feel a stranger. I had discovered the earth I had lost, the stars and the moon of my childhood: my exile was over. . . . I was not only thoroughly Americanized, but, paradoxical as it may seem, was my Old World self again" (Surmelian 1945, 301–3).

As can be seen in this excerpt, the exaltation of America by the Armenians implies much more than the reproduction of the American dream. America symbolizes the revitalization of the old self destroyed by violence. The New World is the new homeland for the national metanarrative founded upon the remembrance of violence. America, beyond being merely a psychological refuge, is the reembodiment of the obliterated old land. The utopian construction of America, which has now become the new fatherland of Armenians who have survived the massacres, is as important an element in the imagination of the nation as the nostalgic remembering of the lost lands. Violence plays an indispensable role in both nostalgic and utopian longing, and in their lived experience as such intense feelings.

National Discourse and the Remembrance of Violence

Recalling the Other is as vital to the formation of the imagined community as recalling violence. This section addresses the "rules of formation" in remembering the perpetrators of the massacres. According to Michel Foucault (1972), rules of formation are the conditions of existence for objects, concepts, and themes within a discourse.[16] Rules of formation also organize the conditions of emergence of an object (such as *nation,* in this case), the form in which its boundaries are drawn, and its relations with other objects. According to Foucault, an object constituted by a discursive formation and its relation to other objects are independent from the reality that exists before discourse. The form of an object, its content, its boundaries, and the plane on which it emerges become concrete only in discourse. In this essay, *rules of formation* refers to the rules that organize who can be remembered as guilty and who can be exempted as innocent in memoirs of Armenians.[17] National discourse leads to the formation of objects with exclusive reference to the idea of national collectivities, regardless of the concrete subjects that are involved in the massacres. That is, the rules of formation attribute guilt and innocence with respect to national belonging.

Despite the internal divisions within the Ottoman Empire, the memoirs at hand construct the perpetrators and the uninvolved in national terms. Survivor memoirs, or the introductions that package and frame them, frequently emphasize that it is the "Turkish nation" that has massacred the Armenians (Bedoukian 1978, preface). Indeed, "the brutal Turks . . . had always planned . . . to kill and finish off the Armenians for good" (Ketchian 1988, 147). This eternal evil plan is one common theme encountered through most memoirs (e.g., Yernazian 1990, 43). According to one narrative, Turks would not be content until they killed all Armenians (Bedoukian 1978, 143–44). This generalization is claimed to be firmly rooted in collective memory, "the continuing saga of generations": "Parents would repeat . . . at dinner or when reminiscing with their many guests" that the Turks have inflicted many pains upon the Armenians and that they always will (Ketchian 1988, 3).

The Other is occasionally constructed as religiously or economically different (e.g., the violators as Muslim, or as poor and nomadic). Nevertheless, these alternative constructions are always translated back into national language, and specific class positions and religious affiliations become the attrib-

---

16. Foucault identifies these elements as objects, concepts, techniques, and ideologies/theories.

17. Julie Taylor (1994) carries out a similar Foucaultian analysis using the concept *regimes of truth.*

utes of specific nationalities. Thus, Mardiganian, a female survivor, addresses the American reader: "I sometimes fear Americans think of us as a nomad people, or as people of a lower class" (1990, 86). Interestingly, survivors consistently picture Turks and Kurds as nomads or poor in almost all of these memoirs. Yet, they picture all Armenians as artisans, merchants, or otherwise rich. The class distinctions within both the Armenian and Turkish communities are ignored.[18] In sum, class or occupation becomes a metaphor for nation.

National discourse, a discourse that leads to the formation of objects (in our case, the agental units of memory) with reference to the idea of nation as a collectivity of people sharing certain characteristics, does allow for exceptions.[19] But with what limitations do the Armenians remember actors in non-national terms? In most of the memoirs, Turks and Kurds who oppose the massacres and who even try to save at least some Armenians from the bloodshed are central actors. Incidents like a Turk saving an Armenian girl from being beaten to death (Ketchian 1988, 32), family friends wanting to hide and save all the members of the neighboring Armenian family (Yervant 1988, 13; Sutherland 1964, 17–18), or a Circassian captain striving to save a whole village under threat (Yernazian 1990, 9) occupy an important affective place in the memoirs. On the other hand, in most of the manuscripts, these anecdotes are handled with interpretations that will not harm a point of view that reduces everything to national essences.

In one of the memoirs, the Kurds help and save some Armenians only because of greed: they get money in return (Aved 1979, 64–65). Similarly, in another account, a group of Turks help, but the narrator remembers thinking that "of course there was a catch somewhere," for "anything involving Turks will have one" (Mardiganian 1990, 123). Men who show some concern for the pains of the Armenians are thought to be of partially Armenian blood (Aved 1979, 81; Ketchian 1988, 38). Turks save as many Armenians as they can after the massacres because they need someone to exploit; after all, they are lazy and

18. There were ordinary farmers, and even highlanders, among the Armenians, as well as artisans and merchants (Feigl 1987, 46–47).

19. As scholars of nationalism have shown (e.g., Brubaker 1996), which characteristics will be emphasized within a set of possible shared attributes (such as language, religion, and region of origin) is a matter of events and political strategies.

cannot produce their own goods (Yernazian 1990, 10). When no recourse is made to such totalizing explanations and good intentions of Kurds and Turks are recognized as that, the sources of virtue and good action are always remembered as *individuals,* and their remembrance modifies neither the image of the Turk nor that of the Kurd. This pattern seems to form the boundaries of the flexibility of national discourse: the massacres are the deeds of the (opponent) nation; the civil behavior belongs to the individuals. Nevertheless, there are points at which the arbitrariness of national discourse becomes apparent, as is the case with all discursive formations.

Beyond National Discourse

The fragility of national discourse becomes clearest when collective units other than the nation emerge in the memoirs, disturbing the totalizing urge in the depiction of the Other. Some of the memoirs do contain hints that there were (organized or unorganized) collectivities that helped Armenians, or at least sympathized with them. During the deportations, some Armenian girls were sold in slave markets. A survivor girl writes that "the ones who were bought by the farmers were destined to work in the fields, and they were the most fortunate, for sometimes the Turkish farmer is kind and gentle" (Mardiganian 1990, 50). In another account, when the Armenians are being deported, they come across a group of farmers. The farmers bow their heads and say "nt, nt, nt," a gesture and an exclamation that act together to show disapproval (Surmelian 1945, 86). In yet another one, a survivor describes a scene where he enters a city together with a group of other Armenians who have survived all the events, where the inhabitants of the city gather and display signs of disapproval and pity (Bedoukian 1978, 56).

Still, the remembered collectivities are unspecified (the farmers of an unknown village) or restricted (as *some* farmers, *some* inhabitants of the city). The only specified collectivity that helped the Armenians is the Kurdish Alevis of Dersim.[20] Dersim, the only region where the heterodox Kurdish Alevi minority prevails over the ethnic and sectarian majority of Anatolia, was character-

---

20. The Turkish thesis develops a totally different position regarding the role of the Dersim Kurds, blaming them for most of the civilian clashes (Halaçoğlu 2002).

ized by periodic peasant resistance against the empire, which manifested itself in the case of the Armenian massacres as a collective will to protect the Armenians. In the memoirs, even the helpfulness of the Dersim Kurds is mentioned in a roundabout manner and by way of implication, as for example when Dersim is recalled as a safe place where Armenians sought refuge (Ketchian 1988, 104), at a time when all people who helped Armenians were being persecuted. There is only one instance in one memoir when Dersim Kurds are remembered explicitly as a helpful collectivity (Mardiganian 1990, 168):

> Beyond these hills was the great Dersim. . . . The inhabitants of the Dersim deserts and wastes are not the vicious type of Kurds who live in the south in the regions to which we had been deported from our homes. The Kurds in the south are nomadic tribes, harsh and cruel. The Dersim Kurds are mostly farmers, and often rebel against their Turkish overlords. They are fanatical Moslems and have their racial hatred of all "unbelievers," as they look upon Christians. But they do not have the lust for killing human beings common in the tribes of the south. To this I owe my life.

National discourse has excluded memories that involve actors other than those specified by the dominant rules of formation. Yet even here—the misunderstandings that mark even such positive remembrances aside—the differential stance of the Dersim population is neutralized and made to fit national discourse through speculations about its Christian and non-Kurdish roots. This suspect attribution is more common when Dersim is discussed in more formal (diplomatic or academic) texts. Despite all these exclusions, the emergence in memory of rare helpful collectivities such as farmers, urbanites, or Alevi Kurds frustrates the totalizing urge of national discourse and unravels the constructed unity, thanks to the recognition of variation in the Other.

Violence and the Collapse of Meaning

Memoirs play a role in making the construction of the nation possible through "remembering" violence, the lost heaven, the longing for the future utopia and the Other. Handling survivor memoirs only in terms of the construction of the nation and of the Other, however, would lead to a conclusion that there is indeed no difference between national historiography and the memory shaped by that historiography. Partially valid though this judgment may be, reducing memory to a mere tool of politics and history would be simplistic. Certain elements in memoirs themselves disrupt meaning in construction; memory is different from history in the way that it erodes the very meaning that history is trying to establish. This difference creates difficulties for the imagination of the nation.

In most of the memoirs, the past and the future are perfectly reconciled by transforming America into a second Armenia; in others, though, there is no easy way of preserving both past and future utopias. In David Kherdian's account, which is more focused on adapting to the future world than reviving the lost Armenian heaven, the massacres are openly mentioned only once in the entire book. They are brought up during the description of a conversation among family members, where the discussion is cut short by one member of the family: "This story has no end" (Kherdian 1981, 181–82). In this memoir, a happy future becomes possible only at the cost of forgetting the past and losing it totally.[21]

Unlike David Kherdian's memoir, most survivor accounts of the New World are disrupted by the past and by violence. In memoirs marked with the will and the determination to grapple with the past, the memory of violence shatters both the past and the present, and makes harmony between them impossible. For example, Mardiganian's recall of the moment when her brother and mother died forms an inseparable part of her perception of the present: "Both mother and Hovnan died with their eyes turned to me, looking into mine! My eyes see them now, every day and every night—every hour, almost—when I look into the new world" (Mardiganian 1990, 161).

Some scholars have noted that sensory memory is potentially disruptive of the unity and totality of narrative memory (Leys 1996; Seremetakis 1994;

---

21. This memoir is the second book of a series, where the first book is titled *Losing Home* and the second *Finding Home*. The difference between the first and the second books is that the lost home is not revived in the second, for it is too painful to be incorporated.

Young 1996).[22] The sensory memory of violence, in the case of the Armenians, disturbs the past, the present, and the future and prevents their smooth articulation in a narrative of losing home and finding it again somewhere else.

This destructive dimension of memory makes functional explanations of the act of remembering even more problematic. Fernando Coronil and Julie Skurski (1991) argue that memory cannot be reduced to function and that its link with the construction of social meaning is more central than its instrumentality. The memoirs analyzed here demonstrate that memories are crucial also in moments when people fail to establish meaning. Almost all of the memoirs, both those written by Armenian survivors and those written by Ottoman and Russian statesmen, try to give meaning to the violence the other side has perpetrated. This rationalization of remembered violence is necessary in order to found or preserve a meaningful symbolic universe. It draws attention to the cultural-psychological import of the act of remembering. In this context, the difference between the two types of memoirs is quite remarkable. The memoirs of the statesmen, like the narratives of historians, are mostly consistent and successful in rationalization, whereas those of the survivors display evident inconsistencies in rationalization. This difference casts doubt on the argument put forth by analysts of memory that both the offender and the offended repress painful memories and build secure lives in which they find peace (Levi 1986, 23–36).

When the rationalization of violence is in question, one can see clear parallels between historiography and "official" memoirs (those of men of state). The Russian general Mayewski, who has been in the regions populated by Armenians, observes that, since Armenians were not oppressed in the villages he has visited, the cause of Armenian rebellions must be "evil" foreign propaganda (Mayewski 1916, 11). Armenians had made the Kurds suffer during these rebellions, and the Kurds took revenge when the circumstances were conducive (89–91). Mayewski's memoir coincides with the Turkish thesis not only in terms of its content (putting the blame on Armenian organizations and the Kurds, rather than on the Turks and the general Armenian popula-

22. There are studies on memory that suggest that the sensory can also create harmony and unity in some instances, while disseminating disruption elsewhere (Kuhn 1995).

tion), but also in its structure of argumentation. The parallelism is especially apparent in the closure of the text and in the definite meaning attributed to violence. Erich Feigl, a historian who sympathizes with the Turkish state, develops a different strategy than that of Mayewski in rationalizing the massacres by focusing more on the violence performed by Armenians. Since Armenians were incited by the Europeans to build a national, independent state on lands where they did not constitute the majority, they had no choice but to resort to violence, wiping out the Turks, and thereby becoming the majority (Feigl 1987, 81–83). The majority of Armenians, by remaining silent in the face of crimes carried out by revolutionaries, deserved to be deported from the area (114–15).

Survivor memoirs do not contradict Armenian historiography in topics such as the central coordination of massacres, their national character, and so on. Yet, when the rationalization of violence is in question, not only is there no absolute coincidence with historiography, each memoir is hardly consistent and coherent within itself. Different authors have different approaches concerning the reasons for the massacres. One common conviction is that Turks always desired to persecute all Christians and "the Armenians knew [this] from past experience" (Yernazian 1990, 43; Ketchian 1988, 147). Another widespread opinion is that the Muslims were launching a holy war and punishing those who believe in the Christian God instead of Allah (Mardiganian 1990, 29, 74). Some believe that their community was being massacred because it was superior to the Turkish nation and the latter could not stand the apparent existence of a superior community, or desired forced intermarriage so that its savage blood would be blended with some noble blood (Ketchian 1988, 11, 38; Mardiganian 1990, 157). Others attributed the violence to a desire for "tasting blood," and acquiring easy wealth, and compensating for attacks the Turks suffered from Christian states (Sutherland 1964, 54–56). In other instances narrators make sense of it all by referring to the teachings of the Qur'an or the place of violence in Muslim tradition (Sutherland 1964, 2; Aved 1979, 62). Apart from the racist tone in some of these constructions, they do not fit the previolence constructions of the accounts themselves, in which Muslims and Christians lived together in peace, the tolerance of Islam being one of the reasons for this peace (Sutherland 1964, xviii; Aved 1979).

Although the memoirs swarm with rationalizations, none of them provide a coherent narrative that exhibits a meaningful continuity between the premassacre lives of Armenians and the massacres.

This same sense of previolence peace, which renders all rationalizations problematic, leads to a shock and an accompanying inability to make sense of the succeeding violence. Most Armenians remember that they were not expecting such an extensive massacre. At each step of the massacres, they reasoned that this was as bad as it could get and that the Turks would not engage in anything worse. According to Mardiganian (1990, 5), especially when the massacres of 1915 started, no one could believe it, since, unlike the massacres of 1894–96, before which some Armenians had resisted paying taxes, Armenians had been giving full support to the government and the army. When news of massacres started to come from other villages, they heard it, talked about it, but did not believe it (Bedoukian 1978, 9). When violence hit home, it made no sense (17). Neither the reasons behind the cruel deeds nor the motivations behind the attempts of some Turks to stop them made sense (Sutherland 1964, 146–48). According to the memoirs, after a certain point the victims started to accept the impossibility of rationalizing violence and the people in deportation convoys stopped fearing, wondering, and crying. They submitted to what they perceived to be their fate.

History and Memory

How should this difference between survivor memoirs and history or official memoirs in the handling of violence be interpreted? Even though scholars have questioned the contrasting of memory and history on the basis of the supposed naturalness of the former and the culturally constructed nature of the latter (Davis and Starn 1989), an opposition founded on similar bases shows up in most of the recent literature. For example, Pierre Nora (1989) proposes that a new kind of memory, *les lieux de memoir,* has taken the place of "natural memory," which history has eradicated. This new memory is still outside history, but it is open to the manipulation of history. For those who want to preserve a more classical form of this opposition (Crane 1997; Samuel 1994), collective memory is an oral revival of the past based on lived experience, whereas history is an artificial and written observation of the past.

When historical truth is in question, the opposition set up between history and memory does not seem to hold. Memories do not make sense by themselves: they gain meaning only when framed by history. In many of the memoirs analyzed here, sections or chapters start with information on the city or village of the survivor (such as its two-thousand-year-old history, its population distribution, etc.) that could only be reached through official means. Even the experienced violence is packaged with historical narrative, which links the moves made by some local official to the balance of forces in the Ottoman capital and on the world scene.

The tight relation between memory and history goes beyond the constant exchange between memory and history. Anastasia Karakasidou (1997), one of the many scholars who draws attention to this exchange, states that historians make use of memories while narrators of memory are influenced by written history. Yet, like other scholars who speak of the history-memory binary, she assumes that history and memory are two separate entities. However, the determination of the parameters of memory by history, their complicity in the same (national) rules of formation, and their critical place in the construction of community, force us to consider the possibility that memory and history are different vectors within the same discursive-strategic plane. History and memory are two modes of remembering that are situated in national discourse. They in turn naturalize national discourse and play into the constitution of national identity.

Given this tight kinship between memory and history, could there be any reason for differentiating one from the other? Although history and memory are vectors of the same plane, there is a small but very important divergence in their modes of operation. Whereas history can incorporate and rationalize violence in a fairly smooth manner, memory does not prevent the irrationality in violence from emerging at the margins of discourse. Gyan Pandey argues that nonstate mass violence is incomprehensible and cannot be incorporated into the narration of modernity and nation. Consequently, nonstate violence, as opposed to state violence, which can be subsumed under the ideal of Progress, is never signified within historical writing but exists in all its bareness in memories (Pandey 1997, 6). When the Armenian massacres are in question, the opposition Pandey sets up between state and nonstate violence is dissolved by the case itself, due to the difficulty in telling the exact institutional and actorial source of violence. The distinction encountered in the case at hand is not the one between state and nonstate violence but rather the difference between signifiable and nonsignifiable violence (Daniel 1996). Whereas history and official memory successfully exclude the nonsignifiable dimension of violence and close meaning, survivor memoirs expose this dimension willy-nilly.

Sensory materials, which generally have no place in the writing of history, keep alive the nightmare of meaninglessness in the memories of the survivors. The power of memory to disrupt established meaning comes partially from this sensory dimension. Although some revisionist historiographers question metanarratives, cause-effect relations, and totalistic-meaning structures, they recommend other mechanisms that would account for chains of events. Even genealogy (Foucault 1984) and subaltern studies (Guha 1988), which are based on the criticism of positivist and narrativist philosophies of history, share with traditional historiography the aim of making sense of history by making events signifiable. Memory, however, carries the nonsignifiable part of life, and especially of violence, in its artery.

Conclusion

This essay analyzes the cultural-political and cultural-psychological aspects of a mass violence that has deeply influenced the lives of millions of people. By analyzing survivor memoirs that lay bare the political nature of remembering, we can see how a specific discursive formation shapes remembering and how memories thus structured play into the imagination and formation of nation.[23] National discourse, though, should not be reduced to nationalism as ideology. It is in fact national discourse itself that makes nationalism as an ideology possible. For example, the text of James Sutherland—one of the survivors who is distinguished from the others in his distance from the nationalist Armenian party, Dashnak, and who emphasizes that he is not a nationalist—

---

23. This essay does not address the question of whether the rules of formation have an effect only on the way memory is represented, or also on the ways in which people actually remember. The material at hand is not enough to conclude whether national discourse shapes the psychological techniques of memory.

operates within the same national discourse as the other texts studied in this essay. Yet, he too remembers in terms of the "nation." Indeed, one need not be a nationalist to be speaking from within national discourse.

The memoirs of survivors and statesmen analyzed here are firmly situated in a historical and political context. Yet, reading the material at hand as a composite of straightforward political statements would still be a mistake. In memory studies, there are prominent examples where memory is reduced to contestation and politics (Swedenburg 1995). The restrictions of such reductionism become most obvious in discussions about nostalgia and utopia. Although both types of longing are liable to political or historical use, they have dimensions that cannot be made sense of solely in instrumental terms. These dimensions, rendered ever the more evident by the sensory remembering of violence, show that memory—which should not be seen as the Other of history or as counterhistory—comprises treasures unknown to history.

8

Polyphony and Geographic Kinship in Anatolia

Framing the Turkish-Greek Compulsory
Population Exchange

Aslı Iğsız

How does one translate a past ordeal when the present context does not have the language or the vocabulary to articulate this event?[1] Roman Jakobson tells us that "an array of linguistic signs is needed to introduce an unfamiliar word" in a new context (1987, 429). This essay proposes to extend Jakobson's argument regarding words to include unfamiliar concepts, such as national identity or despicable ordeals, and their introduction into new contexts. Within this framework, it analyzes how the experiences of the Turkish-Greek population exchange of the 1920s found a conduit for public expression in the 1990s.[2] Two cultural institutions, Kalan Music Productions and Belge Publishing Company, were instrumental in that process, making the first identifiable efforts to bring the experiences of the 1920s population exhange into the public domain. Using linguistic signs, they redefined the relationship between

1. I would like to thank all the cultural professionals who were willing to talk to me on many occasions, and to scholars who answered my questions. Carol Bardenstein, Aslı Gür, Hasan Iğsız, Ayşe Iğsız, and Kader Konuk patiently read successive versions of this paper and provided detailed comments. My greatest debt is to Esra Özyürek for her invaluable feedback and encouragement.

2. For practical reasons, I use the word *culture* in its narrow sense to refer to music, cinema, and literature and their attributes. This is how the terms *cultural sphere, cultural productions, cultural professionals, cultural institutions, cultural establishments, cultural agency,* and *cultural products* should be read.

"Greeks" and "Turks" as a "geographic kinship," thus allowing a reconsideration of the divisive national identities ascribed to each group.[3]

Different sociopolitical contexts translate individuals and their roles differently as nationals, subjects, citizens, comrades, caste members, colonized, minority, and so on, and thus determine an individual's position vis-à-vis a ruling power and to what extent he or she has access to a share of power. While each of these categories de facto sets the terms of relationship among individuals, the categories also assign each individual a political role by positioning them as patriots or citizens. This, of course, can be negotiated or redefined on an individual or collective basis, a process that, in this discussion of cultural institutions, informs the use of the term *agency* to mean the act taken to retranslate individuals and their relationship to one another that goes beyond the official definitions of the Self and the Others.

In defining *agency* in this way, the goal is not to "reduce such acts' meaning to the conscious intentions and deliberations of individuals" in terms of "resistance" (Rapport and Overing 2003, 2). Individual and collective positions and their interrelationships can be multiple and complicated. Thus, considering those who do not "act" to consciously interrupt state-ascribed identities as "active participants of the official discourse" would be too simplistic. In this sense, it is crucial to be aware of varying individual negotiations of such assigned positions and to refrain from disregarding the less visible attempts to undo the state-imposed identificatory practices, such as the teaching of official history in schools, speaking of a national language, and so on, because individuals have multiple ways to give meaning to things around them. Considering these nuances, this essay identifies and illustrates a narrative strategy used by cultural professionals [4] in Turkey to inscribe a new relationship be-

---

3. In identifying the discourse developed in frame narratives analyzed here, Aslı Gür's notion of territorial kinship, explicated in chapter 3 of this volume, has been inspiring. Albeit different, geographic and territorial kinship are related to one another in the way they translate human-human and human-land relationships.

4. For practical reasons, I refer to the musicians, lyric writers, music producers, authors of literary works, translators, and publishers as cultural professionals. These are the human agents of music and literature institutions who produced and circulated the works concerning the Turco-Greek coexistence in Anatolia.

tween the past and present polyphonic Anatolians, a discursive bond that binds individuals across different ethnoreligious and ethnolinguistic attributes—such as "Greek" or "Turkish."[5] The framing narratives used to present the cultural products prepared by Belge and Kalan soften the national contours drawn around people. By relating people to each other through their geographic origin, they imaginatively reconsider and suggest expanding the official identificatory boundaries to embrace all peoples from all backgrounds.

Remembrance and Representation of Things Past

The 1990s witnessed a growing interest in the past in Turkey, especially among the reading public (Neyzi 2002; Özyürek, this volume).[6] History became popular, in part as a result of the efforts of the History Foundation of Turkey, founded in 1991, which aims to involve "ordinary people" in history writing[7] and "endeavors to help the Turkish people form a direct, truly comprehensive and noninstrumentalist relationship with their own history and to make the subject of their own history a field for civic action."[8] In addition, the emergence of three popular history periodicals, *Tarih ve Toplum* (History and Soci-

---

5. The term *polyphony*, originally used by Mikhail Bakhtin (1999), refers to a range and variety of voices, perspectives, and meanings that deny single authorial control. In this essay, I use the word *polyphonic* to describe the multiple voices from past and present Anatolia that are accessible in the Turkish public domain, refuting both the single voice of the state-imagined territory and the single voice of the ethnolinguistic/ethnoreligious homogeneity affixed to the peoples in Turkey.

6. This statement is based on my personal observations of the publishing industry in Turkey and interviews with professionals working for several publishing companies and major bookshops located in Istanbul and Ankara.

7. One example of this is the history-writing competition among high school students organized by the History Foundation of Turkey in Istanbul. Another example is the project guide published under the local-history rubric of the History Foundation's Web page, which defines its goal as "to take the curiosity of locals who are curious about the history of their city or neighborhood one step further and to guide them to join local history groups as actors." For further information see the foundation's Web site, www.tarihvakfi.org.tr.

8. Ibid.

ety), *Toplumsal Tarih* (Social History),[9] and *Popüler Tarih* (Popular History),[10] has manifested a growing interest in the past over the last decade. Finally, there has been a salient increase in the consumption of cultural products that convey collective and individual memory narratives in the form of memoirs, oral history narratives or testimonials, and historical novels. An increased number of books, movies, and music albums have reintroduced the Anatolian past into the Turkish present, bringing the stories of past and present peoples of Turkey to the here and now of the Turkish public domain. Such products have raised retrospective questions about the present, in an attempt to retrieve the hitherto publicly inarticulated stories and to take lessons for the future (Iğsız 2001).

Michel-Rolph Trouillot describes the vernacular use of history as the facts and narratives of both "what happened" and "that which is said to have happened." The first meaning places the emphasis on the sociohistorical process, while the second emphasizes knowledge of that process or a story about that process (Trouillot 1995, 2–3). The boundary between the two is not always clear, as Trouillot reckons. Yet, this statement is complicated when applied to official ideologies and the historiographies they sponsor. The question of "what happened" becomes problematically synonymous with the official version of "that which is said to have happened," implementing a monophonic narrative of the past. *Monophony* is used to describe two phenomena. First, it refers to the official single voice imposed on "that which is said to have happened," not allowing alternative narratives to circulate and raise the question, "What (else) may have happened?" Second, it refers to the single voice of the ethnolinguistic homogeneity affixed to the peoples of the Turkish nation-state territory.

---

9. *Toplumsal Tarih* (Social History) is a publication of the History Foundation of Turkey. During my interview with the editor of the journal, he told me that after the one-hundredth issue, in April 2002, they changed the format by enhancing the visual quality and printing more pictures and shorter articles, and they gave the journal a more popular outlook.

10. *Popüler Tarih* (Popular History) is perhaps the most widely read journal in the market, incorporating ethnographic impressions of journalists in their corpus in addition to historical research.

Until recently, the widest circulating historical account of the transformation from the Ottoman Empire to the Turkish Republic was the official history, perhaps most visible in textbooks.[11] On its Web site, the History Foundation describes the Turkish history education model as "self-praising, isolationist, denying different identities and disregarding the history of Anatolia." Esra Danacıoğlu discusses why official Turkish history writers disregard local identities and how Anatolia became the territory for constructing the homogenizing Turkish national identity (2001, 11–12). She argues that in Turkey the "motherland" is considered sacred, and local (interpretations of) identities are perceived as possible threats that challenge the homogeneity of the nation (12).

Despite the homogenizing narrative of the official history, cultural products have opened retrospective debates over past state practices and have emphasized local cultures in Anatolia in the 1990s. The influx in the production and consumption of such products in the late 1990s and early 2000s manifests a growing tendency in remembering the past tragedies partly staged in Anatolia, such as the compulsory Turkish-Greek population exchange of the 1920s. Documenting and remembering the past through cultural products, rewriting history, collecting mnemonic objects, and recording memory narratives has become a way to decipher silenced "facts" and to render the past polyphony of Anatolia in the public domain. This array of representations, à la Jakobson, of the Greek-Turkish population exchange as an agony and Anatolians as kin through common geography, has invited the public in Turkey today to realize that there are multiple ways in which one could be attached to a land as well as a population. While the texts analyzed in this essay retranslate past and present Anatolians' relationships as kinship, they reiterate the "cultural intimacy" (Herzfeld 1997) shared by people from the same region as geographic kinship. A brief historical overview of the 1923 Greek-Turkish compulsory population exchange is necessary to provide a background for the cultural products analyzed in this essay.

---

11. For views of Turkish youth about Turkish history education, see Tekeli (1998, 192–219).

Who Belongs Where?

Catastrophe and *victory* are two opposing terms that remind the people in Greece and Turkey of the 1922 Asia Minor War. Molded by national(ist) historiographies based on selectively voiced national archive documents, these terms shape the perception and collective memory repertoire around this same event differently in Greece and in Turkey. The 1923 Lausanne peace treaty deployed a compulsory exchange of populations between the two nation-states, forcing the religiously defined minorities to leave their homesteads and homeland. According to Article One of the Convention of Lausanne, as of May 1, 1923, "there shall take place a compulsory exchange of the Turkish nationals of the Greek Orthodox religion established in Turkish territory, and the Greek nationals of Muslim religion established in Greek territory." The population exchange was negotiated internationally, ratified and executed by the League of Nations in accordance with the Treaty of Lausanne. It became the last step taken in the international arena toward homogenizing the Turkish Anatolian demography (Aktar 2000).

However, many accounts of the Greek-Turkish case (e.g., my interviews with first-, second-, and third-generation *mübadils* (exchanged peoples) in both Greece and Turkey, as well as novels) suggest that "homogenization" and the exchange of populations was not as smooth a process as the two states' officials had envisioned. The simplified nationalist notion that equated Greek with Orthodox and Turkish with Muslim did not justly render the exchanged peoples' experiences. The loss of their homesteads and homeland was not the only ordeal the *mübadils* encountered; many were alienated by what they called the "natives" of their "motherland" (Mavrogordatos 1983; Yalçın 1998), the recipient country to which they were now supposedly being returned. *Mübadils* were exchanged based on their religious affiliation,[12] yet many did not speak the language of their new motherland but instead that of the region of

---

12. A Turkish term literally meaning "exchanged," which is used to identify the people who were subjected to the population exchange between Greece and Turkey, interestingly anchoring identification not in a place, in belonging somewhere, or in an ethnic origin, but in a process: that of the exchange.

their geographic origin—that is, of the particular place in Greece or Turkey where each had been born and raised.

Falling out of time, feeling out of context, unable to make sense of the recipient country's realities, which itself was going through radical changes and reforms (see Özyürek's introduction to this volume), all speak to the ordeals some exchanged people experienced. Perhaps these are common experiences to most immigrants or refugees, but what makes the case of the *mübadils* so interesting is the fact that they did not fit into the national-identity paradigm ascribed to them by Greek and Turkish nation-states. Many *mübadils* in Turkey who are now in their late eighties and nineties still identify themselves as "being from . . ." and see their individual geographic origin as a marker of their identity.

How did the exchanged peoples negotiate the tensions between the identity imposed by their mother-state and self-identificatory practices, such as speaking a language, that were at times different from those of their new country?[13] How did their experience mediate the category of *ethnicity* and what other, if any, metaethnic concepts did they resort to in interpreting their own identity? My research indicates that the geographic origin (i.e., the homeland that was now taken away from them) and the memory of it became central to the refugees' self-identification (Iğsız 2001). Despite their religious or at times linguistic affiliations with their new home, many *mübadils* realized that they did not share what the anthropologist Michael Herzfeld calls "cultural intimacy," common frameworks of memory beyond national and ethnic attributes (1997, 13–14) or religion. Putting these experiences of rupture at the center helps convey an indirect critique of national identification practices.

Anthropologist Carol Delaney (1991) argues that in Turkey, procreation is

---

13. In many of the interviews I held with *mübadils* from both Greece and Turkey, the question of language came up, as their mother tongue was not always the same as the one spoken in the motherland. Some Muslims sent to Turkey did not speak a word of Turkish or spoke it improperly, with an accent, and the same was also true for the Orthodox religion practitioners who did not speak Greek, mainly the Karamanli (widely referred to as Turkish Orthodox, which further complicates the issue of who belongs to which category). See Mavrogordatos (1983); Yalçın (1998); and documentaries *To Taxidi* (The Journey; 1998), and *Bir Mübadele Öyküsü* (A Tale of Population Exchange; 2002).

conceptualized through the metaphors of the seed and the soil: while the mother is perceived as the field, the father procures the seed.[14] If the nation-state is constructed by nationalist discourses as the father figure, then it is the paternalistic nation-state that provides citizenship to those who are born under his name. That is to say, it ascribes a national identity, translating individuals into nationals such as Greeks and Turks. In this symbolic framework, the soil is the common origin, the mother from which Anatolians are born even though they do not necessarily carry her name.

The cultural products analyzed here also reflect an extension of identification based on connection with the soil, the place of origin that gave birth to people who spoke different languages and practiced different religions. Hence, these products promote Anatolia as a trope of mother and retranslate individual Anatolians into geographic kin.

Cultural Politics and Geographic Kinship in Narrative Frames

Cultural works are produced and circulated through institutions and their agents; their reception and interpretation are closely linked with the way in which these works are presented to their audience. Mieke Bal points out that "a text does not speak for itself" but rather, "we surround it, or *frame* it before we let it speak at all" (2002, 8; emphasis in original). It is the French narratologist Gérard Genette (1982) who coined the term *paratext* in literature, turning the framing narratives into a powerful tool for (narrative) analysis. He studies auxiliary texts, which he calls paratext, such as the title, the preface, or epigraph accompanying the main text. These shorter texts introduce, frame, and present a text, may lengthen and comment upon it, and ensure and affect its reception. Genette identifies two kinds of paratexts, one located in the same volume as the main text and called peritext, the other, referring to all messages

14. In a book review Leyla Neyzi criticizes Carol Delaney's work because her "rigid interpretation of the ethnographic material through the seed-soil metaphor and the accompanying theory of procreation results in a highly coherent and seamless cultural system" (Neyzi 1994, 213). Although this might be true, the seed and the soil metaphor were inspiring in conceptualizing the discursive practices analyzed in this essay as "geographic kinship."

concerning the text, located outside of the text itself and called epitext (such as interviews, news, etc.).

While peritext is a compelling tool for narrative analysis, it is also a neglected one: most close readings in literary analysis deal with the content of a book or text rather than how it is framed within the same volume of the main text by the institution promoting or printing it. On the other hand, epitexts, without being called as such, have received much attention from scholars studying "representation" and discourse analysis. Gérard Genette, in his later work *Paratexts* (1997), suggests that these framing narratives cannot be considered as paratexts unless they are in complete harmony with the author's intention. This discussion is of secondary value for the purposes of this essay because in fact, regardless of whether a framing narrative is a paratext (epitext or peritext), it represents the main body of a text. It is the institutional politics of this representation (regardless of the author) that reveals cultural agency and operates as a renegotiation of the past in the public domain and a reidentification of individuals from the same geographic origin as kin.[15]

In the 1990s, two cultural institutions, Belge Publishing Company and Kalan Music Productions, hosted and produced cultural works voicing the polyphonic Anatolian past. Interestingly, the names of both cultural corporations speak to the archiving process: one documents literature, and the other one assembles music collections that "remain."[16]

Marenostrum: From Our Sea to "Our" Anatolia

In 1990, Belge Publishing Company initiated a new series, *Marenostrum* (Our Sea). The series opened with the following statement on the first page of the first publication, *Loksandra: Istanbul Düşü*:

15. In some cases, a book's content did not promote peace as much as the book cover suggested. Although this is an interesting tension that needs to be addressed and studied, it is the subject of another study; the limits and the purposes of this essay is to study institutional practices of representation.

16. This is the Turkish language translation of *kalan*.

We are starting our new series *Marenostrum* with *Loksandra: The Istanbul Dream,* written by the Istanbul-born Maria Yordanidou who lived in Batumi and Alexandria and died in November 1989 in Athens, at the age of ninety-two. Marenostrum is a phrase in Latin: When the Romans took possession of the Mediterranean, they called it "our sea." Today we say, "yes, our sea. But our sea belongs to all of us—it is in common to all of us, the Mediterraneans!" The sea where we all have our own share, where we fight, where we fall in love, where we die. The sea which ties us to each other with solid bonds, loaded with memories in common, and which shelters all enthusiasm and extremities. If we consider the Adriatic, the Aegean, the Marmara, and the Black Sea as part of this immense sea, then Maria Yordanidou is one of the writers who best represents this Mediterranean cosmopolitanism in her persona.

Our series will host a real festivity of peoples [in this region]. Our journey began with Yordanidou in Istanbul and will continue with other authors from other port cities, islands, mountains by the sea; it will sometimes lead us to the Balkans, sometimes to the Caucasus. After a promenade in Egypt with Taha Hussein, Tevfik Al Hakim, Nawal Al Sadawi, we will find ourselves in the Durrell's Cyprus, Korfou, Kazancakis' Crete, Henry Miller's Greece, Sciascia's Sicily, Pasolini's Italy. Following our journey in Babel and Odyssea, we will return to Istanbul with Istrati, with *Rum* and Armenian storytellers.[17] The Kurdish love story of Hüseyin Erdem will be followed by Sahar Khalifa's Jerusalem. We will then navigate from Barcelona to the shores of sadness and mountain chains in Morocco. We will meet with the Yugoslav writer Danilo Kiş. While we discover the complex world of Lebanon with Tawfik Awad's Tamima, the Armenian fairy tales will introduce us to a new world.

Marenostrum will be a special series. It will introduce us to ourselves, to each other. This adventure will carry our readers away.[18]

17. Hence, "since 1821, the term *Rum* was used in a device to distinguish a Greek of the Ottoman Empire from one of the independent Greek State, whose citizens are known to Turks as Yunanlı" (Alexandris 1983, 17).

18. All translations from Turkish into English are mine, except for the Kalan framing narratives directly taken from the Kalan Web site, which were originally in English (http://www.kalan.com).

Marenostrum aims to "introduce us to ourselves, to each other." In other words, it first wants to discover who we are. During my interview with him, Ragıp Zarakolu mentioned that their aim as publishers was "to make the stories of Anatolians accessible for the Turkish public" in the cultural public sphere. His late spouse, the co-owner of Belge, Ayşenur Zarakolu, on the other hand, mentioned to me in February 2000 that one of their goals was to challenge official history, "which had been more divisive than unifying." Between 1990 and 2000, when the series was first initiated, *Marenostrum* released more than sixty publications, fifty-eight of which were completely sold out. More than thirty of these books were literary works either translated from Greek or were about the Greeks in Anatolia, most of which explore the population exchange. In fact, the publishing company Belge received the Abdi İpekçi Turkish-Greek Friendship and Peace Prize in 2000 for its *Marenostrum* series, which promoted a "culture of peace and coexistence" among the Greek and Turkish peoples. Osman Bleda, for example, wrote that he translated *Loksandra* in order to contribute to Greek-Turkish friendship. Thus, the language of peace was not always subtle but was also openly stated.

In each publication, the *Marenostrum* statement appears with slight changes from preceding versions, becoming more Anatolian and at times completely detached from the content of the book. Ertuğrul Aladağ's *The Tale of My City: The Traces of the Rum in Muğla,* a novel about the population exchange, appeared in 1993, with a statement that focused on Anatolia instead of on the Mediterranean: *"The Tale of My City* is the new book of the *Marenostrum* series, which aims at revealing the multicultural, multinational, multireligious heritage we have in common in our country. It supports the cultural heritage and coexistence of the Anatolian peoples. Our series justifies the possibility of coexistence. When nationalist and chauvinist claims are at their peak, *Marenostrum* brings back memories from the past, both good and bad, and promotes humane values."

This framing narrative highlights the memories of the refugees of Asia Minor to guide the readers toward reconsidering the possibility of coexistence. Obviously, the cultural professionals who produce *Marenostrum* do not have nationalistic claims against which they adopt a more critical position. With every new cultural production in the series, they aim to gain another lost voice from the Anatolian past: each voice reinscribes an individual into the collective memory in the public domain. This effort becomes another step toward restoring the past polyphony of the land and refuting the nationalist homogeneous and monophonic voice within the Turkish public domain. While these efforts were visible, it is important to note, however, that not all framing narratives presented the cultural products accurately, as the content of the books in question did not always advocate sister/brotherhood among between the Muslims and the Greek Orthodox. In turn, this makes the use of such framing narratives more striking. As to the possible tensions between the books' content and their representation, that is the scope of another study.

In 1995, the framing narrative of another *Marenostrum* publication, *Andonia,* a book by Ertuğrul Aladağ about the Asia Minor *mübadil* experience, revealed a specifically retrospective attitude toward the ethnically defined conflicts of Anatolians:

Ertruğrul Aladağ's *The Tale of My City* (previously published in our series) attracted a large number of readers. Now with *Andonia,* you will read the rest of the story on the other side [of the Aegean]. This is the story of fellow citymen from Muğla, torn apart from their motherland, and their struggles to remake themselves in a new world. This is the grieving history of how those who were "from us" were made into a "from them," which we do not want to see be repeated. Recent tragic experiences and histories show once more how inhuman much ethnic cleansing is and how it belittles societies. If we do not want the past to be remembered with remorse and regrets, then we need to defend coexistence and the common culture; we need to respect other peoples' identities and we need to do this all together.

This statement brings several important points to the reader's attention: first, it introduces the notion of "from us," and second, it promotes the coexistence of "ethnic" groups. What, then, was the criterion that made the Greek Orthodox *mübadil* "from us" if they were ethnically different? I suggest that it is geographic kinship. *Marenostrum* claims that Turks and Greeks of Anatolia shared a common heritage, a cultural intimacy, that rendered them as Anatolians and, thus, as kin.

In *Sekene*'s introduction, for instance, *Marenostrum* openly deploys a discourse of "sister/brotherhood" among the peoples of Anatolia (Aladağ 1997):

> Ertuğrul Aladağ's new work *Sekene* should be considered as an oral history. It demonstrates how identities are constructed and also variable. It draws our attention to the consequences of the tragic population movements and turbulences in Anatolian human geography. Aladağ also gives a crucial message: "The only magic formula to prevent war and overcome bad memories is love." He reminds us of how much we share within this geography; we have common memories and our cultures are similar. . . . This is going to be a special series. With our readers, we will seek for the sister/brotherhood atmosphere, long buried in the darkness of the past. Here, we will construct a spiritual bridge to a common future. Here to construct our sea.

This framing statement guides the reader toward the future and justifies bringing past memories into the present. It invites the reader to be more receptive to Others who share the same geography. While speaking of differences, the *Marenostrum* series does not use a consistent nomenclature but does use a consistent discourse. The *Marenostrum* paratexts advocate that the Anatolian past should be brought to the Turkish present because this will render the past polyphony of the land.

Such emphasis on common geography suggests a culture of coexistence where Anatolia does not signify a national territory but rather a soil that organically relates individuals to each other. The past tragedies of the people connected to each other as geographic kin should thus be voiced in order to construct a common future where Anatolians can coexist. Hence, the retrospective approach of the series: learning from past conflicts will lead Anatolian residents to be more tolerant toward each other.

Geographic Kinship Versus Attributed Identities

The Entrusted Trousseau: People of the Exchange is a collection of oral accounts disguised in novel form—at times creating confusion regarding its genre: the narrators whom the author interviewed are documented with their photographs as if to authenticate their stories, and the whole book is divided into chapters of individual stories about the population exchange. Because of its documentary texture, it has been used as a reference book for the *mübadil* experiences on both sides of the Aegean.

Kemal Yalçın's *The Entrusted Trousseau* was first published in 1998 in the *Marenostrum* series.[19] The novel won the Achievement Prize of the Ministry of Culture in the category of fiction, and the Abdi İpekçi Turkish-Greek Friendship and Peace Prize awarded in the year 2000. Consequently, the second edition of this book was published by a more mainstream publishing company, Doğan Kitap. This suggests two things. First, by the year 2000, the state-sponsored institutions had started to support the cultural products that address past tragedies in Anatolia (although at the time of writing this essay, this was becoming more restricted). Second, major publishing companies also had started to print such cultural products. The success of the cultural products, which created their own reader audience, gained state support in the late 1990s and early 2000 and became a financially lucrative business for publishers.[20]

The first edition of Yalçın's book appears with the following quote, which gives a strong message of geographic kinship. The second edition from Doğan Kitap uses the same statement on the back page—a quote from a non-Muslim Asia Minor *mübadil,* Baba Yorgo from Ayancık: "Look at the beauty of this garden. [Look] at this peach, this plum tree, look at these flowers! Their beauty derives from their togetherness . . . The more different languages, religions, races in a country, the richer it is. . . . These are my last words to you, to inhabitants in Sinop, in Ayancık and to the Turks: There cannot be a garden with only one type of fruit!" The quote emphasizes the differences among people by likening them to different fruits, and it also underlines the fact that these people still belong to the same garden, which is Anatolia.

What makes people different from each other? How do we define what

19. Since the framing statement used by *Marenostrum* in this novel is not different from the first one, I do not include it here. The fact that it did not change suggests that the discourse had become standardized or that it is the author himself who wrote the back cover statement.

20. This support came before the rapprochement between the Greek and Turkish governments. However, with the changing dynamics in Turkey, there seemed to be more directly applied state censorship on cultural products in 2001. See January 2002 issues of the daily newspapers *Milliyet, Radikal, Sabah,* and *Hürriyet* for more information.

many call "ethnicity"? The exchanged people did not necessarily speak what we call today ethnic languages: in other words, not all Greek Orthodox spoke Greek, and not all Muslims from Greece spoke Turkish when they were exchanged, which often resulted in their being called names ("Turkish seed" or "Greek seed") or being alienated from the residents of the recipient country. The religious affiliation did not always seem to be enough for the recipient country's people to accept the newcomers. According to my interviews, for a long time there were no intermarriages, especially in smaller towns and villages, and the exchanged people were singled out, especially in more rural areas. For instance, a Muslim *mübadil,* Refet Özkan, narrates his story: "We did not speak Turkish, our mother tongue was the Rum language. . . . In daily life, in the field, in the garden the natives would humiliate us and call us 'children of the infidel [non-Muslim]!' " (Yalçın 1998, 263).

Özkan continues with an incident when his teacher spat on his face when he realized that he did not speak Turkish (ironically, later, Özkan became a Turkish teacher). Other Muslim *mübadil*s refugees, Salih Tilki and Saliha Korucu, narrate their own stories, how people (the "natives") would call them "creatures," and spread stories about how the exchanged people devoured (ate) men (Yalçın 1998, 208–12, 238).

According to interviews Kemal Yalçın conducted, the Greek Orthodox *mübadil* from Asia Minor received similar reactions from the "natives." Angela Katrini says: "We spoke Turkish. Turkish was our native language. They [the local people] would say 'Turks arrived! These are Turks! The immigrants will take our fields! They should leave!' And they would send their dogs on us [for them to attack us]" (Yalçın 1998, 143).

Another account from Kayserili Karabaş reads: "Because we did not speak the Rum language they would say we were Turks, and they did not give us any woman to marry, nor would they take any woman from us (for the same purpose)" (Yalçın 1998, 81).

In these accounts, it is possible to observe the significance of language in the daily interactions between the exchanged peoples and the natives. It is interesting to observe how in these accounts the newcomers and the locals identified each other according to their place of origin: Turks, *Turkos sporoi* (Turkish seed), *gavur* (infidel), Greek seed, or natives. Religious attributes envisioned as sufficient to homogenize the nation-state by the Greek and Turkish state officials were not necessarily experienced by the people themselves, nei-ther the exchanged people nor the natives. *Mübadil* narratives of homeland and self-identification through geographic origin are significant in terms of revealing their feelings of belonging, at the same time complicating their eth-nic attributes.

Kalan Music and an Ambivalent Genre

Founded in 1991, the Kalan Music Company contributed to voicing the Turk-ish-Greek population exchange by bringing the music component to the pub-lic domain. The company states its goal on its Web page as archiving the music from different regions and pasts of Anatolia. Kalan's approach is conveyed by quotes from the news articles on Hasan Saltık, the owner and founder of the company, described as "the sound missionary of Anatolia" who "archives" Anatolian music.[21] As part of its archiving endeavor, Kalan introduces a new dimension to the folk music genre, recorded in the original languages of the various Anatolian regions, Laz, Pontus, Kurdish, Armenian, Turkish, and Greek, including *rembetiko*.[22]

Rembetika is the Greek underground music of the outlaw. Its origins and definitions are ambivalent. According to Gail Holst, this musical style is an amorphous genre in general.[23] The lyrics can be light, ironic, or sad. The mul-tiple names that define the genre reveal its ambiguous persona: it is called *re-betiko, rembetiko, rebetika,* and *rembetika.* Holst assumes that *rembetika* originated toward the end of the nineteenth century in a number of urban centers where Greeks lived. Around this time musical cafés appeared in towns on both sides of the Aegean where small orchestras played music with both Turkish and Greek traditional instruments.

There is no concrete information regarding the origin of the word *rem-betika,* the music of the *rembet,* the outlaw. Although it is generally assumed to be a Turkish word, *rembetika* does not, at least directly, derive from Turkish since the *mübadils* from Asia Minor brought their own music styles from Ana-

---

21. See *Cumhuriyet,* Feb. 13, 1999; *Hürriyet,* June 13, 1999; and http://www.kalan.com.tr.
22. Interview with Hasan Saltık, Apr. 5, 2000.
23. Personal communication, Mar. 2000.

tolia (Holst 1994, 26–27). Holst argues that even though the "refugees may not have been part of the underworld, they were living on the edge of the Greek society, competing for jobs in poor urban areas, segregated often by language as well as customs from the bulk of the Greek population." Here, Holst draws attention to the cultural intimacy that did not exist between the "refugees" and the natives, as attested by Kemal Yalçın's book showing the alienation of the *mübadil*s in their "motherland" by the natives. It is for this reason that many exchanged people who were musicians joined the *rembet*s or *mange*s in their loosely organized subculture,[24] or were attracted to the hashish-smoking *teké*s to which they were accustomed in Turkey:[25] "Rembetika songs were written by rembetes for rembetes. . . . The rembetis was a man who had a sorrow and threw it out" (Holst 1994, 11–27). It is therefore telling that the name of the music of the "other"—*rembetiko*—is associated with another "other," the Turkish language.

In the Turkey of the 1990s, *rembetika* came to represent the pain and sufferings of the Asia Minor *mübadil*s, of "those who left." This process of representation is illustrated in the framing narratives provided in the album covers of two *rembetika* productions from Kalan, compiled by Muammer Ketencoğlu in 1991 and 1993. These are the first albums in Turkey that reproduced the already existing records of *rembetika* songs in Greek and Turkish. The third *rembetika* album examined here conveys original *rembetika* songs in Turkish translation. It was produced in 1994 by a popular band called Yeni Türkü (The New Song).

Kalan's first *rembetika* album, *Rebetika—Rebetler* (1991), includes the following text on the album cover:

> The *rebets* . . . our old neighbors, most of whose graves are unknown, how can we say *toprağı bol olsun* when they don't even have a soil?[26]
>
> Those who are torn from İzmir came to Paşalimanı, Hiotika in crowds.

24. The *mange*s were men who formed a subculture on the fringe of the society. Many of them were actually in the underworld. The nearest English equivalents are probably "spivs," "wide boys," or "hep-cats" (Holst 1994, 14).

25. *Teké*, or *tekke* in Turkish, literally means a convent of dervishes. Here, however, it also refers to a place, mainly a tavern, where outlaws would go to smoke hashish.

26. *Toprağı bol olsun* (May his grave be broad) is a Turkish phrase used for the deceased. This phrase literally translates as "May his/her earth be plenty."

. . . Those who escaped from fronts in the Afyon War, the Rums from Bergama, Ayvalık, Bornova, Soğukkuyu. . . . For years, they had no work, no food. On this side [of the Aegean] they were humiliated as the "infidel Rum" *(Rum gavuru)* while on the other side they were humiliated as the "Turkish germ" *(Turkos sporos/Türk dölü)*. The population of Greece reached 8.5 million upon their arrival, and in only a few weeks the population increased by one-third. They [our neighbors] were in misery for years. . . .

They lost themselves in alcohol, rebellion, drugs, and music because of hopelessness, but above all because of the pain of the longing for their homeland, because of the nostalgia. . . . They burnt their memories, their longings into songs and ballads. This music is called "rembetika" or "rebetika."

Imagine, what these people must have gone through while listening to it [this music]. . . . Think, what it must be like to have the fear of death at your back, to put your portable belongings in sheets making them into bales. . . . How children would weep. . . . A baby doll (made of cloth) forgotten in a courtyard, kidney beans left on the stove, how the house in which one is born—leave aside getting back—would be lost (forever), not to be seen again. . . . How would one run to left and right, along the cobbled streets.

What kind of a life's music is it that you are listening to? Imagine!

Today what remains from them is the noise (of the streets) of İzmir, of Athens, and the scratched, creaking old records sitting in front of the stores, or on the shelves of the used bookstores. . . .

The old Rum songs that say sorrow in a misty voice and which perhaps bring tears to the eyes.

This framing narrative written by Serdar Sönmez, a cultural professional working for Kalan, depicts *rembetika* exclusively as the music of "those who left us." It invites the audience to listen to the miseries of the Asia Minor *mübadils*. Sönmez suggests that the *mübadils'* miseries are caused by their longing for the homeland, Anatolia, and by their unemployed status in the recipient country. This is why those who left Anatolia became *rembets*, outlaws, outsiders, and wherever they went, either to Greece or to Turkey, they would be considered as outsiders.

The rest of the album's text cites the names of the songs and the musicians who contributed to it. Under the titles of the songs, the reader sees what the song (mostly sung in Greek) is about, and then the geographic lineage, the origin of the musician, and what his or her contribution has been to the *rembetika* style. As this is a collection of original recordings, all musicians are refugees. Like an anthology, the works included in the album reflect the position of the compiler vis-à-vis the work being edited. This "rewriting" (Lefevere 1992) process is revealed in the choice of songs and musicians for the album and in how they represent this music and its musicians: they have connections with Anatolia, and one of the songs is even in Turkish. Likewise, this *rembetika* compilation and its presentation convey geographic kinship among Anatolian peoples, past and present.

Rebetika 2: 1927–1954 (1993) appeared two years after the first one, in 1993. This time both the presentation and the framing narratives were prepared by the musician Muammer Ketencoğlu himself, who compiled *rembetika* songs and produced those albums for Kalan for the first time. Again, the album consisted of a collection of *rembetika* songs recorded between 1927 and 1954.

> Today, the songs of *rebetico* bring new excitement to our people, no matter how belated this has been. It [*rebetico*] offers its poisonous and healing taste to our hearts. Unfortunately (I have a hard time saying "luckily"), we owe these songs to unemployed, poor *manga*s and to people who have been displaced, forced to move from their place and to live in ruins in misery. Just like the other side of any beauty.
>
> The ballads and songs of the Rums from Asia Minor and İzmir, which were open to interaction with Europe, were not different from the ones of the Turks with whom they lived on friendly terms until the 1920s. When they were getting into the boats it was as if it was only their songs that they could take with them. On the other hand, the difficult living conditions around the Piraeus port that developed in the 1850s, created the *manga* subculture that consisted of people who were poor, making fun of all kinds of authority, rebellious, emotional, and unable to do without music and hashish. During the daytime they worked, and at night they went to those small taverns they called *tekke* to play *buzuki* and *bağlama* and get high. Consequently, the exchange of populations between Greece and Turkey is a tragedy caused by what is either called the War of Independence or the Great Disaster, unifying the destiny of the Asia Minor's Rums who lost their homeland and

wealth and became poor, with the disobedient *manga*s from Piraeus. They first sang their songs side by side but separately, and then together, in one voice. The first collection of *rebetico*[27] released approximately six months ago consists of the beginning period of the *rebetico* music represented by the İzmir style. However, especially after the 1930s, the *manga* culture style (also called the Piraeus or the *tekke* style) has become more dominant. Taking this as the point of departure, the whole album that you have in your hands consists of the recordings in the Piraeus style between 1930 and 1950, except for a few distinct examples. I feel deeply moved by being able to share with you some samples of this music, as few as they are.

This production's framing narrative is more elaborate in terms of recognizing the *mangas* style in Piraeus along with the İzmir/Smyrna style of Asia Minor. In other words, *rembetika* is not presented exclusively as the music of those who left Asia Minor.

The production of several *rembetika* albums in such a short period of time implies that there was a demand for it. This is also evident in the fact that Yeni Türkü produced a *rembetika*-style album in translation only a year after the Ketencioğlu-Kalan production, in cooperation with the music company Göksoy, which had not shown an interest in *rembetika* before. Like Kemal Yalçın's *The Entrusted Trousseau,* reprinted by another publishing company, *rembetika* became part of mainstream music in the 1990s.

Unlike the previous *rembetika* albums, *Külhani Şarkılar* by Yeni Türkü is a remade album. The phrase *külhani şarkılar* (songs of *külhani*) emphasizes a boldness used to intimidate others because the word *külhani* carries an intense male, bravado-like connotation. As to the lyrics, they are also rewritten in Turkish; they are not translations. The framing narrative on the album cover reveals the reason why the word *külhani* was chosen to refer to *rembet*s:

> We are in the beginning of the 1900s: the years of the exchange of populations. Muslims in Greece and Christians in Anatolia are forced to migrate

27. Muammer Ketencioğlu prepared three albums of *rembetika*. Here he mentions the first collection that he prepared for Kalan. In this study I discuss three *rembetika* albums prepared in different styles, in order to demonstrate the variety of representations.

collectively from both sides. Both peoples are sent out on a migration of nonreturn, leaving their properties, their homesteads, their habits, and most important above all, their homeland behind. Those who live in the Aegean and İzmir region only take their culture as a relic of the bright days of the past. But their culture is not enough to keep them alive; they find themselves in a big misery. The places where they live are the ghettos. The number of those who can find a decent job is very limited. The places of getting together for the unemployed are *tekke* and *amane* cafes. In those places they relieve their sorrow with hashish, music, and dance. Other important components are, of course, fights, police, and jail. The type of immigrant who lives in the triangle of *tekke,* hashish, and prison is called *rebet,* and their music *rebetika.* We, as Yeni Türkü, translated the terms and found the Turkish equivalent *külhani* and *külhani şarkılar.*

In this album, Yeni Türkü brings the past into the present. It will continue such works in the future. We believe that it is our past that will carry us to our future. Our album, in this sense, is a proposition.

Both the translation and the text render *rembet*s as exclusively male, suggesting the confusion between *manga* and *rembet*s. In Turkish, *külhani* is never used for women. Holst explains that the *manga* style of Piraeus was highly male dominated. The Smyrna/İzmir style, brought to Greece by the Asia Minor refugees, on the other hand, included women as *rembete*s (Holst 1994, 42–44).

Hence, by calling "rembets" *külhani,* Yeni Türkü refers to the original meaning and remasculinizes the genre. The cover of the album includes a sketched moustache, despite which, however, there are female vocals in the album—this attests to the lack of clarity as to what this term and the music really mean. *Külhani Şarkılar* is the first *rembetika* album released in Turkey that aims to establish geographic kinship relations between Greeks and Turks through the lyrics, rewritten in Turkish by Cengiz Onural. The lyrics of the last two songs directly narrate the experience of the refugees (those who fled before the exchange) and of the people taking part in the population exchange. They appear on the cover with the following words: "Look what this *bağlama*[28]

28. A *bağlama* is a musical instrument with three double strings played with a plectrum. This instrument is also used in *rembetika*-style music.

says in the hands of the remarkable Tsaous; the *zeybeks*[29] chose a side; and listen [to this music] in Smyrna. One day Tsaous migrated during one of the (armed) conflicts. They say his face never smiles in the *els*[30] of Piraeus. The night burns our chest. Are these stars of ice? Or (is it that) the stars in Piraeus are less than (the ones in) my Smyrna?"

The other song, "Old Friends," reads:

> Two people on two opposite shores; their eyes, shadowed with a delicate sorrow, the same song in their tongue, hazy with the same *rakı*.[31] Who would believe they are enemies? The love for homeland has neither language nor religion. Once you are born it burns your heart. If it is our destiny to be neighbors from now on, how can one not cry to this enmity of ours? The house I am born in, old friends, our neighborhood: Bosporus still decorates my dreams, Istanbul is a habit of old days, disregard that I am (now) coming from Athens.

These two songs, particularly the second one, assert a geographic kinship between the exchanged peoples. The rewritten lyrics[32] narrate the nostalgia for a homeland that houses its present and past peoples: They sing the same song, they drink the same beverage, and they belong to the same region. This statement cuts across notions of ethnicity as, according to the songs, "homeland has neither religion nor language boundaries." In other words, being from the same homeland unifies people. Religion and language, on the other hand, separated the exchanged peoples: first from the people in their homeland, and then from those in their recipient culture. The two songs by Yeni Türkü suggest that people from the same geography share deeper connections than language and religion that came to define the "ethnic" boundaries in the international order of the twentieth century.[33]

---

29. Zeybek is the name of a tribe formerly inhabiting some districts near İzmir/Smyrna. In Turkey today, *zeybek* is the symbol of the Aegean, of İzmir region in particular.

30. The Turkish word *el* denotes "hand," as well as "foreign (lands)" in English.

31. Rakı is an alcoholic drink made of anise, consumed both in Turkey and Greece.

32. Interview with Muammer Ketencioğlu, Feb. 2000.

33. Interestingly, these two songs do not exist in the cassette tape versions of the album, but only in the CD version. I could not find which came out first, and why there was a differ-

Discursive practices promoting kinship ties among Anatolians extend to the past, present, and future. The paratexts demonstrate an attempt to transcribe publicly the personal stories of the *mübadil* and to translate Anatolians as geographic kin. What brings these peoples closer than simple intimacy is having been born in Anatolia. The belief iterated by Carol Delaney, that it is not only seed and blood but also the field conceptualized as a womb, provides a space to conceptualize the soil of Anatolia as such: a discursive womb.

Conclusion

The past is intricately woven by complex narratives of events and experiences. When being exposed or subjected to "happenings" collectively, individuals also experience everything in their own way. So, where to begin? Which tales to pick, whose stories to tell to "make" history? In Turkey over the last decade the past has been reconfigured with the shift that articulates individual stories in the public domain. This essay recounts the discursive practices of a publishing company and a music company that enabled a space to make the stories of the *mübadil*s "public," and discusses how representations of the 1923 Greek-Turkish population exchange convey the past polyphony of Anatolia, inviting its present residents to engage in a public dialogue (by listening to music and reading literature) with their geographic kin—the past Anatolian people.

Cultural professionals who bring the past polyphony of Anatolia into their works reconceptualize the human geography of Turkey. They represent peoples from Asia Minor as bound to each other by their geographic origin: Anatolia becomes a metaphorical mother who embraces all of her "children," past and present regardless of their ethnoreligious and national affiliations. While cultural products render the polyphony of Anatolia by acknowledging the past and the stories of the people who once lived there, they also convey their separation from Asia Minor as a tragedy. This establishes the language and the vocabulary to translate the ordeal of the Greek-Turkish forced migra-

---

ence. As arbitrary as the removal of these songs on the exchange might be, this also demonstrates the role of cultural producers in the production of cultural works.

tion into the present and locates the individual and collective sufferings caused by this event on the "map." The politics of framing narratives reveals that the ways in which these cultural products are presented to their audience are an attempt to renegotiate homogeneously ascribed identities.

The cultural institutions analyzed in this essay produce such cultural works that archive the narratives of the Greek-Turkish population exchange and make them public as an alternative repository for the past against official history. This initiative is visible in how the framing narratives examined here suggest an institutionalized attempt to make the audience conscious of their "organic" ties to all Anatolians. The emphasis of these frame narratives on geographic kinship ties undermines the divisiveness of religion and ethnicity, and underlines the possibility of a multiple coexistence in the same land.

By bringing the Asia Minor *mübadil* memory narratives of homeland into the Turkish cultural sphere, the cultural products voice or represent the past peoples from the same homeland. The memory narratives and songs are fluid, but once they are included in a cultural production, they solidify. As they are recorded and stored, they turn into archives for an audience to return to and verify the evidence of the past.[34]

Interviews with the cultural professionals point at the shifts in the political reception of their works: the owner of Kalan, Hasan Saltık, for instance, was prosecuted for the Kurdish album *Newroz* that he prepared at the end of the 1980s. However, during the late 1990s many Turkish bureaucrats offered Kalan albums as gifts to their foreign colleagues. State policies and cultural politics do not necessarily overlap, and in the case of the cultural politics induced through framing narratives as analyzed here, cultural products can (re)introduce and/or (re)shape certain concepts and ways of thinking about these concepts. The pertinent question to ask here would be: for whom? Who consumes these products?

My survey of cultural professionals in publishing companies and book and music shops in the summer of 2003 denotes that there is not a clear por-

34. This tendency of recording is also visible in the Economic and Social History Foundation's oral history project entitled *Tarihe Bin Canlı Tanık* (One Thousand Witnesses to History), marketed with the slogan "Kaybetmiyoruz Çünkü Kaydediyoruz" (We do not lose because we record).

trait of the present and target public audience. In most instances the responses were estimates of a readership or audience with "more leftist tendencies and curiosity and tolerance towards other cultures, or members of the religiously defined minorities themselves." The late Ayşenur Zarakolu identified the Marenostrum readers as "people addicted to reading and learning about the realities, past and present tragedies of this geography." However, at this point, it is difficult to draw any conclusions. The audience of these products is the subject of another study.

The final question to think about regards the timing of these products: why now? Anthropologist Leyla Neyzi explains the recent "rediscovery of history" among Turks with disillusionments caused by modernity (2002, 139–43). Although this might be one of the reasons, numerous cultural professionals I interviewed thought that competing nationalisms in the world and in contemporary Turkey are the most important reasons why these professionals turned to "history." They wanted to remind their audiences that nationalism caused tragedies such as partitioned lands, forced migrations, and massacres all around the world and in Turkey, such as the Greek-Turkish population exchange. By doing so, the cultural professionals warned their audience against the brutal results to which present nationalisms can lead.

The professionals who author the framing narratives analyzed here exploit different narrative strategies to develop a culture of peace, to gain recognition of the differences between peoples residing in Anatolia, and to promote mutual tolerance and coexistence. The representations in the 1990s of the 1923 Greek-Turkish population exchange opened a retrospective platform to contest homogenizing practices and air tensions between state-imposed identity and self-identification. As those representations transform the rhetoric of Anatolia from a homogeneous nation-state territory into a homeland and a mother, they also renegotiate and put into question the translation of individuals into homogeneously defined "ethnies." The frame narratives instead construct and suggest a different model for coexistence in which peoples are related to each other through their place of origin.

The music and film producers, publishers, and translators and the awards given for their work make bold political statements retrospectively, and successfully open a new space to rethink ethnic and national boundaries. Framing narratives suggest that memories of the past carry the public in Turkey toward the future. Thus, in recollecting past tragedies in Anatolia and reconsidering ethnic divisions, new ways are proposed to think about the contemporary ethnic problems in Turkey, and offer a discursive model of coexistence.

References

Index

References

Abélès, Marc. 1990. *Anthropologie de l'état*. Paris: Armand Colin.

Abu el-Haj, Nadia. 2001. *Facts on the Ground: Archaeological Practice and Territorial Self-Fashioning in Israeli Society*. Chicago: Univ. of Chicago Press.

Ağaoğlu, Adalet. 1990. *Ölmeye Yatmak* (Lying Down to Die). Istanbul: Remzi Kitabevi.

Akar, Rıdvan. 1999. *Aşkale Yolcuları, Varlık Vergisi, ve Çalışma Kampları* (Passengers to Aşkale, Wealth Tax, and Work Camps). Istanbul: Belge.

Akçam, Taner. 2004. *From Empire to Turkish Republic: Turkish Nationalism and the Armenian Genocide*. London: Zed Books.

Akın, Nur. 1992. "Osman Hamdi Bey, Âsâr-ı Atika Nizamnamesi ve Dönemin Koruma Anlayışı üzerine" (On Hamdi Bey, Regulations Regarding Antique Buildings, and the Protection Approach of the Era). In *Osman Hamdi Bey ve Dönemi* (Osman Hamdi Bey and His Era), edited by Zeynep Rona, 233–39. Istanbul: Tarih Vakfı Yurt Yayınları.

Akşit, Elif. 2001. "Yürümek" (Walking). In *Hatırladıklarıyla ve Unuttuklarıyla Türkiye'nin Toplumsal Hafızası* (Social Memory in Turkey: Things Remembered and Forgotten), edited by Esra Özyürek, 301–24. Istanbul: İletişim.

Aktar, Ayhan. 2000. *Varlık Vergisi ve Türkleştirme Politikaları* (Wealth Tax and Turkification Policies). Istanbul: İletişim Yayınları.

Akurgal, Ekrem. 1970. *Ancient Civilizations and Ruins of Turkey*. Istanbul: Mobil Oil Türk A.Ş. Yayınları.

———. 1997. *Anadolu Kültür Tarihi* (History of Anatolian Culture). Ankara: Tübitak Popüler Bilim Yayınları.

Aladağ, Ertuğrul. 1993. *Kentimin Öyküsü: Muğla'da Rum İzleri* (The Story of My City: Greek Remains in Muğla). Istanbul: Belge Yayıncılık.

———. 1995. *Andonia*. Istanbul: Belge Yayıncılık.

———. 1997. *Sekene*. Istanbul: Belge Yayıncılık.

Alexandris, Alexis. 1983. *The Greek Minority of Istanbul and Greek-Turkish Relations, 1918–1974*. Athens: Centre for Asia Minor Studies.

Altınay, Ayşe Gül. 2000. "Ordu-Millet-Kadınlar: Dünyanın İlk Kadın Savaş Pilotu Sabiha Gökçen" (Army-Nation-Women: World's First Aviation Pilot, Sabhia Gökçen). In *Vatan Millet Kadınlar* (Homeland Nation Women), edited by Ayşe Gül Altınay, 246–79. Istanbul: İletişim Yayinlari.

Anderson, Benedict. 1983. *Imagined Communities: Reflections on the Origin and Spread of Nationalism.* London: Verso.

Anderson, June. 1998. *Return to Tradition: The Revitalization of Turkish Village Carpets.* San Francisco: California Academy of Sciences; Seattle: Univ. of Washington Press.

Antze, Paul, and Michael Lambek, eds. 1996. *Tense Past: Cultural Essays in Trauma and Memory.* London: Routledge.

Appadurai, Arjun. 1986. *The Social Life of Things.* Cambridge: Cambridge Univ. Press.

———. 1996. *Modernity at Large.* Minneapolis: Univ. of Minnesota Press.

Appadurai, Arjun, and Carol Breckenbridge. 1988. "Why Public Culture?" *Public Culture* 1, no. 1: 5–10.

Arı, Kemal. 1995. *Büyük Mübadele* (The Big Population Exchange). Istanbul: Tarih Vakfı Yurt Yayınları.

Asaf, Mehmed. 1982. *1909 Adana Ermeni Olayları ve Anılarım* (Armenian Events of Adana and My Memories). Ankara: Türk Tarih Kurumu.

Aşkın, Turgut. 1999. *Bergama'da Eski Halk Giysileri Takılar İnanışlar* (Traditional Garments, Jewelry, and Beliefs in Bergama). Izmir: Alkan Okul Yayınevi.

Atasoy, Sümer. 1983. "Anadolu Medeniyetleri Müzesi" (Anatolian Civilizations Museum) and "Turkiye'de Müzecilik" (Museums in Turkey). In *Cumhuriyet Dönemi Türkiye Ansiklopedisi* (Encyclopedia of Turkey in the Republican Era), 6:1464–68. Istanbul: İletişim Yayınları.

Atlıhan, Şerife. 1993. "Traditional Weaving in One Village of Settled Nomads in Northwest Anatolia." *Oriental Carpet and Textile Studies* 4:77–88.

Audi, Robert. 2003. *Epistemology: A Contemporary Introduction to the Theory of Knowledge.* London: Routledge.

Aved, Thomas. 1979. *Toomas, the Little Armenian Boy: Childhood Reminiscence of Turkish Armenia.* Fresno, Calif.: Pioneer Publishing.

Aydemir, Şevket Süreyya. 1966. *İkinci Adam: İsmet İnönü* (The Second Man: İsmet İnönü). Istanbul: Remzi Kitabevi.

Baer, Marc. 2000. "Turkish Jews Rethink 500 Years of Brotherhood and Friendship." *Turkish Studies Association Bulletin* 24, no. 2: 63–74.

Bahloul, Joelle. 1996. *The Architecture of Memory: A Jewish-Muslim Houshold in Colonial Al-*

geria, 1937–1962. Translated by Catherine du Peloux Menage. Cambridge: Cambridge Univ. Press.

Bahrani, Zainab. 1998. "Conjuring Mesopotamia: Imaginative Geography and a World Past." In *Archaeology under Fire: Nationalism, Politics and Heritage in the Eastern Mediterranean and Middle East,* edited by Lynn Meskell, 159–74. New York: Routledge.

Bakhtin, Mikhail. 1984. *Problems of Dostoevsky's Poetics.* Edited and translated by Caryl Emerson. Minneapolis: Univ. of Minnesota Press.

———. 1996. *The Dialogic Imagination.* Austin: Univ. of Texas Press.

Bal, Mieke. 2002. *Traveling Concepts in the Humanities: A Rough Guide.* Toronto: Univ. of Toronto Press.

Bal, Mieke, Jonathan Crewe, and Leo Spitzer, eds. 1999. *Acts of Memory: Cultural Recall in the Present.* London: Univ. Press of New England.

Balandier, Georges. 1971. *Sens et puissance: Les dynamiques sociales.* Paris: PUF.

Bali, Rıfat. 1999. *Cumhuriyet Yıllarında Türkiye Yahudileri: Bir Türkleştirme Serüveni (1923–1945)* (Turkish Jews in the Republican Years: An Adventure of Turkification). Istanbul: İletişim Yayınları.

———. 2001. "Toplumsal Bellek ve Varlık Vergisi" (Social Memory and Wealth Tax). In *Hatırladıklarıyla ve Unuttuklarıyla Türkiye'nin Toplumsal Hafızası* (Social Memory of Turkey: Things Forgotten and Remembered), edited by Esra Özyürek, 87–126. Istanbul: İletişim Yayınları.

Bardenstein, Carol. 1999. "Trees, Forests, and the Shaping of Palestinian Collective Memory." In *Acts of Memory: Cultural Recall in the Present,* edited by Mieke Bal, Jonathan Crewe, and Leo Spitzer, 148–71. London: Univ. Press of New England.

Bartu, Ayfer. 1997. "Reading the Past: The Politics of Cultural Heritage in Contemporary Istanbul." Ph.D. diss., Univ. of California, Berkeley.

———. 1999a. "Who Owns the Old Quarters? Rewriting Histories in a Global Era." In *Istanbul: Between the Global and the Local,* edited by Çağlar Keyder, 31–45. Lanham, Md.: Rowman and Littlefield.

———. 1999b. "Archaeological Practice as Guerilla Activity in Late Modernity." *Journal of Mediterranean Archaeology* 12, no. 1: 91–95.

———. 2000. "Where is Çatalhöyük? Multiple Sites in the Construction of an Archaeological Site." In *Towards Reflexive Method in Archaeology: The Example at Çatalhöyük,* edited by Ian Hodder, 101–9. Cambridge: McDonald Institute for Archaeological Research; London: British Institute of Archaeology at Ankara.

Bayatlı, Osman. 1944a. *Bergama'da Köyler: Eğrigöl.* Izmir: Meşher Matbaası.

————. 1944b. *Bergama'da Köyler: Pınarköy, Narlıca, Tepeköy, Yalnızev* (Villages in Bergama: Pınarköy, Narlıca, Tepeköy, Yalnızev). Izmir: Güneş Yayınevi.

————. 1945a. *Bergama'da Köyler: Bölcekköy* (Villages in Bergama: Bölcekköy). Izmir: Güneş Yayınevi.

————. 1945b. *Bergama'da Köyler: Tırmanlar* (Villages in Bergama: Tırmanlar). Izmir: Güneş Yayınevi.

Bayburtluoğlu, İnci. 1991. "Müze Belgelerine Göre Kuruluşundan Günümüze Kadar Anadolu Medeniyetleri Müzesi" (Anatolian Civilizations Museum from Its Foundation to Today According to Museum Documents). *Ankara Dergisi* 1, no. 2: 96–124.

Baydar, Oya, and Feride Çiçekoğlu. 1998. *Cumhuriyet'in Aile Albümleri* (Family Albums of the Republic). Istanbul: Tarih Vakfı Yurt Yayınevi.

Baykam, Bedri. 1997. *Gözleri Hep Üzerimizde* (His Eyes Are Always Over Us). Ankara: Ümit Yayınları.

Bedoukian, Kerop. 1978. *The Urchin: An Armenian's Escape*. London: J. Murray.

Benhabib, Seyla. 1999. "Models of Public Space: Hannah Arendt, the Liberal Tradition, and Jürgen Habermas." In *Habermas and the Public Sphere*, edited by Craig Calhoun, 73–98. Cambridge: MIT Press.

Benjamin, Walter. 1969. "Some Motifs in Baudelaire." In *Illuminations*, 155–200. New York: Harcourt.

Bennett, Tony. 1995. *The Birth of the Museum: History, Theory, Politics*. London: Routledge.

Ben-Yehuda, Nachman. 1995. *The Masada Myth: Collective Memory and Mythmaking in Israel*. Madison: Univ. of Wisconsin Press.

Berdahl, Daphne. 1999. *Where the World Ended: Re-unification and Identity in the German Borderland*. Berkeley: Univ. of California Press.

Berik, Günseli. 1987. *Women Carpet Weavers in Rural Turkey*. Geneva: International Labour Office.

Berkes, Niyazi. 1988 [1964]. *The Development of Secularism in Turkey*. New York: Routledge.

Berktay, Halil. 1983. *Cumhuriyet İdeolojisi ve Fuat Köprülü* (The Republican Ideology and Fuat Köprülü). Istanbul: Kaynak Yayınları.

Bertaux, Daniel, ed. 1981. *Biography and Society*. Thousand Oaks, Calif.: Sage.

Bertaux, Daniel, and Martin Kohli. 1984. "The Life Story Approach: A Continental View." *Annual Review of Sociology* 10:215–37.

Black, David. 1985. *The Atlas of Rugs and Carpets*. London: Tiger Books International.

Bodnar, John. 1992. *Remaking America: Public Memory, Commemoration, and Patriotism in the Twentieth Century.* Princeton, N.J.: Princeton Univ. Press.

Böhmer, Harald. 1983. "The Revival of Natural Dyeing in Two Traditional Weaving Areas of Anatolia." *Oriental Rug Review* 3, no. 9: 2.

————. 2002. *Koekboya Natural Dyes and Textiles: A Colour Journey from Turkey to India and Beyond.* Ganderkesee, Germany: Remhöb Verlag.

Bora, Tanıl. 1999. "Istanbul of the Conqueror: The 'Alternative Global City' Dreams of Political Islam." In *Istanbul: Between the Global and the Local,* edited by Çağlar Keyder, 31–46. Lanham, Md.: Rowman and Littlefield.

Boswell, David, and Jessica Evans. 1999. *Representing the Nation: A Reader.* London: Routledge.

Bourdieu, Pierre. 1977. *Outline of a Theory of Practice.* Translated by Richard Nice. Cambridge: Cambridge Univ. Press.

Bourdieu, Pierre, and Alain Darbel. 1990. *The Love of Art: European Art Museums and Their Public.* Translated by C. Beattie and N. Merriman. Stanford, Calif.: Stanford Univ. Press.

Bourdin, Alain. 2000. *La question locale.* Paris: Presses Universitaires de France.

Boyarin, Jonathan. 1992. *Storm from Paradise: The Politics of Jewish Memory.* Minneapolis: Univ. of Minnesota Press.

————. 1994. *Remapping Memory: The Politics of Timespace.* Minneapolis: Univ. of Minnesota Press.

Boym, Svetlana. 2001. *The Future of Nostalgia.* Boston: Harvard Univ. Press.

Bozdoğan, Sibel. 2001. *Modernism and Nation Building: Turkish Architectural Culture in the Early Republic.* Seattle: Univ. of Washington Press.

Bozdoğan, Sibel, and Reşat Kasaba. 1999. *Rethinking Modernity and National Identity in Turkey.* Seattle: Univ. of Washington Press.

Braude, Benjamin, and Bernard Lewis, eds. 1982. *Christians and Jews in the Ottoman Empire: The Functioning of a Plural Society.* New York: Holmes and Meier.

Brubaker, Rogers. 1996. *Nationalism Reframed: Nationhood and the National Question in the New Europe.* Cambridge: Cambridge Univ. Press.

Brüggermann, Werner, and Harald Böhmer. 1983. *Rugs of the Peasants and Nomads of Anatolia.* Munich: Kunst and Antiquitäten.

Buğra, Ayşe. 2002. "Political Islam in Turkey in Historical Context: Strengths and Weaknesses." In *Politics of Permanent Crisis: Class, Ideology, and State in Turkey,* edited by Neşecan Balkan and Sungur Savran, 107–44. New York: Nova Science Publishers.

Butler, Judith. 1997. *The Psychic Life of Power: Theories in Subjection.* Stanford, Calif.: Stanford Univ. Press.

Byatt, Antonia Susan. 2002. *On Histories and Stories: Selected Essays.* Cambridge, Mass.: Harvard Univ. Press.

Calhoun, Craig , ed. 1998. *Social Theory and the Politics of Identity.* Cambridge, Mass., and London: Blackwell.

Canbolat, Fatma, ed. 2001. *Boğazköy'den Karatepeye Hititbilim ve Hitit Dünyasının Keşfi Sergi Kataloğu* (Hittitology from Boğazköy to Karatepe and the Discovery of the Hittite World Exhibition Catalog). Istanbul: Yapı Kredi Yayınları.

Casey, Edward. 1987. "The World of Nostalgia." *Man and World* 20: 361–84.

Castaneda, Quetzil. 1996. *In the Museum of Maya Culture: Touring Chichen Itza.* Minneapolis: Univ. of Minnesota Press.

Ceci, Stephen, and Elizabeth Loftus. 1994. " 'Memory-work': A Royal Road to False Memories." *Applied Cognitive Psychology* 8:351–64.

Chakrabarty, Dipesh. 2000. *Provincializing Europe: Postcolonial Thought and Historical Difference.* Princeton, N.J.: Princeton Univ. Press.

Chatterjee, Partha. 1993. *Nation and Its Fragments: Colonial and Postcolonial Histories.* Princeton, N.J.: Princeton Univ. Press.

———. 2000. "Two Poets and Death: On Civil and Political Society in the Non-Christian World." In *Questions of Modernity,* edited by Timothy Mitchell, 35–48. Minneapolis: Univ. of Minnesota Press.

Chernykh, E. N. 1995. "Postscript: Russian Archaeology after the Collapse of the USSR." In *Nationalism, Politics and the Practice of Archaeology,* edited by Philip L. Kohl and Clare Fawcett, 139–48. Cambridge: Cambridge Univ. Press.

Çınar, Alev. 2001. "National History as a Contested Site: The Conquest of Istanbul and Islamist Negotiations of the Nation." *Comparative Studies in Society and History* 34, no. 2:364–91.

Cohen, Abner. 1979. "Political Symbolism." *Annual Review of Anthropology* 8:87–113

Cohen, Jeffrey H. 1998. "Craft Production and the Challenge of the Global Market." *Human Organization* 57, no. 1: 74–82.

Conkey, Meg, and Ruth Tringham. 1995. "Archaeology and the Goddess: Exploring the Contours of Feminist Archaeology." In *Feminisms in the Academy,* edited by D. Stanton and A. Stewart, 199–247. Ann Arbor: Univ. of Michigan Press.

Coronil, Fernando, and Julie Skurski. 1991. "Dismembering and Remembering the Nation: The Semantics of Political Violence in Venezuela." *Comparative Studies in Society and History* 33, no. 2:288–337.

Courbage, Youssef, and Philippe Fargues. 1997. *Christians and Jews under Islam.* Translated by Judy Mabro. London: I. B. Tauris.

Crane, Susan. 1997. "Writing the Individual Back into Collective Memory." *American Historical Review* 102, no. 5:1372–412.

Dadrian, Vahakn N. 1999. *Warrant for Genocide: Key Elements of Turko-Armenian Conflict.* New Brunswick, N.J.: Transaction.

————. 2003. *The History of the Armenian Genocide: Ethnic Conflict from the Balkans to Anatolia to the Caucasus.* New York: Berghahn Books.

Danacıoğlu, Esra. 2001. *Geçmişin İzleri: Yanıbaşımızdaki Tarih İçin Bir Kılavuz* (The Remainders of the Past: A Guide for History Right Next to Us). Istanbul: Tarih Vakfı Yurt Yayınları.

Daniel, Valentine. 1996. *Charred Lullabies: Chapters in an Anthropology of Violence.* Princeton, N.J.: Princeton Univ. Press.

Darga, Muhibbe. 1992. *Hitit Sanatı* (The Hittite Art). Istanbul: Akbank Yayınları.

Davis, Natalie, and Randolf Starn. 1989. "Introduction: Memory and Counter-Memory." *Representations* 26:1–6.

Davison, Andrew. 1998. *Secularism and Revivalism in Turkey: A Hermeneutic Reconsideration.* New Haven, Conn.: Yale Univ. Press.

Delaney, Carol. 1991. *The Seed and the Soil: Gender and Cosmology in Turkish Village Society.* Berkeley: Univ. of California Press.

Dirks, Nicholas. 1990. "History as a Sign of the Modern." *Public Culture* 2:25–32.

Duncan, Carol. 1995. *Civilizing Rituals: Inside Public Art Museums.* London: Routledge.

Duncombe, Stephen. 2002. *Cultural Resistance Reader.* New York: Verso.

Dündar, Fuat. 2001. *İttihat ve Terakki'nin Müslümanları İskan Politikası (1913–1918)* (The Muslims of Order and Progress and Settlement Politics [1913–1918]). Istanbul: İletişim Yayınları.

Eco, Umberto. 1979. *The Role of the Reader: Explorations in the Semiotics of Texts.* Bloomington: Indiana Univ. Press.

Edensor, Tim. 1998. *Tourists at the Taj: Performance and Meaning at a Symbolic Site.* London: Routledge.

Eley, Geof. 1999. "Nations, Publics, and Political Cultures: Placing Habermas in the Nineteenth Century." In *Habermas and the Public Sphere,* edited by Craig Calhoun, 289–339. Cambridge, Mass.: MIT Press.

Elias, Norbert. 1991. *The Symbol Theory.* London: Sage.

Erdoğan, Necmi. 2000. "Kalpaksız Kuvvacılar: Kemalist Sivil Toplum Kuruluşları" (Kuvvaists Without Hats: Kemalist Civil Society Organizations). In *Türkiye'de Sivil Toplum ve Milliyetcilik* (Civil Society and Nationalism in Turkey), 235–64. Istanbul: İletişim Yayınları.

Ersanlı, Büşra. 2003. *İktidar ve Tarih: Türkiye'de "Resmi Tarih" Tezinin Oluşumu (1929–1937).* Istanbul: İletişim Yayınları.

Feigl, Erich. 1987. *Bir Terör Efsanesi* (A Legend of Terror). Istanbul: Milliyet Yayınevi.

Fentress, James, and Chris Wickham. 1988. *Social Memory.* Oxford, Basil Blackwell.

Ferro, Marc. 2002. *Les tabous de l'histoire.* Paris: Nil Editions.

Foucault, Michel. 1970. *The Order of Things: An Archaeology of the Human Sciences.* London: Tavistock.

———. 1972. *Archaeology of Knowledge.* New York: Harper and Row.

———. 1977. *Discipline and Punish: The Birth of the Prison.* New York: Pantheon Books.

———. 1984. "Nietzsche, Genealogy, History." In *The Foucault Reader,* edited by Paul Rabinow, 76–100. New York: Pantheon Books.

Fraser, Nancy. 1999. "Rethinking the Public Sphere: A Contribution to the Critique of Actually Existing Democracy." In *Habermas and the Public Sphere,* edited by Craig Calhoun, 109–42. Cambridge, Mass.: MIT Press.

Gellner, Ernest. 1983. *Nations and Nationalism.* Oxford: Blackwell.

Genette, Gérard. 1982. *Palimpsestes: La littérature au second degré.* Paris: Seuil.

———. 1997. *Paratexts: Thresholds of Interpretation.* Cambridge: Cambridge Univ. Press.

Ger, Güler, and Fabian Faurholt Csaba. 2000. "Consumption, Globalization, and the Other: Cultural Production and Authenticity in a Post-traditional World." *Advances in Consumer Research* 27:131.

Gillis, John, ed. 1994. *Commemorations: The Politics of National Identity.* Princeton, N.J.: Princeton Univ. Press.

Gimbutas, Marija. 1991. *The Civilization of the Goddess: The World of Old Europe.* New York: Harper Collins.

Glassie, Henry. 1993. *Turkish Traditional Art Today.* Bloomington: Indiana Univ. Press.

Göçek, Müge. 2003. "Reconstructing the Turkish Historiography on the Armenian Massacres and Deaths of 1915." In *Looking Backward, Moving Forward: Confronting the Armenian Genocide,* edited by Richard G. Hovannisian, 209–30. New Brunswick, N.J.: Transaction.

Göle, Nilüfer. 1996. *The Forbidden Modern: Civilization and Veiling.* Ann Arbor: Univ. of Michigan Press.

Guha, Ranajit. 1988. "On Some Aspects of the Historiography of Colonial India." In *Selected Subaltern Studies,* edited by Ranajit Guha and Gayatri Chakravorty Spivak, 37–44. New York: Oxford Univ. Press.

Gülalp, Haldun. 1999. "Political Islam in Turkey: The Rise and Fall of the Refah Party." *Muslim World* 89, no. 1:22–41.

————. 2001. "Globalization and Political Islam: The Social Bases of Turkey's Welfare Party." *International Journal of Middle East Studies* 33, no. 3:433–48.

Güney, Yılmaz. 1984. "Message de Cineaste Yilmaz Guney." In *Le crime de silence,* edited by Gerard Chailand and Alice Aslanian-Samuelian. Paris: Flammarian.

Gupta, Akhil, and James Ferguson, eds. 1999. *Culture, Power, Place: Explorations in Critical Anthropology.* Durham, N.C., and London: Duke Univ. Press.

Gür, Asli 2001. "Anatolian Civilizations Discourse: Popular Representation of Turkey's Past and Present Through Archaeological Artifacts." Paper presented at Annual Middle East Studies Association Meeting, San Francisco.

————. 2004. "Political Excavations of the Anatolian Past: Articulations of Nationalism and Archaeology in Turkey." Unpublished manuscript.

Gürbilek, Nurdan. 1992. *Vitrinde Yaşamak: 1980'lerin Kültürel İklimi* (Living on the Window: The Cultural Climate of the 1980s). Istanbul: Metis Yayınları.

Gurney, Oliver Robert. 1990. *The Hittites.* 2nd ed. New York: Penguin.

Habermas, Jurgen. 1991. *The Structural Transformation of the Public Sphere: An Inquiry into a Category of Bourgeois Society.* Translated by Thomas Burger. Cambridge, Mass.: MIT Press.

Halaçoğlu, Yusus. 2002. *Facts on the Relocation of Armenians.* Ankara: Turkish Historical Society.

Halbwachs, Maurice. 1992 [1950]. *On Collective Memory.* Translated and edited by L. A. Cose. Chicago: Univ. of Chicago Press.

Hall, Stuart. 1991. "The Local and the Global: Globalization and Ethnicity." In *Culture, Globalization, and the World-System: Contemporary Conditions for the Representation of Identity,* edited by Anthony King, 19–40. Binhamton, N.Y.: State Univ. of New York at Binghamton.

————. 1997. "The Work of Representation." In *Representation: Cultural Representations and Signifying Practices,* edited by Stuart Hall, 13–64. London: Sage.

Hall, Stuart, and Paul Du Gay, eds. 2002. *Questions of Cultural Identity.* London: Sage.

Hamilakis, Yannis. 1999. *"La trahison des archéologues?* Archaeological Practice as Intellectual Activity in Postmodernity." *Journal of Mediterranean Archaeology* 12, no. 1:60–79.

Hamilton, Carolyn. 2000. "Faultlines: The Construction of Archaeological Knowledge at Çatalhöyük." In *Towards Reflexive Method in Archaeology: The Example at Çatalhöyük,* edited by Ian Hodder. Cambridge: McDonald Institute for Archaeological Research; London: British Institute of Archaeology at Ankara.

Hassan, Fekri A. 1997. "Beyond the Surface: Comments on Hodder's 'Reflexive Excavation Methodology.' " *Antiquity* 71:1020–25.

Hawley, Walter A. 1918. *Asia Minor.* London: John Lane.

Heper, Metin. 1998. *İsmet İnönü: The Making of a Turkish Statesman.* Leiden: Brill.

Herzfeld, Michael. 1997. *Cultural Intimacy: Social Poetics in the Nation-State.* New York: Routledge.

———. 2004. *The Body Impolitic: Artisans and Artifice in the Global Hierarchy of Value.* Chicago: Univ. of Chicago Press.

Hetherington, Kevin. 1996. "The Utopics of Social Ordering: Stonehenge as a Museum Without Walls." In *Theorizing Museums: Representing Identity and Diversity in a Changing World,* edited by Sharon MacDonald and Gordon Fyfe, 153–76. Oxford: Blackwell.

Hirschon, Renee. 1998. *Heirs of the Greek Catastrophe.* New York: Berghahn Books.

———, ed. 2003. *Crossing the Aegean: An Appraisal of the 1923 Compulsory Population Exchange Between Greece and Turkey.* New York: Berghahn Books.

Hobsbawm, Eric J. 1995 [1987]. *The Age of Empire, 1875–1914.* London: Abacus.

Hobsbawm, Eric, and Terence Ranger. 1983. *The Invention of Tradition.* Cambridge: Cambridge Univ. Press.

Hodder, Ian. 1991. *Reading the Past: Current Approaches to Interpretation in Archaeology.* 2nd ed. New York: Cambridge Univ. Press.

———, ed. 1996. *On the Surface: Çatalhöyük, 1993–1995.* Cambridge: McDonald Institute for Archaeological Research; London: British Institute of Archaeology at Ankara.

———. 1997. " 'Always momentary, fluid and flexible': Towards a reflexive excavation." *Antiquity* 71:691–700.

———. 1998. "The Past as Passion and Play: Çatalhöyük as a Site of Conflict in the Construction of Multiple Pasts." In *Archaeology under Fire: Nationalism, Politics and Heritage in the Eastern Mediterranian and Middle East,* edited by Lynn Meskell, 124–39. New York: Routledge.

———. 1999. *The Archaeological Process: An Introduction.* Oxford: Blackwell.

———, ed. 2000. *Towards Reflexive Method in Archaeology: The Example at Çatalhöyük.* Cambridge: McDonald Institute for Archaeological Research; London: British Institute of Archaeology at Ankara.

Holst, Gail. 1994. *Road to Rembetika: Music of a Greek Sub-culture, Songs of Love, Sorrow and Hashish.* Limni: Harvey & Co.

Houston, Christopher. 2001a. *Islam, Kurds and the Turkish Nation State.* Oxford: Berg.

————. 2001b. "Brewing of Islamist Modernity: Tea Gardens and Public Space in Istanbul." *Theory, Culture, and Society* 18, no. 6: 77–97.

Hovannisian, Richard G. 1967. *Armenia on the Road to Independence, 1918.* Berkeley: Univ. of California Press.

————, ed. 1998. *Remembrance and Denial: The Case of the Armenian Genocide.* Detroit: Wayne State Univ. Press.

Hutton, Patrick. 1993. *History as an Art of Memory.* Hanover and London: Univ. Press of London.

Huyssen, Andreas. 1995. *Twilight Memories: Marking Time in a Culture of Amnesia.* London: Routledge.

Iğdemir, Uluğ. 1973. *Ellinci: Yılında Türk Tarih Kurumu* (Turkish History Institution on Its Fiftieth Anniversary). Ankara: Türk Tarih Kurumu Basımevi.

Iğsız, Aslı. 2001. "Synesthetics of Homeland in the Motherland: Sensescapes in Memory Narratives of Asia Minor Refugees." Paper presented at the Middle East Studies Association Meeting, San Francisco.

İnan, Afet. 1933. "Atatürk'ün Tarih Tezi" (The History Thesis of Atatürk). *Belleten* 3, no. 10: 243–66.

Ivy, Marilyn. 1995. *Discourses of the Vanishing: Modernity, Phantasm, Japan.* Chicago: Univ. of Chicago Press.

İzgi, Ömer. 2001. "Turks and Armenians: The Ottoman Experience." In *The Armenians in the Late Ottoman Period,* edited by Türkkaya Ataöv, 1–21. Ankara: Turkish Historical Society.

Jakobson, Roman. 1987. "On Linguistic Aspects of Translation." In Roman Jakobson, *Language in Literature,* edited by Krystyna Pomorska and Stephen Rudy. Cambridge, Mass.: Belknap Press.

Jelavich, Barbara. 1983. *The History of the Balkans.* New York: Cambridge Univ. Press.

Jevremovic, George. 1988. "Rug Farming in Anatolia." *Oriental Rug Review* 8, no. 4:7–11.

Jewsiewicki, Bogumil. 1986. "Collective Memory and the Stakes of Power." *History in Africa* 13:195–223.

Jusdanis, Gregory. 1991. *Belated Modernity and Aesthetic Culture: Inventing National Literature.* Minneapolis: Univ. of Minnesota Press.

Kabaklı, Ahmet. 1998. "Atatürk ve Atatürkçüler" (Atatürk and Atatürkists). *Yeni Türkiye* 23–24:679–685.

Karabayır, Mehmet. 2001. *Geçmişten Günümüze Çumra* (Çumra from the Past to Today). Çumra: Beledlyesi Yayinlari.

Karakasidou, Anastasia. 1997. *Fields of Wheat, Hills of Blood: Passages to Nationhood in Greek Macedonia, 1870–1990.* London: Univ. of Chicago Press.

Kepel, Gilles. 1994. *Revenge of God: The Resurgence of Islam, Christianity, and Judaism in the Modern World.* Translated by Alan Braley. University Park, Pa.: Penn State Univ. Press.

Ketchian, Bertha Nakshian. 1988. *In the Shadow of the Fortress: The Genocide Remembered,* edited by Sonia I. Ketchian. Cambridge, Mass.: Zoryan Institute for Contemporary Armenian Research and Documentation.

Keyder, Çağlar. 1999a. "The Setting." In *Istanbul: Between the Global and the Local,* edited by Çağlar Keyder, 3–30. Lanham, Md.: Rowman and Littlefield.

———. 1999b. *Istanbul: Between the Global and the Local.* New York: Rowman and Littlefield.

Kherdian, David. 1981. *Finding Home.* New York: Greenwillow Books.

Kinross, Lord. 1965. *Atatürk: A Biography of Mustafa Kemal, Father of Modern Turkey.* New York: William Morrow.

Koçak, Cemil. 1986. *Türkiye'de Milli Şef Dönemi (1938–1945): Dönemin İç ve Dış Politikaları üzerine Bir Araştırma* (The National Chief Period in Turkey (1938–1945): Research on the Internal and External Affairs During the Period). Istanbul: Yurt Yayınları.

Koğacıoğlu, Dicle. 2003. "Political Party Dissolutions by the Constitutional Court of Turkey: Judicial Delimiting of the Political Domain." *International Sociology* 18, no. 1:258–76.

Kohl, Phillip L., and Clare Fawcett, eds. 1995. *Nationalism, Politics and the Practice of Archaeology.* Cambridge: Cambridge Univ. Press.

Koşay, H. Zübeyir. 1979. "Ankara Arkeoloji Müzesi'nin İlk Kuruluş Safhası ile İlgili Anılar" (Memoirs about the Foundation of the Ankara Archeological Museum). *Belleten* 43, no. 170:309–12.

Kuhn, Anette. 1995. *Family Secrets: Acts of Memory and Imagination.* New York: Verso.

Kundera, Milan. 1980. *The Book of Laughter and Forgetting.* Translated by Michael Henry Helm. New York: Penguin.

Landreau, Anthony N. 1978. *Yörük: The Nomadic Weaving Tradition of the Middle East.* Pittsburgh, Pa.: Carnegie Institute.

LaRoche, Cheryl J., and Michael L. Blakey. 1997. "Seizing Intellectual Power: The Dialogue at the New York African Burial Ground." *Historical Archaeology* 31, no. 33:84–106.

Layoun, Mary N. 2001. *Wedded to the Land? Gender, Boundaries, and Nationalism in Crisis.* Durham, N.C.: Duke Univ. Press.

Lefevere, André. 1992. *Translation, Rewriting and the Manipulation of Literary Fame.* London: Routledge.

Lefort, Claude. 1988. *Democracy and Political Theory.* Minneapolis: Univ. of Minnesota Press.

Levi, Primo. 1986. *The Drowned and the Saved.* New York: Summits Book.

Lewis, Bernard. 1968. *The Emergence of Modern Turkey.* London: Oxford Univ. Press.

Leys, Ruth. 1996. "Traumatic Cures: Shell Shock, Janet and the Question of Memory." In *Tense Past,* edited by Paul Lantze and Michael Lambek, 103–45. New York: Routledge.

Linde, Charlotte. 1986. "Private Stories in Public Discourse: Narrative Analysis in the Social Sciences." *Poetics* 15:183–202.

Lindsay, Stephen, and Don Read. 1994. "Psychotherapy and Memories of Childhood Sexual Abuse: A Cognitive Perspective." *Applied Cognitive Psychology* 8:281–338.

Lowenthal, David. 1985. *The Past Is a Foreign Country.* Cambridge: Cambridge Univ. Press.

Macdonald, Sharon, and Gordon Fyfe, eds. 1996. *Theorizing Museums: Representing Identity and Diversity in a Changing World.* Cambridge: Blackwell.

Macqueen, James G. 1986. *The Hittites and Their Contemporaries in Asia Minor.* New York: Thames and Hudson.

Magnarella, Paul. 1979. *The Peasant Venture.* Boston: G. K. Hall.

Mango, Andrew. 1999. *Atatürk.* London: John Murray.

Marchese, Ron. 2003. "The Use of Amulets in Turkish Life." *Textile Museum Journal* (Spring): 35–48.

Marchese, Ron, and Marlene Brue. 1998. "Brokers of the Textile Tradition: The Case of the Shopkeepers in Modern Turkey." In *Creating Textiles: Makers, Methods, Markets,* 165–74. Proceedings of the Sixth Biennial Symposium of the Textile Society of America, Inc. New York: Textile Society of America.

———. 1999. "World Markets and Their Impact on Turkish Weaving: Understanding Cultural Transformation." *Anatolica* 25:243–50.

Marcus, George. 1995. "Ethnography in/of the World System: The Emergence of Multi-Sited Ethnography." *Annual Review of Anthropology* 24:95–117.

Mardiganian, Aurora. 1990. *Ravished Armenia.* J.C. and A. Fawcett.

Mason, Wilton. 1985. "DOBAG Revisited." *Oriental Rug Review* 5, no. 5:2–4.

Mavrogordatos, George. 1983. *Stillborn Republic: Social Coalitions and Party Strategies in Greece, 1922–1936.* Berkeley: Univ. of California Press.

Mayewski, [General]. 1916. *Les massacres d'Armenie de Russie a Van Puis a Erzeroum.* Petersburg: Imprimerie Militaire.

McCarthy, Justin. 2001. "The Population of the Ottoman Armenians." In *The Armenians in the Late Ottoman Period,* edited by Türkkaya Ataöv, 65–85. Ankara: Turkish Historical Society.

McQueen, James G. 1986. *The Hittites and Their Contemporaries in Asia Minor.* New York: Thames and Hudson.

Mellaart, James. 1967. *Çatal Hüyük.* London: Thames and Hudson.

Mellaart, James, Belkıs Balpınar, and Udo Hirsch. 1989. *The Goddess from Anatolia.* Milan: Eskenazi.

Melson, Robert. 1992. *Revolution and Genocide: On the Origins of the Armenian Genocide and the Holocaust.* Chicago: Univ. of Chicago Press.

Meskell, Lynn. 1995. "Goddesses, Gimbutas and 'New Age' Archaeology." *Antiquity* 69:74–86.

———, ed. 1998. *Archaeology under Fire: Nationalism, Politics, and Heritage in the Eastern Mediterranean and the Middle East.* London: Routledge.

Mickelwright, Nancy. 1986. *Women's Dress in 19th Century Istanbul: Mirror of a Changing Society.* Philadephia: Univ. of Pennsylvania Press.

Miller, Donald E., and Lorna Touryan Miller. 1993. *Survivors: An Oral History of the Armenian Genocide.* Berkeley: Univ. of California Press.

Mitchell, W.J.T., ed. 1981. *On Narrative.* Chicago: Univ. of Chicago Press.

Monceau, Nicolas. 2000. "Cumhuriyet'in 75. Yıldönümü ve Osmanlı Devleti'nin 700. Kuruluş Yıldönümü: Geçmişin ve Bugünün Modernliğini Kutlamak" (Celebrating the Modernity of Yesterday and Today: The 75th Anniversary of the Republic and the 700th Anniversary of the Ottoman Empire). In *Türkiye'de Sivil Toplum ve Milliyetçilik* (Civil Society and Nationalism in Turkey), 505–47. Istanbul: İletişim.

Nairn, Tom. 1997. *Faces of Nationalism: Janus Revisited.* London: Verso.

Navaro-Yashin, Yael. 1999. "The Historical Construction of Local Culture: Gender and Identity in the Politics of Secularism Versus Islam." In *Istanbul: Between the Global and the Local,* edited by Çağlar Keyder, 59–75. New York: Rowman and Littlefield.

———. 2002. *Faces of the State: Secularism and Public Life in Turkey.* Princeton, N.J.: Princeton Univ. Press.

Neyzi, Leyla. 1994. Review of *The Seed and the Soil: Gender and Cosmology in Turkish Village Society,* by Carol Delaney. *American Ethnologist* 21:212–13.

———. 2002. "Sabbateanism, Identity, and Subjectivity in Turkey." *Comparative Studies in Society and History* 44, no. 1:137–58.

Nora, Pierre, ed. 1986. *Les lieux de mémoire: La nation I-II-III.* Paris: Éditions Gallimard.

————. 1989. "Between Memory and History: *Les lieux de memoire.*" *Representations* 26 (Spring): 7–25.

————. 1996. "General Introduction: Between Memory and History." In *Rethinking the French Past: Realms of Memory,* edited by Pierre Nora, 1–20. Translated by Arthur Goldhammer. New York: Columbia Univ. Press.

O'Bannon, George. 1990. "A Visit to Ayvacık." *Oriental Rug Review* 10, no. 6:6–9.

Olshan, Marc. 1991. "The Opening of Amish Society: Cottage Industry as Trojan Horse." *Human Organization* 50, no. 4:378–84.

Özdalga, Elizabeth. 1998. *The Veiling Issue, Official Secularism, and Popular Islam in Modern Turkey.* Richmond, Surrey: Curzon.

Özdoğan, Mehmet. 1992. "Arkeolojide Çağdaşlaşma ve Türk Arkeolojisini Bekleyen Tehlikeler" (Modernization and Archeology and Dangers Awaiting Turkish Archeology). In *Osman Hamdi Bey ve Dönemi* (Osman Hamdi Bey and His Era), edited by Zeynep Rona, 192–200. Istanbul: Tarih Vakfı Yurt Yayınları.

————. 1998. "Ideology and Archaeology in Turkey." In *Archaeology under Fire: Nationalism and Politics and Heritage in the Eastern Mediterranean and Middle East,* edited by Lynn Meskell, 111–24. New York: Routledge.

Ozouf, Mona. 1984. In *Les lieux de mémoire,* edited by Pierre Nora, 139–66. Paris: Gallimard.

————. 1988. *Festivals and the French Revolution.* Cambridge, Mass.: Harvard Univ. Press.

Öztürkmen, Arzu. 2001. "Celebrating National Holidays in Turkey: History and Memory." *New Perspectives on Turkey* 25:47–75.

Özyürek, Esra. 2000. "Mecliste Başörtüsü Düğümü" (The Head Scarf Knot in the Parliament). In *Vatan, Millet, Kadınlar* (Homeland, Nation, Women), edited by Aysegül Altınay, 339–57. Istanbul: İletişim Yayınları.

————. 2004a. "Miniaturizing Atatürk: Privatization of the State Imagery and Ideology in Turkey." *American Ethnologist* 31, no. 3:374–91.

————. 2004b. "Wedded to the Republic: Public Intellectuals and Intimacy Oriented Publics in Turkey." In *Off Stage/On Display: Intimacies and Ethnographies in the Age of Public Culture,* edited by Andrew Shryock, 101–30. Stanford, Calif.: Stanford Univ. Press.

————. 2006. *Nostalgia for the Modern: State Secularism and Everyday Politics in Turkey.* Durham, N.C.: Duke Univ. Press.

Paksoy, İsmail Günay. 1992. "Bazı Belgeler Işığında Osmanlı Devleti'nin Kültür Mirası Politikası üzerine Düşünceler" (Meditations on the Politics of Ottoman Cultural Heritage Based on Some Documents). In *Osman Hamdi Bey ve Dönemi*

206 | References

(Osman Hamdi Bey and His Era), edited by Zeynep Rona, 201–21. Istanbul: Tarih Vakfı Yurt Yayınları.

Pamuk, Orhan. 1994. *The Black Book*. Translated by Güneli Gün. London: Faber and Faber.

Pandey, Gyan. 1997. "Violence—'Out There': Memories of Partition." Paper presented to the Advanced Studies Center of the International Institute, Univ. of Michigan.

———. 1998. "Memory, History and the Question of Violence: Reflections on the Reconstruction of Partition." Deuskar Lectures, delivered at the Center for Studies in Social Sciences, Calcutta.

———. 2001. *Remembering Partition: Violence, Nationalism and History in India*. Cambridge: Cambridge Univ. Press.

Parla, Taha. 1985. *The Social and Political Thought of Ziya Gökalp, 1876–1924*. Leiden: Brill.

———. 1991. *Türkiye'de Siyasi Kültürün Resmi Kaynakları* (The Official Sources of Political Culture in Turkey). Vols. 1 and 2. Istanbul: İletişim Yayınları.

Peroomian, Rubina. 2003. "New Directions in Literary Responses to the Armenian Genocide." In *Looking Backward, Moving Forward: Confronting the Armenian Genocide*, edited by Richard G. Hovannisian, 157–80. New Brunswick, N.J., and London: Transaction.

Prager, Jeffrey. 1998. *Presenting the Past: Psychoanalysis and the Sociology of Misremembering*. Cambridge, Mass.: Harvard Univ. Press.

Ramaswamy, Sumathi. 2001. "Remains of the Race: Archaeology, Nationalism, and the Yearning for Civilization in the Indus Valley." *Indian Economic and Social History Review* 38, no. 2:105–45.

Rapport, Nigel, and Joanna Overing. 2003. *Social and Cultural Anthropology: The Key Concepts*. London: Routledge.

Robertson, Jennifer. 1991. *Native and Newcomer: Making and Remaking a Japanese City*. Berkeley: Univ. of California Press.

Rofel, Lisa. 1999. *Other Modernities: Gendered Yearnings in China after Socialism*. Berkeley: Univ. of California Press.

Rosaldo, Renato. 1989. "Imperialist Nostalgia." *Representations* 26 (Spring): 107–22.

Rountree, Kathryn. 2001. "The Past is a Foreigners' Country: Goddess Feminists, Archaeologists, and the Appropriation of Prehistory." *Journal of Contemporary Religion* 16, no. 1:5–27.

———. 2002. "Goddess Pilgrims as Tourists: Inscribing the Body Through Sacred Travel." *Sociology of Religion* 63, no. 4:475–96.

Rowlands, Michael. 1994. "The Politics of Identity in Archaeology." In *Social Construction of the Past: Representation as Power,* edited by G. C. Bond and A. Gilliam, 129–43. London: Routledge.

Roy, Oliver. 1994. *The Failure of Political Islam.* Cambridge: Harvard Univ. Press.

Ryan, Mary P. 1999. "Gender and Public Access: Women's Politics in Nineteenth-Century America." In *Habermas and the Public Sphere,* edited by Craig Calhoun, 73–98. Cambridge: MIT Press.

Sakallıoğlu, ümit Cizre. 1996. "Parameters and Strategies of Islam-State Interaction in Republican Turkey." *International Journal of Middle East Studies* 28, no. 2:231–51.

Sakayan, Dora. 1997. *An Armenian Doctor in Turkey.* Montreal: Arod Books.

Saktanber, Ayşe. 1997. "Formation of a Middle-Class Ethos and Its Quotidien: Revitalising Islam in Urban Turkey." In *Space, Culture and Power,* edited by Ayşe Öncü and Petra Weyland, 140–56. London: Zed Books.

Samuel, Raphael. 1994. *Theaters of Memory: Past and Present in Contemporary Culture.* London: Verso.

Savage, Kirk. 1994. "The Politics of Memory: Black Emancipation and the Civil War Monument." In *Commemorations: The Politics of National Identity,* edited by John R. Gills, 127–49. Princeton, N.J.: Princeton Univ. Press.

Scott, James C. 1985. *Weapons of the Weak: Everyday Forms of Peasant Resistance.* London: Yale Univ. Press.

Seremetakis, Nadia, ed. 1994. *The Senses Still: Perception and Memory as Material Culture in Modernity.* Boulder, Colo.: Westview.

Shankland, David. 1996. "Çatalhöyük: The Anthropology of an Archaeological Presence." Chap. 18 in *On the Surface: Çatalhöyük, 1993–1995,* edited by Ian Hodder. Cambridge: McDonald Institute for Archaeological Research; London: British Institute of Archaeology at Ankara.

———. 2000. "Villagers and the Distant Past: Three Seasons' Work at Küçükköy, Çatalhöyük." Chap. 14 in *Towards Reflexive Method in Archaeology: The Example at Çatalhöyük,* edited by Ian Hodder. Cambridge: McDonald Institute for Archaeological Research; London: British Institute of Archaeology at Ankara.

Shankland, David, Cemil Bezmen, and Judith Bunbury. 1995. "The Turkish Museum Service." Preliminary Research Report sponsored by the Rockefeller Foundation.

Shaw, Wendy M. K. 2003. *Possessors and Possessed: Museums, Archaeology, and the Visualization of History in the Late Ottoman Empire.* Berkeley: Univ. of California Press.

Shaw, Stanford, and Ezel Kural Shaw. 1977. *History of the Ottoman Empire and Modern Turkey.* Cambridge: Cambridge Univ. Press.

Shirinian, Lorne. 1998. "Survivor Memoirs of the Armenian Genocide as Cultural

History." In *Remembrance and Denial: The Case of the Armenian Genocide,* edited by Richard G. Hovannisian, 292–309. Detroit: Wayne State Univ. Press.

Silberman, Neil Asher, ed. 1989. *Between Past and Present: Archeology, Ideology and Nationalism in the Modern Middle East.* New York: Henry Holt.

————. 1995. "Promised Lands and Chosen Peoples: The Politics and Poetics of Archaeological Narrative." In *Nationalism, Politics and the Practice of Archaeology,* edited by Philip L. Kohl and Clare Fawcett, 249–62. Cambridge: Cambridge Univ. Press.

Silverman, Kaja. 1996. *The Threshhold of the Visible World.* London: Routledge.

Smith, Anthony D. 1986. *The Ethnic Origins of Nations.* Oxford: Blackwell.

Solmaz, Gürsoy. 1995. *Yaşayanların Dilinden Erzurum-Sarıkamış-Kars'ta Ermeni Zulmü* (Armenian Oppression in Erzurum-Sarıkamış-Kars from the Perspective of Those Who Experienced It). Van: Yüzüncü Yıl Üniversitesi Yayınları.

Somers, Margaret, and Gloria Gibson. 1994. "Reclaiming the Epistemological 'Other': Narrative and the Social Construction of Identity." In *Social Theory and the Politics of Identity,* edited by Craig Calhoun, 37–99. Oxford: Blackwell.

Sotiriou, Dido. 1982. *Benden Selam Söyle Anadolu'ya* (Say Hi to Anatolia). Istanbul: Alan Yayınları.

Spooner, Brian. 1986. "Weavers and Dealers." In *The Social Life of Things,* edited by Arjun Appadurai, 195–235. Cambridge: Cambridge Univ. Press.

Starrett, Gregory. 2003. "Violence and the Rhetoric of Images." *Cultural Anthropology* 18, no. 3:398–428.

Stewart, Kathleen. 1988. "Nostalgia—a Polemic." *Cultural Anthropology* 3, no. 3:227–41.

Stirling, John. 1950. *Turkish Village.* New York: John Wiley and Sons.

Stokes, Martin. 2000. " 'Beloved Istanbul': Realism and the Transnational Imaginary in Turkish Popular Culture." In *Mass Mediations: New Approaches to Popular Culture in the Middle East and Beyond,* edited by Walter Armburst, 224–42. Berkeley: Univ. of California Press.

Stoler, Ann Laura, and Karen Strassler. 2000. "Castings for the Colonial: Memory Work in 'New Order' Java." *Comparative Studies in Society and History* 42, no. 1:4–48.

Stronza, Amanda. 2001. "Anthropology of Tourism: Forging New Ground for Ecotourism and Other Alternatives." *Annual Review of Anthropology* 30:261–83.

Sturken, Marita. 1997. *Tangled Memories: Vietnam, the AIDS Epidemic, and the Politics of Remembering.* Berkeley: Univ. of California Press.

Suleiman, Susan Rubin, ed. 1998. *Exile and Creativity: Signposts, Travelers, Outsiders, Backward Glances.* Durham, N.C.: Duke Univ. Press.

Suny, Ronald. 2001. "Religion, Ethnicity, and Nationalism: Armenians, Turks, and the End of the Ottoman Empire." In *God's Name: Genocide and Religion in the Twentieth Century,* edited by Omer Bartov and Phyllis Mack, 23–61. New York: Berghahn Books.

Surmelian, Leon Z. 1945. *I Ask You, Ladies and Gentlemen.* New York: E. P. Dutton.

Sutherland, James Kay. 1964. *The Adventures of an Armenian Boy.* Ann Arbor, Mich.: Ann Arbor Press.

Swedenburg, Ted. 1995. *Memories of Revolt: The 1936 Rebellion and the Palestinian National Past.* Minneapolis: Univ. of Minnesota Press.

Taylor, Julie. 1994. "Body Memories: Aide-Memoirs and Collective Amnesia in the Wake of the Argentine Terror." In *Body Politics: Disease, Desire and the Family,* edited by Michael Ryan and A. Gordon. Boulder, Colo.: Westview.

Tekeli, İlhan. 1998. *Tarih Bilinci ve Gençlik: Karşılaştırmalı Avrupa ve Türkiye Araştırması* (History Consciousness and Youth: Comparative Europe and Turkey Research). Istanbul: Tarih Vakfı Yurt Yayınları.

Thomas, Nicholas. 1991. *Entangled Objects: Exchange, Material Culture, and Colonialism in the Pacific.* Cambridge: Harvard Univ. Press.

Thompson, Jon. 1986. "A Return to Tradition." *Hali* 8, no. 2: 14.

Toprak, Binnaz. 1981. *Islam and Political Development in Turkey.* Leiden: Brill.

Trigger, Bruce. 1995. "Romanticism, Nationalism, and Archaeology." In *Nationalism, Politics and the Practice of Archaeology,* edited by Philip L. Kohl and Clare Fawcett, 263–79. Cambridge: Cambridge Univ. Press.

Trouillot, Michel-Rolph. 1995. *Silencing the Past: Power and the Production of History.* Boston: Beacon.

Tuğal, Cihan. 2002. "The Islamist Movement in Turkey: Beyond Instrument and Meaning." *Economy and Society* 31, no. 1:85–111.

Türköz, Meltem. 2001. "The Social Life of the State's Fantasy: Turkish Family Names in 1934." Paper presented at the Middle East Studies Association Meeting, San Francisco.

Urry, John. 1995. *Consuming Places.* London: Routledge.

Volkan, Vamık, and Norman Itzkowitz. 1984. *The Immortal Atatürk: A Psychobiography.* Chicago: Univ. of Chicago Press.

Warner, Michael. 2002. "Publics and Counterpublics." *Public Culture* 14, no. 1:49–90.

White, Jenny. 1999. "The Islamic Chic." In *Istanbul: Between the Global and the Local,* edited by Çağlar Keyder, 77–91. Lanham, Md.: Rowman and Littlefield.

———. 2002. *Islamist Mobilization in Turkey: A Study in Vernacular Politics.* Seattle: Univ. of Washington Press.

www.returntotradition.com. Web site of the San Francisco dealer who markets DOBAG rugs.

www.wordweb.org/sacredjo.

Yalçın, Kemal. 1998. *Emanet Çeyiz: Mübadele İnsanları* (Entrusted Trousseau: Peoples of the Exchange). Istanbul: Belge Yayınları.

Yener, Aslıhan, Harry Hoffner, and Simrit Dhesi. 2002. *Recent Developments in Hittite Archaeology and History.* Winona Lake, Ind: Eisenbrauns.

Yernazian, K. Eprahim. 1990. *Judgment onto Truth.* New Brunswick, N.J.: Transaction.

Yerushalmi, Yosef Hayim. 1982. *Zakhor: Jewish History and Jewish Memory.* Seattle: Univ. of Washington Press.

Yervant, John. 1988. *Needle, Thread, and Button.* New Brunswick, N.J.: Zoryan Institute.

Yıldız, Ahmet. 2001. *"Ne Mutlu Türküm Diyebilene": Türk Ulusal Kimliğinin Etno-Seküler Sınırları (1919–1938)* ("How Happy Is the One Who Can Say I am a Turk": Ethno-Secular Boundaries of the Turkish National Identity). Istanbul: İletişim Yayınları.

Yordanidou, Maria. 1990. *Loksandra: İstanbul Düşü* (Loksandra: An Istanbul Dream). Istanbul: Belge Yayınları.

Young, Allan. 1996. *Bodily Memory and Traumatic Memory: Cultural Essays in Trauma and Memory,* edited by Paul Antze and Michael Lamber, 89–102. New York: Routledge.

Zürcher, Erik Jan. 1998. *Turkey: A Modern History.* London: I. B. Tauris.

Index

Italic page number denotes illustration.

Other titles in Modern Intellectual and Political History of the Middle East